THE VETERANS' PRACTICAL PRIMER:

GETTING YOUR BENEFITS

BY

KEN HUDNALL

OMEGA PRESS
EL PASO, TEXAS

Other Works by Ken Hudnall

FICTION

<u>Manhattan Conspiracy</u>
Blood On The Apple
Capital Crimes
Angel of Death

<u>The Darkness Series</u>
When Darkness Falls
Fear the Darkness

Even Paranoids Have Enemies

NON-FICTION

<u>The Occult Connection</u>
UFO's, Secret Societies and Ancient Gods
The Hidden Race

No Safe Haven: Homeland Insecurity

<u>Spirits of the Border</u>
The History and Mystery of El Paso Del Norte
The History and Mystery of Fort Bliss, Texas
The History and Mystery of the Rio Grande
The History and Mystery of New Mexico
The History and Mystery of Colorado

The Veterans Practical Primer: Getting Your Benefits

OMEGA PRESS
An imprint of Omega Communications

For Information Address:

Omega Press
5823 N. Mesa, #823
El Paso, Texas 79912
Or
http://www.kenhudnall.com

FIRST EDITION

Printed in the United States of America

DEDICATION

As with all of my efforts, I must first give thanks to the greatest support any veteran, or writer, can have, my wife Sharon. However, unlike most of my books, there are a number of others that I must also thank for the creation of this book.

To Congressman Silvestri Reyes for his assistance in bringing my own struggle with the Department of Veterans Affairs to a successful conclusion. He arranged a personal meeting between myself and Carl Lowe, the Director of the Waco Region. After some initial unpleasantness, I found Mr. Lowe to be a man of integrity and more importantly, a man of his word. He, like all regional directors is faced with a monumental job and there are only so many hours in the day. It is unfortunate that every veteran cannot have a face to face meeting with the decision authorities. This would stop much of the confusion.

The Department of Veterans Affairs employs thousands of individuals, the vast majority of whom are good, caring, decent people who want to do the best that they can for those who have given so much to serve this great country. However, as in every organization there is a small percentage of employees who are full of their own importance and take delight in denying the requests of veterans. It seems that this power that they are able to exercise over others in some way makes up for their inability to exercise power in any other fashion. It is truly these individuals who have make this book both necessary and possible.

The Department of Veterans Affairs publishes dozens of pamphlets about how to submit claims and obtain various benefits. However these pamphlets do not take into consideration the human elements. As an example, most veterans have no idea how to prove a condition that is not documented in their medical records. Only a small percentage of veterans have ever heard of the Board of Veterans Appeals and even fewer have heard of the U.S. Court of Appeals for Veterans Claims. Most give up when their initial claim is denied.

When there is secrecy and a lack of knowledge, there is normally resentment in those who the system ignores. The VA by its very nature has large numbers of veterans attempting to obtain benefits at the same time. In order to allow the decision authorities the time they need to make decisions on various claims, Regional telephone numbers are unlisted and many things are done behind closed doors. Unfortunately, this leads to anger and resentment on the part of the veteran. Hopefully, this book will help the veteran understand the system just a little better.

6\Getting Your Benefits

PART ONE

UNDERSTANDING THE
DEPARTMENT OF VETERANS AFFAIRS

Mission Statement Of The Department Of Veterans Affairs

"To care for him who shall have borne the battle and for his widow and his orphan."

These words, spoken by Abraham Lincoln during his Second Inaugural Address, reflect the philosophy and principles that guide VA in everything that it does, and are the focus of the agency's endeavors to serve the veterans of this Nation and their families.

CHAPTER ONE

You and The Department of Veterans Affairs

No matter who you are or how much you love military life, at some point in your life, you will be forced to put the uniform in the closet and retire. So looking to the future, you are ready to leave the military service after a successful career and you are looking forward to the many benefits that the law says are available to you through the Department of Veterans Affairs. Obtaining these benefits should be a piece of cake for someone who has managed to build a successful career in an occupation as difficult as that of soldier, right? Well, not necessarily so. I have heard many former soldiers proclaim that the benefits being denied them are theirs by law. However, no matter what they do they are denied.

Unfortunately, it is a sad fact that just because the law gives you an entitlement to a certain benefit from the Department of Veterans Affairs it does not follow that you will actually receive the benefit in question. Confusing? Well, you are not alone in believing that the system is totally confusing and arbitrary.

The problem is that these benefits that the law stipulates that the veterans are entitled to receive are not automatically bestowed on the recipient, no matter how deserving that recipient might be. Regulations that have been put in place in order to govern the granting of veterans' benefits make it very clear that these benefits must only be awarded after the veteran establishes his or her eligibility and a medical review performed by a physician employed by the Department of Veterans Affairs determined that the veteran meets the specific requirements for those benefits. This seems very clear, but in actuality, it is about as clear as mud.

The system works because of the personnel that process the paperwork and determine exactly what benefits the applicant might be entitled to receive. While the vast majority of these VA employees are well intentioned, dedicated workers who actually do want what is best for the veteran, there are unfortunately, a number of faceless paper processors are able to act as they see fit, answerable to no one but another faceless paper processor. Many of these faceless cogs in the mysterious wheel have not even served in the military and as a result, have little actual understanding of what the veteran has gone through prior to them receiving the veteran's file and the application for benefits.

To successfully receive the requested benefits, it takes a veteran who is knowledgeable and able to work his way through a system that many times does not even follow its own rules and has the ability to laugh at the law. If you think that the Internal Revenue Service is above the law, wait until you understand the system that has been put in place to take care of this nation's veterans.

Now I am not saying that every veteran will have difficulties in obtaining benefits through the Department of Veterans Affairs, but I am saying that many times the veteran will not be aware of all of the benefits to which he (or she) may be entitled or even how to properly apply for these benefits. If the application and the supporting paperwork are filled out incorrectly, this is as bad as never applying in the first place. There are also a number of benefits that will only be made available if the veteran specifically asks for them. So how is the veteran to know that these benefits exist? This is where research comes into play.

Know Your Opponent

Do not misunderstand me, the VA is there for the veteran. However, the benefits are not freebies, you must apply for the desired benefits, establish that you meet the requirements for the benefits you desire and above all, be patient. For me it works best to view the faceless raters as opponents in a great game. It is my job to place the raters in the position that they must grant my request. I do this by styling my application in such a fashion that they have no alternative but to grant it.

The first rule taught in the military is that you need to know your adversary. However, it seems that when a veteran leaves the service, that he or she totally forgets all of this training and the importance of preparation. Entering the civilian world is just like going into the military, you need to learn the ropes, so to speak and certainly how to work the system. There is always a "go to" guy (or gal) in every organization, military or civilian, and it is important that this person be found within the VA system. Even on an informal basis, this person can give you pointers necessary to achieve success.

It is surprising, and very unfortunate, that so many veterans, who as defenders of our freedoms left nothing to chance in conducting a military operation would depend on faceless bureaucrats to determine what benefits they are entitled to receive as a result of their military service. Just because the veteran is no longer on active duty does not mean that the need for careful preparation is no longer applicable.

It would also be surprising to many to find out that not all of the employees of the Department of Veterans Affairs have spent even one day in the military and yet these people are sometimes charged with making determinations regarding whether or not someone's condition is service connected and how much of an impact the condition in question has on the daily life of the veteran in question. Even more surprising, these people are not physicians and yet they have the authority to over rule or even ignore medical determinations made by trained physicians.

This is something like asking a blind man to determine how long a piece of wood might be or how deep a color a blue wall should be painted. What is the frame of reference to be used by the decision maker? Unfortunately, this lack of experience on the part of the rater can play a major role in the final decision. Because it is very possible that the rater that handles your claim for benefits may never have served in the military, it is incumbent upon you as the veteran to paint as complete a picture as possible during the application process about what your medical problem is, how it came about and what affects it is having on your life..

Just as the military preaches knowing your opponent, it is just as important that the veteran become very familiar with the laws, regulations, programs and guidelines used the Department of Veterans Affairs in determining eligibility for the various benefit programs available. This knowledge can mean the difference between success and failure in one of the most important operations you will conduct during your lifetime. By this I am referring to the benefits that you as a veteran can obtain for yourself and your family from this country. This is especially true if you have come out of your military service with a physical or mental disability.

There is no guidebook for laymen covering the many laws that pertain to the granting of benefits from the Department of Veterans Affairs. I have seen applications for benefits submitted by veterans that simply say, "My back hurts." Depending on the completeness of the veteran's military medical records, this simple statement could be sufficient for the benefits requested to be granted or hopelessly inadequate. In a perfect world, such a short concise statement would be sufficient however, normally this is not the case. The applicant's reliance on the benevolence of "the system" to work with such little information is similar to betting your entire bankroll on one roll of the dice and hoping for the best.

With an experienced, well-trained, dedicated rater who is very familiar with military life and a complete military medical record such a simple statement, as "my back hurts" might be enough to result in a proper, fair decision. However, it must be remembered that the rater is committing funds and is, or should be, very careful in making such a determination. Depending on a veteran's age at the time a disability rating is assigned, this commitment could run into several hundred thousand dollars over time.

To insure that only those veterans who qualify receive government benefits, there is a very detailed analysis that must take place. The analysis of this application would be

(1) Did something occur on active duty that could or would have resulted in a back injury? and

(2) Did the veteran seek treatment for the problem while on active duty? and

(3) Is the incident and the treatment documented in the military medical record? and

(4) To what level is the injury?

This is the logical analysis that should be undertaken in regarding to a claim such as "my back hurts" or any claim, for that matter. It should also be remembered that the decisions are being made by human beings and humans are not perfect. Sometimes, the decisions made regarding the granting or denying of benefits are not even logical, but once made, these decisions have the force of law, whether or not the decision maker even knew what he or she was talking about. One of the reasons that it is very important to try and insure a successful decision in regard to the initial application for benefits is that not even a court of law may overturn the decision of a VA rater, even if the decision is clearly totally illogical and wrong.

It is also important for the veteran to know that the law does say that when you receive a decision from the Department of Veterans Affairs (VA) that you will also be made aware of the laws upon which this decision was based. Though it would be logical for the applicant to be made aware of the various laws before applying, the policy is to include a list of the applicable laws used to arrive at the decision with the decision itself. This is somewhat like you being brought to trial and not finding out until the trial is over what you are charged with or what defenses you might have raised on your own behalf.

What I have written to this point makes the system sound like a nightmare, doesn't it? Well, there is some good news – most of the employees of the Department of Veterans Affairs are good intentioned, caring individuals who truly want to do the best that they can for the veteran. Most of those working at the operational level are former military and understand the problems faced by the veteran in dealing with such a massive paper mill. However, those at the higher levels of the system are usually career bureaucrats who, more often than not, look at the veterans as problems to be ignored.

In defense of this attitude, however, it is a sad fact that unfortunately, there are those who served this country who try to obtain benefits for which they are not entitled. Conversely, from time to time you will run into those career bureaucrats who believe that their word is (or should be) law and often they make decisions based upon political expediency or their own personal bias rather than what is right. These are the ones who are more concerned with CYA (covering their back side) rather than following the spirit, or even the letter, of the rules.

These are the ones who have forgotten the purpose of the Department of Veterans Affairs and are more concerned with their own enrichment than they are the problems of the veterans. These are the ones that the system really does not need, but getting rid of them is almost impossible as they are deeply entrenched, sort of like a tick on a dog.

During my over 20 years of dealing with the VA I have met both types. I have been afforded priceless assistance above and beyond the call of duty and I have also been lied to by senior employees of the VA when the truth would have actually served them better. I have learned of certain of my records being destroyed so that the raters in question would look good to their superiors and I have dealt with people who have made it clear that if I gave them any trouble, I would never get the benefits that I sought even if I could establish that I was entitled to them.

I know that it sounds unreasonable, but I have had some VA officials inform me that they would personally make sure my application was turned down. It is with these less than honorable individuals in mind that I write this book. No one should have to go through what I have gone through and my case is not one of the worst that I have seen.

As an example of how extreme a situation can become within the VA system, I ran across a lady in a VA Canteen cafeteria not too long ago who was almost in tears after a meeting with an officer at the VA. Her husband was in the hospital for the third time in only a few months with a condition that was believed, by his physicians, to be service connected and she was at the VA trying to get his benefits approved in order to allow the government to pay the cost of his expensive medical treatments.

The poor lady had just met with a VA employee who said very callously that the treatment needed by the husband was very expensive and frankly, if the VA stalled in approving the benefits, that her husband would probably die and the government would save the cost of his care and he (the speaker) would be considered as being very frugal with the government's money. So what if a veteran's family was reduced to poverty and his wife to a nervous wreck and a widow? At least the person she had seen at the VA would look good to his superiors and would probably get promoted. But was this why the VA was created?

In my own case, after I was determined to be 100% disabled, I applied for the Vocational Rehabilitation Program. I had been in the program once before, but now that I was found to be medically unable to perform the duties of that occupation for which I had trained any longer[1], the laws governing this program made it very clear that I was entitled to retraining for an occupation that I could perform with my disabilities. The laws, rules and regulations regarding the vocational rehabilitation program are some of the most detailed and well written that I have encountered.

However, the person who had to approve my reentry into the program did not want to give that approval since his boss might wonder why he had allowed me a second entry into the program. After all, he said, he needed to cover his ass (there's that CYA again) so he did not get into any trouble. Then, in

---

[1] I was finally determined to be a 100% disabled after two hospital stays for a "minor" problem.

spite of denying my application, he urged me to appeal the decision he had just made, as he made no secret of the fact that he believed that I was correct. His statements reminded me somewhat of the logic that Alice ran into when she went down the rabbit hole.

So here was a very peculiar, but not unique, situation that many veterans have told me that they have encountered. Though the person who had the authority to approve my reentry into the program agreed with me that I was entitled to reentry, and the applicable laws and medical evidence clearly supported my request, he was not granting my request. As he said, what else did I have to do with my time except deal with the bureaucratic maze he was putting me into when I was forced to appeal his incorrect and illogical decision? I might or might not get what I was requesting once I appealed his decision, but either way it came out, he would look good to his superiors who determined such things as promotions and raises.

I talked to his boss about this situation but this individual laughingly dismissed my complaint out of hand. It was his personal opinion, contrary to both the law and the medical determinations from the VA, itself, that I had to have some skill that I could use to earn a living and therefore, I did not need retraining. The mere fact that his personal opinion had no place in such a decision was not something that he even considered. He also paid no attention to the law since after all, in his mind, his word was law.

Such is the power of the government bureaucrat that these two individuals could ignore VA medical determinations and even the very laws governing the VA without fear of punishment as long as they denied the requested benefits. As it was explained to me, if I managed to get someone higher to reverse their decision and they are called to explain their reasons for making such an incorrect decision, they would only have to say that they erred on the side of conserving scarce government resources.

In the illogical world of the bureaucrat, if these two had granted my request and were later challenged by someone higher, then they might have to actually defend a decision. Taking a stand for what was right rather than just agreeing with their superiors would show their superiors that they are not a team player and this determination might affect their personal raises and promotions. Is this what the VA is all about?

This practice of the VA employees being concerned only with their own advancement at the expense of the veteran,, I believe, must stop and it can only stop if the veteran knows the laws and government regulations as well as, or better than, the VA employee with whom he or she must deal. It is time that the Department of Veterans Affairs concerned itself more with the problems of the veterans than the problems of the employees.

CHAPTER TWO

Benefits for Military Veterans

So to begin this education that I believe is needed by each and every veteran, let us look first at and try to understand the organization known as the Department of Veterans Affairs.

Today, the United States has the most comprehensive system of assistance for its veterans of any nation in the world. Caring for its veterans has been a corner stone of military service in this country since the earliest days of the American colonies.

Records show that the concept of caring for the military veterans of this country goes back to as early as 1636. At this time, the citizens of Plymouth Colony were at war with the Pequot Indians. Those who were injured during the various battles that took place prior to the end of this conflict were concerned about their ability to survive on their own once their period of service ended. In order to reward those who had risked their lives to defend the colony, the citizens of Plymouth colony passed a law that mandated that disabled soldiers would be taken care of by the colony.

During the American Revolution the Continental Congress encouraged enlistments by providing pensions for soldiers who were disabled during the conflict. While the central government guaranteed financial payments to those who were injured while in uniform, medical and hospital care given to veterans was provided by the individual States and the communities in which they lived. This resulted in some veterans receiving very good care and others receiving little or no care.

In 1811 in an attempt to rectify this inequity, the first domiciliary and medical facility for veterans was authorized by the Federal Government. After the American Civil War, the Nation's veterans' assistance program was expanded to include benefits and pensions not only for veterans, but also their widows and dependents.

It was also after the Civil War that many State veterans homes were established. Since domiciliary care was available at all State veterans homes, incidental medical and hospital treatment was provided for all injuries and diseases, whether or not of service origin. Indigent and disabled veterans of the Civil War, Indian Wars, Spanish-American War, and Mexican Border period as well as discharged regular members of the Armed Forces were cared for at these homes.

In 1917, Congress was faced with the burden of ensuring proper care for all of the young men who enlisted as a result of the United States' entry into World War I. After much thought some of the new programs authorized for America's veterans included disability compensation, insurance for both those on active duty as well as veterans, and vocational rehabilitation for the disabled.

By the 1920s, the various benefits available to this country's veterans were administered by three different Federal agencies: the Veterans Bureau, the Bureau of Pensions of the Interior Department, and the National Home for Disabled Volunteer Soldiers. The requirement to work with all three federal agencies in order to receive the available benefits caused a great deal of confusion and red tape for the veteran and raised a number of questions regarding the need for a central agency.

To remedy this situation, the establishment of what became known as the Veterans Administration came in 1930 when Congress authorized the President to "consolidate and coordinate Government activities affecting war veterans." The three component agencies became bureaus within the Veterans Administration. Brigadier General Frank T. Hines, who directed the Veterans Bureau for seven years, was named as the first Administrator of Veterans Affairs, a job he held until 1945.

The VA health care system has grown from 54 hospitals in 1930, to include 171 medical centers; more than 350 outpatient, community, and outreach clinics; 126 nursing home care units; and 35 domiciliaries. VA health care facilities provide a broad spectrum of medical, surgical, and rehabilitative care. The responsibilities and benefits programs of the Veterans Administration grew enormously during the following six decades.

World War II resulted in not only a vast increase in the veteran population, but also in large number of new benefits enacted by the Congress for veterans of the war. The World War II GI Bill, signed into law on June 22, 1944, is said to have had more impact on the American way of life than any law since the Homestead Act more than a century ago. Further educational assistance acts were passed for the benefit of veterans of the Korean Conflict, the Vietnam Era, Persian Gulf War, and the All-Volunteer Force.

In 1973, the Veterans Administration assumed another major responsibility when the National Cemetery System (except for Arlington National Cemetery) was transferred to the Veterans Administration from the Department of the Army. The Agency was charged with the operation of the National Cemetery System, including the marking of graves of all persons in national and State cemeteries (and the graves of veterans in private cemeteries, upon request) as well and administering the State Cemetery Grants Program.

The Department of Veterans Affairs (VA) was established as a Cabinet-level position on March 15, 1989. President Bush hailed the creation of the new Department saying, "There is only one place for the veterans of America, in the Cabinet Room, at the table with the President of the United States of America."

This is nice sounding talk, but unfortunately, the system is not operated by the President, but by faceless paper pushers who feel that they are accountable to no one. The higher profile of the agency and the additional funding that came as a result only allowed the faceless ones to increase their ranks and burrow deeper into the marrow of the system.

A Smooth Transition

As I referenced earlier, the best soldier sometimes makes the worst veteran. This is primarily because the best soldier is one that skips various steps that would help him or her make a smooth transition into life as a veteran in order to continue to perform his or her job duties. The soldier who is eager to take off the uniform for the last time, on the other hand, normally spends a great deal of time finding out what steps to take in order to maximize the benefits available as a result of having served in the military. The goal of this book is to make the reader who happens to be a good soldier, also a good veteran.

In order to have a smooth transition from active duty to the VA system, there are a number of things that the active duty soldier **must** accomplish prior to leaving the service. Failure to accomplish these steps will have very long reaching affects that can sometimes be very detrimental to the individual receiving all veterans' benefits to which he or she is entitled. For this reason, Part Two will deal with **Active Duty Musts**. It should be clearly understood that there is no going back and correcting an oversight once the soldier has left active duty and entered the VA system.

To give a very clear example of what can happen if these things are not accomplished, when I left the military, it was known that there was some type of problem with my knees and back, but the military medical personnel were not sure what the problem might be. As I out processed, I was on crutches the entire time. I kept asking for the Orthopedist to examine my left knee, but he was too busy to take the time to do this, he merely extended the profile he had previously issued.

During my separation physical the examining physician refused to annotate on the out processing physical that I was on crutches since this was not, in his opinion, a permanent problem. I had been out of the service for less than two weeks when a civilian orthopedist[2] properly diagnosed my knee and back

---

[2] This orthopedist was a nationally known sports medicine expert who was well familiar with such problems as I was suffering.

problems. When this information was communicated to the Reserve Component that I was now a part of, it was determined that I should be returned to active duty temporarily to have the military address the issues.

The Orthopedist that had been treating me on active duty confirmed the diagnosis once he read he new medical reports and stated that had he known the correct diagnosis, that the conditions that I actually had should have resulted in my being placed on the Temporary Disability Retired List[3] rather than being allowed to ETS. He told me that it was still possible to get this done, but for this to have happened, the medical authorities at Martin Army Community Hospital at Fort Benning, Georgia would have to admit that they had made a mistake.

It should not surprise anyone to know that the Hospital Command refused to admit that an error in diagnosis had been made and told me that I was out so I could get screwed as far as they were concerned. I should go to the VA.

I had legal recourse at that point in time, but I was not aware of it and those I went to within the military system either were not aware of the avenues open to me or had a vested interest in lying to me. This included the Inspector General at the Martin Army Hospital. He very openly lied, both to me and to his own superiors (so as to not make the Army look bad), and it was later found that he had made others change their stories to support his personal beliefs. Of course, the Army failed to do anything about it.

I lost very valuable benefits since I did not know the system. Now I do know the system and you should too.

---

[3] This will be discussed in a later chapter.

PART TWO

ACTIVE DUTY MUSTS

CHAPTER THREE

OUT PROCESSING MUSTS

The steps that are taken during the out processing periods as you leave each duty stations and when you finally leave the service for the last time are so important to the smooth in-processing into the Department of Veterans Affairs system that I am going to take things somewhat out of order so that I can cover these issues early in the outline of this book. Many of the steps that I will outline apply to both those simply leaving the service as well as those retiring from the service. There are certain important distinctions, but I will cover them in some detail.

In-and Out-Processing:

Department of Defense (DOD) Regulations requires that all Active Duty personnel attend both In- and Out-processing programs and that these programs include information on TRICARE[4] benefits. As the active duty individual moves between installations, there is an out processing requirement at the old duty stations and an in processing requirement at the new duty station. Most of the in processing programs include such information as how to access health care at the military treatment facility (MTF) and in the community and how to resolve problems accessing health care.

In addition, at most installations the In- and Out-processing checklists include stops at the TRICARE Service Center. The old region will cover you for urgent and emergency care until you enroll at the new region, or for up to thirty days from the day you out-process from your old location, whichever comes first. You should not dis-enroll from your old region when you out process. When you transfer your enrollment to your new duty location, you will be automatically dis-enrolled from your old location.

---

[4] TRICARE is the Active Duty and Retired Medical Coverage Program.

TRICARE

Enrollment in TRICARE Prime includes completion of an enrollment form, assignment of a PCM and enrollment in the Defense Enrollment Eligibility Reporting System (DEERS). All beneficiaries, including Active Duty (all Active Duty are required to enroll in TRICARE Prime, family members may choose their health plan option), must complete an enrollment form in order to be in TRICARE Prime. You have up to 30 days from your out-processing date to enroll in your new location in order to continue your family members' TRICARE Prime coverage.

Medical Record Control:

Your medical records jacket should contain a complete picture of your health status from the day you entered the military. One of your jobs as you go through the process necessary to leave a former duty station is for you to get your medical records from your PCM team or central records at the Post Hospital and take it to your final out-processing appointment.

While the record is in your possession, check it to make sure that every illness or injury that occurred at the duty station you are leaving is documented thoroughly. Sometimes if an injury is treated in the field by the unit medic, the report will fail to make its way to your medical record. This can have very negative effects on your request for benefits as you get older and all of the injuries that happened while on active duty begin to take their toll.

You might also copy the medical record so that you now have one in your possession. Make it a point to keep it updated as you make visits to the medical facilities. This way you can determine if any medical reports are missing from your official record. It is the military medical record that will be used by the VA to determine your eligibility for benefits.

It is regulation for officers and senior NCOs to carry their medical records to their next duty stations and the records are normally sent to the next duty station for enlisted. However, no matter what your status is, make sure that you have a copy of that record in your possession at all times. It can be a lifesaver.

Scheduling appointments while in transit to your new base:

As you travel from your old duty station to the new duty station, situations may arise where you, or your dependents, need medical care. Only seek care for acute problems or emergencies, as routine care is not covered by TRICARE. You will have to pay for such non-emergency appointments. However, even if the appointment is considered non-emergency and you must pay, make sure that you have a copy of any medical reports resulting from these appointments in your possession and insist that such reports be placed in your military medical file.

While the treatment came from a non-military facility, the injury or illness that required the treatment still happened on active duty and as such may have a bearing on your VA benefits.

From a practical standpoint, if at all possible use a military facility if available. As a Prime enrollee you have priority at any military treatment facility in any region. However, make sure that a copy of any medical reports generated from any such visits makes it way to your military medical file.

If there are no military facilities available to you, then you may use a civilian provider but must call your PCM or Health Net 1-877-874-2273 for authorization. Follow all instructions to ensure claim is paid if the matter is covered.

Claims While in Transit:

If you are seen by a TRICARE network provider (authorized per above), they will submit a claim for payment to Health Net. If you are seen by a non-network provider (but approved by TRICARE) you may be asked to pay the bill in full at the time of treatment. You can then submit a claim for reimbursement. If you are seen by a non-network provider (who is not approved by TRICARE) you are responsible for payment in full.

Submit all claims to:

Health Net Federal Services, Inc.
c/o PGBA, LLC/TRICARE
P.O. Box 870141
Surfside Beach, SC 29587-9741

Always Get Authorization

Avoid Point of Service charges: Prime enrollees are charged a Point of Service fee ($300/$600 deductible, 50% of billed charges) if they receive care from a civilian provider without getting prior authorization.

Prescription Options While In Transit:

Situations may arise where you need prescriptions filled while in transit. If there is a Military Treatment Facility nearby, these prescriptions can be filled free of charge if the medication is on the formulary

Network Pharmacy: Call the local managed care support contractor for a listing of network pharmacies (Giant, CVS, Eckert, etc) in that area. You must show your TRICARE or military ID card. Prime enrollees pay for the medicine up front and submit the claim to TRICARE Region 1 for reimbursement.

National Mail Order: Order ahead for a 90-day supply of maintenance medications. Prime pays $3/$9. Forms available at your local TRICARE Service Center

Locating a TRICARE Service Center/MTF at new assignment:

Contact the local Managed Care Support Contractor to locate a military facility, network provider or pharmacy in your new region.
TRICARE North: 1-877-874-TRICARE (2273)
TRICARE South: 1-800-444-5445
TRICARE West: 1-888-west

Dis-enrolling from your current PCM:

When you enroll at your next facility you will automatically be dis-enrolled from your PCM. If you move to an area that has no military bases, then you will be dis-enrolled before leaving.

WHETHER YOU ARE TREATED IN THE MILITARY OR BY A CIVILIAN MEDICAL FACILITY, GET A COPY OF ALL RECORDS GENERATED BY THE VISIT AND MAKE SURE COPIES GET INCLUDED IN BOTH YOUR PERMANENT MEDICAL RECORD AND YOUR PERSONAL COPY OF YOUR MEDICAL RECORD.

CHAPTER FOUR

WHEN YOU OUTPROCESS FOR THE LAST TIME

ETS Out-processing

The military, in its infinite wisdom has a formalized process for everything. While the time that these programs may require seems excessive, they are extremely important to your future ability to obtain benefits from the VA and other federal agencies. For this reason, no matter how useless the briefing about future medical care may seem when you are 22 years old and in perfect health, go to the briefings. You have no idea what the future will bring as a result of medical problems that do not bother you now but may be severe problems in the future.

TIMELINE

The Army has a program for those leaving the service that is called the Army Career and Alumni Program (ACAP). Participation in this program is mandatory. The ACAP process consists of:

- Pre-Separation Benefits Briefing (mandatory) that is held at least 90 days prior to start of terminal leave or ETS.

- ETS Transition Briefing (mandatory) that is held at least 90 days prior to separation.

- Schedule Separation Physical (or obtain a waiver[5]) from CTMC (mandatory) between 30 and 120 days before start of terminal leave or ETS.

---

[5] More on this later.

- Determine if you are taking terminal leave and/or permissive TDY. Complete a DA31 and turn it in to your unit for approval.

- After unit approval, the Soldier must bring a copy of the DA31 to the Transition Point at least 45 days before start of the leave/PTDY.

- Determine if eligible for extended medical benefits and/or separation pay.

- Ask a Transition Point employee when your orders should be ready.

- The Soldier must personally pick up the orders from the ETS section in the Transition Point and schedules Initial Interview Appointment.

- Go to Transportation to arrange for furniture pick up or a do it yourself (DITY) move.

- Go to Housing if you live in government quarters and schedule a date for quarters termination. If you decide to hire a cleaning team, make arrangements at Housing.

- Get TA-50 cleaned at Quartermaster Laundry to get it ready for turn in to CIF.

- Pick up clearing papers 10-12 working days before start of terminal leave or PTDY.
  - Be in Duty Uniform
  - Bring four copies of your orders
  - Bring four copies of your DA31.

- Go to your CTMC or the Post Hospital (where your medical records are kept) and request to have a copy of your medical records made.

- Begin clearing the installation and your unit.

- Attend your Initial Interview Appointment at the Transition Center.
  - Be in Duty Uniform
  - Bring clearing papers, your DA31, and your orders
  - Bring documentation of awards or schools that are not on your ERB or 2-1

- Finish clearing the installation and your unit.

- Clear Finance and Travel on the day of Final Out.

- Clear Central Clearing Agency (CCA) on day of Final Out. They will verify you have cleared all agencies on both clearance forms before signing off.
  - Be in Duty Uniform
  - Bring Installation and Unit Clearance Forms
  - Bring CIF turn-in verification
  - Bring Quarters Termination verification

- Attend Final Out Appointment in Transition Center.
  - Be in Duty Uniform
  - Bring ACAP Pre-Separation Checklist, DD-Form 2648
  - Bring completed Installation Clearance Form stamped by CCA.
  - Bring completed Unit Clearance Form stamped by CCA.

* Bring VA claim form and physical (or waiver[6])

Sign out at Unit

FINAL OUT APPOINTMENT

Before leaving the Transition Center, you should have:

Verified the real DD-214 and signed all 8 copies.
- If not taking leave, you will be given the #1 and #4 copies of your DD-214.
- If taking leave or PTDY you will sign for the #4 copy and the #1 copy will be mailed to you the first working day after your ETS.

Received instructions about your ID cards.
- If not taking leave, you will turn in your ID card and the ID cards of your family members.
- If taking leave or PTDY, you will be given an envelope to mail all ID cards back to your final duty station.

Received a discharge certificate, if your reserve obligation has been completed. If you have not completed your reserve obligation, St. Louis will mail it to you upon its completion.

---

[6] This VA claim form in one of the most important documents that you will ever fill out. This claim form is the beginning of your entry into the VA system.

Received paperwork for a Reserve ID Card if you have an obligation to join a Reserve or Guard unit.

Received Transition Assistance ID cards for you and your family members, if eligible.

Received an information sheet on Safeguarding your DD-214.

Received a memo with a copy of your orders, DA-31, and stamped clearing papers stapled to it. Bring the memo, with attachments, to your unit to sign out of your final duty station.

Re-enter the civilian world.

REMEMBER: THIS IS THE LAST TIME YOU WILL HAVE ANY SORT OF CONTROL OVER YOUR MILITARY MEDICAL RECORDS. MAKE SURE THAT THEY ARE COMPLETE AND THAT YOU HAVE A COPY. THESE RECORDS AND YOUR DD 214 ARE YOUR KEY TO YOUR VA BENEFITS.

CHAPTER FIVE

THE ARMY CAREER AND ALUMNI PROGRAM (ACAP)

The Army Career and Alumni Program (ACAP), which is required by law, explains benefits and entitlements available to former soldiers upon separation from the US Army. The ACAP briefing can be scheduled one year before ETS, two years before retirement, or prior to deployment if the Soldier is affected by a Stop-Loss policy.

It is best to complete the ACAP process, which includes the ACAP briefing, resume' assistance and help in searching for employment, 90 days prior to separation. Soldiers schedule their Pre-Separation Briefing at the ACAP Center.

This program is considered so important to successful re-integration into civilian life that soldiers appearing for Final Out at the Transition Point or Retirement Services cannot be cleared unless they bring DD Form 2648, the Pre-Separation Counseling Checklist showing they received the ACAP Pre-Separation Briefing.

This is the basic information given to the soldier about a mandatory briefing that they must go through in order to get out of the service. But is it important, or just another program that someone at the Department of Defense thought would be good for the soldiers or is it really beneficial? This may come as a surprise, but it is actually a good thing.

INDIVIDUAL TRANSITION PLAN

The return to civilian life is, after all, your transition. Without a plan, you can quickly lose control of the process. Just as it took you some time to adjust to being in the military, the return to civilian life can also cause some severe disruptions in your life. As a result, the Military determined that a soldier making this transition needs their own individual transition plan.

Returning to civilian life is a complex undertaking. Many steps must be taken, and many questions must be answered. Transition assistance staff, personnel office staff, relocation specialists, education counselors, and many others can help, but only you and your family can make the critical decisions that must be made. A good beginning is for each departing Service member to develop an Individual Transition Plan (ITP).

The ITP is your game plan for a successful transition back to civilian life. It is a framework you can use to fulfill realistic career goals based upon your unique skills, knowledge, experience, and abilities. It is not a Department of Defense form. It is something you create by yourself, for yourself.

The ITP identifies likely actions and activities associated with your transition. You can determine what these might be through consultation with your Transition Counselor and using a document called the Pre-separation Counseling Checklist, DD Form 2648 (to access and download the form, go to: http://web1.whs.osd.mil/forms/DD2648.PDF). This Pre-separation Guide will help you work through the nine headings listed on the Pre-separation Counseling Checklist. The checklist allows you to indicate the benefits and services about which you wish to receive additional counseling as you prepare your ITP. You will then be referred to subject experts who will gladly answer any questions you may have. Work through each element on the checklist, but select for further exploration only those resources that are appropriate for you.

Some Terminology and Notes on Your New Status

Congress originally granted different separation benefits for three sets of separatees:-

- Eligible Involuntary Military Separation,

- Special Separation Benefit (SSB), and

- Voluntary Separation Incentive (VSI) separatees.

However, the original benefit package for each type of separation was changed in FY 1993, when Congress passed legislation that equalized the benefits among all three groups. This legislation is retroactive; therefore Eligible Involuntary, all SSB, and all VSI separatees now get the same benefits, regardless of their separation date. Retirees continue to receive special benefits that reflect their additional years of service.

It is also helpful to understand the difference between "discharge" and "separation" and the difference between "transition benefits" vs. "transition services":

Discharge: Complete severance from all military status gained by the enlistment or induction concerned.

Separation: A general term that includes discharge, release from active duty, release from custody and control of the Armed Forces, transfer to the Individual Ready Reserve, and similar changes in active or reserve status.

Transition Benefits: Certain involuntarily separated members are eligible for transition benefits. Eligibility for transition benefits depends on the nature and characterization of a member's discharge.

Transition Services: All separating members within 180 days of separation or retirement are eligible for transition services. Eligibility for services is not affected by length or character or service.

If you are uncertain about your future plans, now is the time to obtain all the assistance and information you need. Professional guidance and counseling are available at your Transition Office as are workshops, publications, information resources, automated resources, and government programs. Take advantage of each one that pertains to your unique situation. It is your Individual Transition Plan: It is your responsibility and your life.

Pre-separation Counseling: Your Best Beginning

Some people say that military life isn't easy. Leaving the military isn't easy either. As you separate from military service, you must make numerous decisions, follow many procedures, and fill out a variety of forms-all to help make sure your transition is a smooth one.

Your first step in the separation process is to go to your installation's Transition Office. Each Service has its own way of doing things; so too with the Transition Offices. In most cases, you will find the Transition Office located inside your installation's Family Center:

• Army: Army Career and Alumni Program Center

• Air Force: Family Support Center

• Navy: Fleet and Family Support Center (Navy personnel should make an appointment with their Command Career Counselor for a pre-separation counseling interview at least 180 days prior to separation)

• Marines: Career Resource Management Center (CRMC)/Transition & Employment Assistance Program Center.

Step 1. Schedule Your Pre-separation Counseling Appointment

Your pre-separation process needs to begin as soon as possible. Schedule your pre-separation counseling appointment at least 180 days prior to your separation at your installation Transition Office. It takes time to prepare for an effective transition. Public Law 101-510 requires pre-separation counseling (completion of DD Form 2648) to occur no later than 90 days prior to separation; therefore, if you have not had an appointment within 90 days of separation, call the Transition Office or your Navy Command Career Counselor and schedule a visit immediately. However, it is strongly recommended that you set up your pre-separation counseling appointment at least 180 days prior to separation.

At this meeting, the Transition Office will:

- Assist you in developing an individual needs assessment.

- Identify helpful relocation resources.

- Offer immediate and long-range career guidance.

- Provide benefits counseling.

- Refer you to other service providers for any additional assistance you may require.

Step 2. Review the Pre-separation Counseling Checklist

Your Transition Counselor will walk you through the Pre-separation Counseling Checklist which is one of the most helpful documents you will be asked to complete. It helps ensure that you will receive the necessary assistance and advice to benefit fully from the wide range of services and entitlements available to you. The checklist is required by law to be filed in your personnel record.

Step 3. Draft Your Individual Transition Plan

You have several options on how to develop your ITP. Information on how to do so is available through the Transition Office. You may choose to use your Pre-separation Counseling Checklist as the basis for developing your own unique ITP.

Once you have created your ITP, show it to your Transition Counselor. The counselor will refer you to the appropriate subject expert or enroll you in the most helpful pre-separation programs. Maximum participation in this process by you and your spouse is encouraged. Use the Transition Assistance Program Eligibility chart along with individual counseling to assist you in determining what resources are available to you and your family.

Many professionals in the personnel industry have published guides on career change. These show that everyone undergoing a career transition seems to go through the same seven fundamental stages.

Phase One: <u>Assessment</u>

Who am I? What talents and experiences do I possess? Why would someone want to hire me?

In this phase, document your portfolio of knowledge, experience, skills, talents, and abilities. For starters, create a list using your personal Verification of Military Experience and Training (VMET) document, DD Form 2586. This document is available to you online at http://www.dmdc.osd.mil/vmet. Contact your supporting Transition Office for assistance if you are unable to access the VMET On-Line Web site. Your VMET outlines the training and experience you received during your military career. It is designed to help you, but it is not a resume. Add anything else you can think of to this list. In essence, you are now creating an "asset bank" from which you can draw later when called upon to write a resume or attend a job interview. If you need help, use the professional guidance available through your local installation Transition Office or Education Center. Or refer to the self-help section of your local library or bookstore for useful career planning books.

The investment you make now in conducting your assessment is very valuable. It will bring the "professional you" into clearer focus, and it will have a major impact in making and implementing your career decisions.

Phase Two: <u>Exploration</u>

What are the current and emerging occupational areas that are attractive to me? Do these jobs coincide with my values and aptitudes? How do I find such jobs?

With your assessment in hand, you probably have some ideas about what you want to do. Now is not the time to limit your opportunities. Expand the list of job titles and career paths that appeal to you. Broaden your geographic horizons to include several places where you might like to pursue your career. Many resources are available to help you explore your expanded set of options. Do your homework.

The Transition Office can help you focus on jobs that employers need to fill today and will need to fill in the near future. Transition staff can help you identify the geographic areas that have opportunities in your fields of interest.

Your state employment office is another good resource during this phase, offering such services as job interviewing; selection and referral to openings; job development; employment counseling; career evaluation; referral to training or other support services; and testing. It can lead you to information on related jobs nearby and can introduce you to the Department of Labor database, DOD Job Search which has listings of thousands of jobs across the nation.

Many other assets are available; your Transition Office can tell you about them. Use the library too; the Reference Section has helpful publications.

Phase Three: Skills Development

How do I prepare myself to be an attractive candidate in the occupational areas that I have chosen? Do I need additional education or training?

As you continue through the exploration phase, you may find some interesting opportunities for which you feel only partially equipped. Your local Transition Office and Education Center can help you determine the academic credentials or vocational training programs you will need and how to acquire them.

The Sailor/Marine American Council on Education Registry Transcript (SMART) document is also available at https://www.navycollege.navy.mil. This document can help you identify our current academic credits and assist you with continuing your education.

Phase Four: Trial Career Programs

Do I have the aptitude and experience needed to pursue my occupational interests? Are there internships, volunteer jobs, temporary services, or part-time jobs where I might try out the work that interests me?

To learn about intern programs, inquire at your Transition Office your local civilian personnel office, or the state employment office. Some government-sponsored programs, such as obtaining teaching credentials, can provide income and training in exchange for guaranteed employment. Check local and base libraries and the education office for books containing intern program information. Temporary agencies are also a great way to become familiar with a company or industry. Explore internship possibilities with private employers: Many companies have such programs but do not advertise them. Don't necessarily turn down an interesting volunteer position. Volunteering increases your professional skills and can sometimes turn into a paid position.

Phase Five: *The Job Search*

How do I identify job requirements and prospective companies, find networks and placement agencies, and generally increase my knowledge and experience in the job market? How do I write a resume, develop leads, conduct an interview, and complete a job application?

Once you have selected your future career, you must now begin the challenge of finding work. Millions of people are hired all across the country every year. Employee turnover opens up existing positions, and entirely new jobs are created every day. Nevertheless, the job market is competitive. The best way to improve your odds is to play your best hand: Seek the opportunities for which you are best prepared.

Work hard at finding a job. Network! The vast majority of jobs are filled by referrals, not the want ads. Use your network of friends, colleagues, and family; as well as the job listings provided by your installation's Transition Office, the local personnel office, or even the nearest community college. Take advantage of job-hunting seminars, resume-writing workshops, and interviewing techniques classes too. Attend job fairs and talk to as many company representatives as possible.

Phase Six: <u>Selection</u>

How do I select the right job?

Although it might be tempting, you don't have to take the first job that comes along. Consider the type of work, location, salary and benefits, climate, and how the opportunity will enhance your future career growth. Even if you take the first job offer, you are not necessarily locked into it. Some experts say employers are biased against hiring the unemployed. A shrewd move might be to look for a job from a job. Take a suitable position-and then quickly move on to a better one.

Phase Seven: <u>Support</u>

How do I make a smooth transition to a new career?

For your transition to be truly successful, you should manage the personal affairs side of your career change with the same professionalism and care as your job search. Things like out-processing, relocation, financial management, taking care of your family, and coping with the inevitable stress are important too. Your ITP provides an opportunity to integrate these issues with the career-oriented activities that are the central focus of your transition effort.

Think of your transition as a journey. The Individual Transition Plan is your map. Use it to chart your course and set your destination. You choose the best route; select the landmarks that will be important to you. This document, the Pre-separation Guide, serves as your guidebook, offering insight and information as you travel along your route. Use the Transition Office as a trusty compass to guide you in the right direction. Throughout your journey, you remain in charge of where you are going and how you will get there.

You have been in the military for a number of years, and you are now making the transition back to civilian life. Understanding stress and coping with it are essential skills you will need to get through this difficult time.

A. Leaving the Military Challenges Your Identity

You have worked hard to become Sergeant Smith, Petty Officer Lee, or Captain Jones. When asked what you do, you have often replied, "I'm in the Army (Air Force, Navy, or Marines)." And everybody around you knew what you meant. Now you must start over as a civilian. Now you are just plain Bob, John or Alice. The identity that was your assurance of acceptance is now gone.

Changing careers is a stressful undertaking, perhaps even more so for those leaving military service after many years. For example, a doctor goes to school for eight years and carries the title for the rest of his or her life. A Service member, however, may have worked for 30 years to achieve a rank or grade, but upon leaving the Armed Forces, he or she leaves this rank behind-and with it, a large portion of his or her identity.

Some people easily find new identities; others may never find them. And still others may feel that they will never find them. Transition is traumatic and stressful, but it also opens up a whole range of possibilities. If you approach your transition as an opportunity to grow, you will have already taken a giant step toward reestablishing your identity.

B. What Is Stress?

Everybody knows what stress feels like. But what is it really? The experts tell us that stress is a real state of being. It is not an attitude; it is not a sign of being unable to handle things. Stress is a physical response, which, if left unchecked, can lead to mental and physical exhaustion and illness.

Natural stress in our lives is considered good. It allows our bodies to respond to danger. You know the expression, "Fight or flight." Unnatural stress comes from continued threats or dangers over which we have no control. The body is alert for long periods of time with no chance to relax. It is important to remember that the body, like any good machine, begins to wear out if it runs in high gear for too long.

In his book, *Winning Life's Toughest Battles*, Dr. Julius Segal outlines three broad categories of very stressful events. These are:

• Events that lead to the loss of a special relationship, such as divorce

• Events you cannot control that make you feel helpless, such as an accident

• Events with lasting consequences, such as a terminal illness or the loss of your job

Transitioning from the military often has aspects of all three categories. In a sense, you lose many special relationships by losing the daily interaction with your co-workers. If you are not choosing to leave the military on your own, you may feel that you are helpless and that the situation is beyond your control. Transition, obviously, has permanent consequences. When you lose your job, by choice or not, your entire life changes in many ways. Clearly, leaving the military for civilian life can be one of the most stressful events you will ever face.

The Stress-Health Connection

It is important to look for signs of stress overload. Some symptoms of stress overload include:

• Constant fatigue

• Headaches

• Trouble sleeping or sleeping too much

• Stomach problems

• More frequent colds or other illnesses

• Smoking or drinking more than usual

• Feeling nervous

• Being irritable or angrier than you want to be

• Desire to be alone, away from other people

• Inability to eat or eating more than usual

If you are suffering from some of these symptoms, it is likely they are stress related. You may want to consider professional assistance.

Stress can also cause other more serious medical problems that may well be considered service connected. These medical problems must be documented by medical professionals in order to bring them under the purview of the VA.

The "Grieving Process" Is Normal

Research has shown that most people go through major life changes in stages. These stages are present in a wide variety of major life traumas:

• Denial: "This is not really happening," or "This is not happening to me."

• Anger: Directed either at yourself or at others.

• Depression: Often accompanied by a sense of helplessness.

• Acceptance: This is the turning point, when you begin to accept the situation as it is.

• Resolution: Begin to take the steps necessary to return to a normal state.

Proceeding through each step is normal, and the process cannot be rushed. Often however, people may progress out of a stage and then drop back into it. If uncontrolled, the bouncing back and forth between stages can continue for a long time. As you make your transition to civilian life, look for these stages in yourself and acknowledge your movements from one step to the next.

Coping With Transition-Related Stress

The experiences of thousands of Service members who have recently separated suggest that this transition is likely to be stressful for you and your family. Previous transitioners have found several tactics extremely important in dealing with the stress related to separation from the military:

• **Get going**: It is your transition; no one can do it for you. Work through the grieving process and do not procrastinate. Put your situation in perspective and get on with your life. After all, you are not the first person to go through transition, and you will not be the last. You'll do okay too.

• **Sell yourself**: Sell yourself: You have a great product-YOU! So sell yourself! Now is not the time to be modest about your accomplishments. No one will come looking for you unless they know you are available. Once you let them know, you will find many people who will help you.

• **Work at it**: Work at planning your transition as if it were a job. However, if you spend every waking hour working on it, you will burn out. Take time for yourself and your family.

• **Lighten up**: This is probably the most important piece of advice. Do not lose your sense of humor. An upbeat disposition will see you through.

• **Keep your family involved**: Your family has a large stake in your transition. They are experiencing many of the same feelings, worries, and uncertainties as you are. Do not keep your plans to yourself; get your family involved in this process. Let them in on your plans and ask for their input throughout the process. It's their life too.

• **Volunteer**: Consider doing volunteer work. Your charitable actions will help others and assist you in getting to know the community beyond the military installations and enhance your networking.

• **Take a change management course**: Consider taking a change management course before stress appears, or at the first signs of stress.

A smooth and painless re-entry into the civilian world is as important to your health and well being. Like anything else, this takes preparation and consideration. Do not rush through it, but take your time and do it right.

CHAPTER SIX

THE SEPARATION PHYSICAL

A separation physical is not mandatory (except for retirees), but it is highly recommended. This separation physical is the last opportunity that you as a soldier will have to make sure that your medical history from your military service is complete. You must also make sure that the medical history section of the physical exam form includes information on every injury and illness that happened to you during your military career. If an injury or illness is not listed and addressed by the physician conducting the separation physical exam, then the VA will be hesitant to grant service connection for the problem. They will take the position that since it wasn't addressed during the separation physical that it was not a problem.

As an example, during my separation physical, the physician failed to mention that I was on a medical profile and walking with the aide of crutches. He also misdiagnosed the problems with my knees and back as being a very minor condition. As a result, the VA used the physical exam to deny me service connected benefits for several conditions for a number of years.

WHEN IS A DOCTOR NOT A DOCTOR?

Once I discovered how important the separation physical was to my future benefits and that the physical that I had undergone was less than adequate, I began to research the qualifications of the physician that had conducted the physical. I discovered that he was from Romania, brought to this country under Operation Paperclip[7] at the end of World War II and that he had probably never

---

[7] This program was created by the CIA to allow the Agency to bring people into this country who had information about the Russian military. Werner Von Braun was also

completed medical school. He had been a medical corpsman with the German Army during World War II and been captured by the Russians. He had spent a number of years treating captured German General Officers before being released from a Russian POW Camp. He was then brought to this country under the auspices of the Central Intelligence Agency in return for his vast knowledge regarding the Russian military.

I also discovered that he had been thrown out of every hospital he had ever been associated with due to his lack of competence in his own medical specialty. A Federal Court had found that he had been properly excluded from a hospital due to his lack of expertise. In spite of all of these problems, the Army hired him as an Eye, Ear, Nose and Throat Specialist, but after a number of problems, assigned him to do physicals.

I took this information to the VA in order to overcome the damage caused by the slipshod physical. However, to my surprise, the VA refused to even consider this information, claiming that a physical was a physical and that any doctor could properly perform a physical. I then went to the Army Department of Medicine in Washington DC to ask the military address the lack of qualifications of this particular military physician. To my shock, I was told that until the mid-1980s, there was no requirement that an individual even be a physician in order to practice medicine in the Army. All it required for anyone to practice medicine in the military was certification from the Chief of Military Medicine that the individual in question was competent to practice medicine. I was told that the military could even certify me to practice medicine and it would be legal. I still have periodic problems with the VA over this physical exam, all caused by this man's incompetence.

DEMAND THAT YOUR PHYSICAL EXAM BE THOROUGH AND COMPLETE – MAKE SURE THAT YOU HAVE THE PHYSICIAN'S NAME.

POINTS OFF FOR SPELLING

As petty as it sounds, many times the VA rating personnel demonstrate a talent for being literal that defies logic. As a case in point, I was hospitalized for several days while on active duty with a rather rare problem[8] called Tietze's Syndrome. This condition is caused by a viral infection that I contracted while serving on active duty in South America and it is permanent.

The first time the condition flared up, I was taken to a military hospital with what was diagnosed as appendicitis. Luckily, the surgeon was somewhat

---

brought into this country under Operation Paperclip. As part of the acclimation process, the individual was allowed to choose their own career.

[8] This condition is rare in the United States, but it is seen often in other countries. Tietze was the name of the German physician who first studied this viral infection.

familiar with the condition and correctly determined that I was not having an attack of appendicitis. However, though the surgeon was familiar with the condition, his spelling left something to be desired. In my medical records, he spelled the condition as TseTse's[9] Syndrome. For a number of years the VA refused to grant service connection for this problem since I had not been assigned to Africa and clearly did not have sleeping sickness.

Now this was a silly position for the VA to take as my hospitalization for this condition was thoroughly documented in my military medical records. It was also clear from my medical records that I contracted this infection while serving on active duty. However, the VA rater would not budge from the initial determination that I could not be service connected for sleeping sickness since I had never served in Africa.

Tiring of this silliness, I finally had to do a fully blown legal brief, supported by medical articles discussing the condition known as Tietze's Syndrome as part of my appeal and instruct the VA on exactly what this condition was and the normal after affects suffered by someone who had contracted this ailment. Even then, the granting of service connection was done very begrudgingly and I was given a zero rating.

Since that time I have spent a week in a local hospital for what was believed to be a heart attack. I was in such pain that I was given Nitro for my heart and morphine for the pain. After six days flat on my back and approximately $100,000.00 in medical tests[10] an older doctor that had spent a lot of time in Mexico and had seen cases of Tietze's Syndrome, walked into my room and told me to go home, I was fine.

Another Use for the Separation Physical

While a separation physical is not mandatory for most personnel, there are a number of indicators of how important the Army believes that this physical can be to the soldier. One of the clearest indicators of how important the separation physical is viewed is the requirement that soldiers who elect NOT to take a separation physical must obtain a waiver (Form 57, with attached DA form 2697) from CTMC. Both forms require signature by a physician's assistant or a physician. However, if you fail to take a separation physical you are trusting to luck that your medical record is complete and fully documents every health or medical problem you experienced while on active duty. It also assumes that you

---

[9] The TseTse fly is found generally in Africa and carries the dreaded sleeping sickness. For years, the VA has insisted that I do not have sleeping sickness. They are correct, but they have continued to miss the point.

[10] Even after all of these tests, the only thing that the medical staff was sure of was that I was not pregnant and they were only sure of this since I am a male. They were diligently looking for evidence of the heart attack that they knew that I had suffered.

will never again be bothered by problems that began on active duty and thus have no need to involve the VA in your future medical care.

This is not the time to be macho. If you had any medical or mental problems while in the service, make sure that you list them in the medical history section of the physical exam form. Bring them to the physician's attention. It will pay you dividends later.

Exams for separation physicals must be accomplished between 30 and 120 days prior to start of terminal leave (or ETS date, if no leave is taken). To schedule a physical, call CTMC.

When Soldiers appear for a separation physical they should bring a **_COMPLETE_** list of all medical conditions, illnesses, and injuries for which they were treated while on active duty. This would not be a requirement unless the military was aware that it was possible for some things not to be properly documented in the service medical record.

As I have said a number of times, it is very possible that reports on conditions for which you received treatment in the field may not have made their way to your medical file. Such oversights are especially common in combat zones. You can have your leg blown off on a landmine, but if there is not report in your medical file referencing this injury, as far as the VA is concerned, it did not happen.

I was once medivaced from a remote jungle location for heat stroke, however, due to the seriousness of my condition, instead of returning me to garrison for treatment, I was taken to the closest military medical facility, which was a lightly staffed medical clinic located at a very small military base in South America. I spent most of a day being treated before being released to return to my unit.

Though I am told I almost died in this incident, no report of this incident ever made it to my permanent medical file. The paperwork was lost somewhere between the small remote medical facility and my military medical records. Thus when I applied to the VA for benefits for residuals of Heat Stroke I found that I had no evidence in my military medical record that the event had even taken place. It took me a number of years to get service connection for residuals of heat injury.

If you are aware of such oversights or omissions, try and make sure that the physician conducting your separation physical makes note of the event, or condition so that there is at least some record in your file. In my case, the physician said that he would annotate my physical exam form with the fact that I had suffered heat stroke but he failed to do so.

A clerk at CTMC will tell you when your separation physical should be ready for you to pick up. The Soldier must personally pick up the physical at CTMC and bring it to the Transition Point for the Final Out appointment.

Soldiers appearing for Final Out at the Transition Point cannot be cleared unless they bring either a completed separation physical or a waiver (with DA form 2697) signed by a physician or physician's assistant.

A Word About Your Medical Records

A soldier's military medical record is the property of the US Government, not the Soldier. You will not be allowed to leave the final duty station with your original medical record. Whether you are retiring or leaving the service through separation, the original medical record will be forwarded to either the VA or the records center in St. Louis, MO for processing by the appropriate agency. It is very likely that you will never see your original military medical record again. Therefore, it is of primary importance that no matter what else may be happening that the soldier makes sure that he or she gets a complete copy of their medical record before they leave the final duty station.

At least ten working days before ETS (or ten days before starting terminal leave/permissive TDY), Soldiers who want a copy of their medical records must go to the TMC or hospital where their records are kept and request to have a copy made. Just prior to Final Out, the original health record is transported to the Transition Point for subsequent transfer to either the Personnel Records Center in St. Louis or a VA Hospital. Only the CTMC or hospital can copy medical records.

From a practical standpoint, if these original medical records are lost or destroyed, all evidence of your illnesses and injuries that occurred while on active duty are gone.

ALWAYS KEEP A COMPLETE COPY OF ALL MEDICAL RECORDS!

CHAPTER SEVEN

PERMISSIVE TDY

Certain soldiers are eligible for permissive TDY in conjunction with their terminal leave. However, this Permissive TDY (PTDY) is an authorization, not an entitlement. The commander does not have to approve PTDY if he or she determines that the soldier is needed for operational purposes. The Installation Commander or Activity Commander is the approving authority.

Even though you may be on the way out of the service, being on TDY means that you are still a member of the military. As a result, working at Civilian Employment while on PTDY is prohibited.

PTDY in conjunction with transition leave is only authorized for Soldiers not eligible to reenlist that meet certain criteria:

- Soldier is flagged and cannot reenlist due to PT failure or overweight

- Soldier has too much time for grade (RCP)

- Soldier has bar to reenlistment (see exceptions below)

Soldiers are not eligible for PTDY in conjunction with transition leave if:

- They are eligible for reenlistment

- They have declined an assignment and signed a DCSS statement

- They are barred for reenlistment for declining to attend PLDC or BNOC

- Separation is due to AWOL, Lost Time, or other adverse conditions

- Soldier has declined to go to a promotion board

If authorized for RCP, up to 20 days PTDY in conjunction with transition leave may be approved.

If authorized for reasons other than RCP, no more than 10 days PTDY in conjunction with transition leave may be approved.

If a Soldier signs a DCSS statement or is barred for declining PLDC, BNOC, etc., or a promotion board, even if flagged for other reasons, she/he is ineligible for PTDY in conjunction with Transition Leave. These are voluntary actions and DA has determined that they override all other reasons for transition.

Permissive TDY in conjunction with transition leave can only be authorized if a Soldier's individual circumstances meet criteria above.

How To Apply For Permissive TDY

Soldier completes a Request for Permissive TDY form and attaches it to a Leave Request form (DA-31).

Only one DA-31 is needed, and it is prepared as follows:
- Check the "PTDY" box and the "Other" block.
- "Terminal leave" is typed on the blank line.
- The amount of leave accrued through the Soldier's ETS date will be put in the "accrued leave" block.
- In the next block will be the amount of leave the Soldier plans to take.
- Leave can only be taken in whole days. Half days will be paid.
- The entire time-period will be entered in block 10 (begin day PTDY starts, include leave days, through ETS date).
- In the "Remarks" section, list what days are PTDY and what days are chargeable as leave.

One smart move, if you are granted permissive TDY is to immediately have a complete physical by a civilian physician. If something shows up during this physical, immediately report it to the military. Remember, you are still a member of the military even though you are on Permissive TDY. If you have a medical problem while on TDY make it a matter of record. It will pay dividends.

CHAPTER EIGHT

CLEARING THE INSTALLATION

One of the last things that a soldier must do before leaving the military is clear the installation. This is done through the execution of the Installation Clearance Record and Unit Clearance Record (DA Form 137-1). The forms can usually be picked up at the Installation Central Clearance Agency (CCA) ten (10) working days before start of transition leave or permissive TDY (PTDY) taken in conjunction with PCS, ETS, or retirement.

If no transition leave or TDY is taken, clearance records can be picked up ten working days prior to the actual PCS, ETS, or retirement date. Soldiers pending elimination receive clearance forms as soon as the elimination is initiated with the commander's memorandum to clear without published orders.

Soldiers pending PCS[11] will have two appointments at CCA. The Initial PCS appointment at CCA will be at 1300 five working days prior to departure. The Final PCS appointment at CCA will be a walk-in on the last working day before departure.

Soldiers become exempt from duty rosters and routine duties 10 working days prior to ETS, PCS, or retirement.

Clearing time for transfer from one unit to another on post is normally one duty day plus time required to turn in or be issued CTA-50 clothing and equipment, if required. This may be extended by the Commander in the case of Soldiers without privately owned vehicles that must use government transportation.

---

[11] Permanent change of station.

Soldiers will be required to report to one formation each day during the clearance period unless excused by proper authority. This allows the Commander/1SG to monitor the progress of soldiers' clearance.

Soldiers will be free to use time not required to clear military agencies to accomplish medical and administrative requirements, conclude personal affairs, and prepare for movement.

Only the unit commander or his/her representative can sign the Commander/1SGs signature on the Unit Clearance Record. When the unit commander is clearing the installation clearance records will be signed by his rater or rater's authorized Deputy/XO.

Officers in the grade of Colonel (06) and above may designate a representative to clear the installation for them. However, these officers must personally clear their family quarters or bachelor quarters (BOQ) and arrange for shipment of household goods.

All Soldiers must clear their hand receipts and/or property books prior to their final CCA appointment.

Soldiers transitioning from active duty must clear the Central Issue Facility within ten calendar days prior to their anticipated date of departure from the installation. Commanders will initiate a report of survey within five days of being notified that a soldier has failed to clear CIF.

Soldiers being administratively separated from the Army must complete installation clearance prior to reporting to the Transition Point for processing. CIF must be cleared as soon as possible after notification that a Soldier is being processed for administrative separation.

Soldiers conducting themselves improperly during out processing will be returned to their unit for corrective action.

Soldiers pending separation under certain Chapters will require an escort during out processing. Escorts will be of equal grade or higher (minimum E4) than the soldier being separated.

All soldiers are generally required to be in proper military uniform while clearing the Installation, to include final clearance at CCA.

After Soldiers clear CCA and the Transition Center or Retirement Services they must sign out through their unit before leaving the installation.

CHAPTER NINE

MILITARY SEPARATION CODES

Every organization has its own private language known only to those who are members in good standing. So to does the US Military have a way of letting others know many things about you that might be illegal if done openly, to include confidential medical information that would normally be considered to be covered by the Privacy Act. The meaning of these separation codes is also kept confidential, not even the soldier is made aware of what the codes mean that are placed on his documents.

The Military makes this information available to others through a series of Military Separation Codes that can be found in your military records. The soldier is given no explanation of these codes, but the information contained within may well be important. Not only are these codes contained in your military records but they may be annotated on various military separation documents. If the wrong code is placed on your separation documents it can have a serious effect on your future plans and in fact deny you VA benefits.

These codes are subject to change, and, more importantly, the Department of Defense will no longer allow the military services to release the meanings of these codes to either the soldier in question or the general public. Study your documents and know the meaning of everything that pertains to you or your military career. Failure to do this can come back to haunt you later. The below definitions were obtained before this prohibition went into effect.

B70 -   Death, Battle Casualty - Navy

B79 -   Death, Battle Casualty - Navy

BDK -   Security reason

BFS -   Good of the Service, conduct triable by court martial

BHJ -   Unsuitability (Reason Unknown)

BHK -   Unsuitability, substandard performance

BKC -   See BRA

BLC -   Homosexuality

BLF -   Drug use

BLM - Unfitness (Reason Unknown)

BML - Homosexuality

BMN - Unsuitability (Reason Unknown)

BNC -   Misconduct, Misconduct, moral or professional dereliction or in interests of national security

BRA -   Engaged or attempted to engage in, or solicited another to engage in homosexual act(s)

BRB -   See JRB, BKC

BRC -   See JRC, BKC

CBL -   Unsuitability (Reason Unknown)

DCH -   Early Release - To teach

DER -   Disability - Non EPTS - No Severance Pay

DFS -   Good of the Service, conduct triable by court martial

DLC -   Homosexuality

EKD -   AWOL, Desertion

ELPAC - Entry Level Performance & Conduct

FBC -   Other

FBK -   Expiration of Term of Service

FBL -   Expiration of Term of Service

FCM -   Conscientious Objector

FDF -   Pregnancy

FDG -   Parenthood

FDL -   See JDL

FFT -   Physical standards, no disability

FGM - To accept commission

FHC - In lieu of discharge

FHG - Serving under suspended sentence to dismissal

FKD - AWOL, Desertion

FND - Miscellaneous reasons (Unqualified resignation)

GDK - Security reason

GFN - Released for Conditions Existing Prior to Service

GFT - Unqualified for Active Duty - Other

GFV - Unqualified for Active Duty - Other

GHF - Other

GHJ - Unsuitability (Reason Unknown)

GHK - Unsuitability (Reason Unknown)

GJB - Court Martial

GKA - Discreditable Incidents - Civilian or Military

GKB - Civil Court conviction

GKC - Homosexuality

GKD - AWOL, Desertion

GKE - Financial Irresponsibility

GKG - Fraudulent Entry

GKH - Lack of Dependent Support

GKK - Drug use

GKL - Sexual Perversion

GKQ - No listing at this time.

It should be noted that all of those who receive the GK Series separation codes are generally seen as ineligible for re-enlistment.

GKS - AWOL, Desertion

GLB - Discreditable Incidents - Civilian or Military

GLC - Homosexuality

GLF - Drug use

GLG - Financial Irresponsibility

GLH -   Lack of Dependent Support

GLJ -   Shirking

GLK -   Unsanitary Habits

GLL -   Sexual Perversion

GMB - Character or Behavior Disorder

GMC - Enuresis

GMD - Inaptitude

GMF - Sexual Perversion

GMG - Alcoholism

GMH - Financial Irresponsibility

GMJ -   Motivational problems

GMJ -   Shirking

GMK - Character or Behavior Disorder

GML - Homosexuality

GMM - Drug use

GMN - Unsuitability (Reason Unknown)

GMP - Unsanitary Habits

GNC -   Misconduct (Reason Unknown)

GPB -   Drug use

H21 - H23 - Death, Non-Battle, Other (USMC)

H25 - H59 - Death, Non-Battle, Other (USMC)

H31 -   Death, Non-Battle, Other (USMC)

H4G -   Death, Non-Battle, Other (USMC)

H51 -   Death, Non-Battle, Other (USMC)

H61 - 1169 - Death, Battle Casualty - Marine

HBF -   Early Release - To attend school

HCR -   No listing at this time.

HDF -   Pregnancy

HDK -   Security reason

HFT -   Unqualified for Active Duty - Other

HFV - Unqualified for Active Duty - Other

HGH - No definition for this code at this time

HHJ - Unsuitability (Reason Unknown)

HJB - Court Martial

HKA - Discreditable Incidents - Civilian or Military

HKB - Civil Court conviction

HKD - AWOL, Desertion

HKE - AWOL, Desertion

HKE - Financial Irresponsibility

HKG - Fraudulent Entry

HKH - Lack of Dependent Support

HKJ - Shirking

HKK - Drug use

HKL - Sexual Perversion

HKQ - No information on file

HLB - Discreditable Incidents - Civilian or Military

HLC - Homosexuality

HLF - Drug use

HLG - Financial Irresponsibility

HLH - Lack of Dependent Support

HLJ - Shirking

HLK - Unsanitary Habits

HLL - Sexual Perversion

HMB - Character or Behavior Disorder

HMC - Enuresis

HMD - Inaptitude

HMF - Sexual Perversion

HMG - Alcoholism

HMJ - Motivational problems

HMM - Drug use

HMN - Financial Irresponsibility

HMN - Unsuitability (Reason Unknown)

HMP - Unsanitary Habits

HNB - Character or Behavior Disorder

HNC - Misconduct (Reason Unknown)

HPD - No information at this time

HRC - Homosexuality

HRG - No information at this time

HWL - Homosexuality

J11 – USAF Other

JBB - Involuntary discharge, age, USAF

JBB - Other

JBC - Other

JBD - Retirement - 20 - 30 Years Service

JBH - Other

JBK - Expiration of Term of Service

JBK - Involuntary discharge at end active obligated service, USN - Enlisted

JBM - Early Release - Insufficient time left in service after returning from overseas or other duty

JBM - Within 3 months of end active obligated service, USN - Enlisted

JCC - Early Release - Reduction in authorized strength

JCC - General demobilization. Reduction in authorized strength, USN - Enlisted

JCM - Conscientious Objector

JCP - Other, Alien not lawfully admitted

JDA - Fraudulent entry

JDF - Pregnancy

JDG - Parenthood

JDJ - Early Release - In the national interest

JDK - Security reason

JDL - Withdrawal of ecclesiastical endorsement

JDM - Early Release - Other

JDN - Lack of jurisdiction (other than void enlistment)

JDP - Breach of Contract

JDR - Early Release - Other

JDR - Strength reduction. first term airman, USAF

JDT - USN, USMC, Failure to meet minimum qualifications for Retention

JED - Early Release - Insufficient Retainability

JEH - USAF Expeditious Discharge

JEM - Army Trainee Discharge

JEM - USAF Expeditious Discharge

JEM - USN, USMC Failure to meet minimum qualifications for Retention

JET - Army Trainee Discharge

JET - USAF Trainee Discharge (See also JGA)

JFA - No description at this time.

JFB - Minority, Underage

JFBI - Physical disability that existed prior to entry. was revealed by Marine during enlistment processing and was waived by AFEES or higher headquarters, USMC

JFC - Enlisted/reenlisted/extended/inducted in error/ Erroneous Enlistment or Induction

JFC1 - Erroneous enlistment; a medical board determined that Marine failed to meet required physical standards for enlistment. Marine was not aware of defect and defect was not detected or waived by AFEES, USMC

JFF - Secretarial Authority

JFG- (1 - 7) - USMC Other, for the Good of the Service

JFG (9) - USMC Trainee Discharge

JFG (B) - USMC Expeditious Discharge

JFG - Army, Navy, USAF Discharge by competent authority w/o Board Action. (Failure to resign - failed to meet entrance physical requirement)

JFL -   Physical Disability - Severance Pay or Juvenile Offender

JFL -   Physical disability. entitled to severance pay., USN - Officers

JFL1 - Physical disability with severance pay, USAF

JFL2 - Physical disability that existed prior to service but was aggravated by the Service, with severance pay, USAF

JFM -   Physical disability existing prior to entry on active duty established by physical evaluation board proceedings. Not entitled to severance pay. USN - Enlisted

JFM -   Physical disability existing prior to service as established by physical evaluation board. Not entitled to severance pay., USN Officers

JFM -   Released for Conditions Existing Prior to Service

JFM2 - Physical disability that existed prior to entry, disability was unknown by Marine but was detected and waived by AFEES or higher headquarters, USMC

JFM3 - Physical disability that existed prior to entry for any reason not falling within the purview of JFM1 or JFM2, USMC

JFN -   Physical disability existing prior to service as established by medical board, not entitled to severance pay., USN - Officers

JFN -   Released for Conditions Existing Prior to Service

JFN1 - Physical disability determined by a medical board that existed prior to entry, disability was revealed by Marine during enlistment processing and waived by AFEES or higher headquarters, USMC

JFN2 - Physical disability determined by a medical board that existed prior to entry, disability was unknown to Marine but detected and waived by AFELS or higher headquarters, USMC

JFN3 - Physical disability determined by a medical board that existed prior to entry; any reason not falling within the purview of JFN1 or JFN2, USMC

JFP -   Misconduct (Reason Unknown) or Disability not in the line of duty

JFR -   Disability - Non EPTS - No Severance Pay

JFR - Physical disability not existing prior to entry on active duty established by physical evaluation board processing. Not entitled to severance pay., USN - Enlisted

JFR1 - Physical disability that existed prior to service and not aggravated by the Service, without severance pay, USMC

JFS - See KFS

JFT - Unqualified for Active Duty - Other

JFU - Positive Urinalysis

JFV - Physical condition, not a disability, interfering with performance of duty, USN - Enlisted

JFV1 - Discharge because of a physical condition which is not disabling. involuntary, USMC

JFV5 - Medical board determination of obesity, USMC

JFV6- Discharge because of a physical condition which is not disabling (Pseudofolliculitis Barbae), USMC

JFX - Personality disorder (See also JMB)

JFW- Erroneous enlistment; Medical condition disqualifying for military service, with no medical waiver approved.

JG7 - Army, Navy, USMC Failure to meet minimum qualifications for Retention

JG7 - USAF Trainee Discharge

JGA- Entry level status performance and conduct or entry level status performance - pregnancy

JGB - Failure of selection for permanent promotion

JGB - Failure to select for promotion. not retirement eligible, USN - Officers

JGC - Failure to select for promotion. not retirement eligible, USN - Officers

JGC1 - Failure of selection for promotion, USAF

JGF - Failure to meet minimum qualifications for Retention

JGH - Army, Air Force Expeditious Discharge

JGH - USN, USMC Failure to meet minimum qualifications for Retention

JHD - Disqualified from officer candidate training physical, USN - Enlisted

JHD - Navy Expeditious Discharge

JHD - Other

JHE - Failure to meet minimum qualifications for Retention

JHF - Failed to meet course standards

JHJ - Army, USMC, USAF Unsuitability (Reason Unknown)/Unsatisfactory performance

JHK - Unsuitability, substandard performance

JHM - Misconduct (Reason Unknown)

JIV - Unqualified for Active Duty - Other

JJB - Court Martial

JJC - Court Martial, Desertion

JJD - Court Martial, Other

JKA - Discreditable Incidents - Civilian or Military

JKB - Civil Court conviction

JKC - Homosexuality

JKD - AWOL, Desertion

JKE - Financial Irresponsibility

JKF - Army, Navy Air Force AWOL, Desertion

JKG - Fraudulent Entry

JKH - Lack of Dependent Support

JKJ - See JHJ

JKK - Character or Behavior Disorder (see also JPC)

JKK - Drug use

JKL - Sexual Perversion (see also JPD)

JKL - Shirking

JKM - Misconduct, pattern of misconduct (See also JKE)

JKN - Misconduct, minor disciplinary infractions (See also JKF)

JKQ - Misconduct, commission of a serious offense (See also JKH)

JKV - Unsanitary Habits

JLB - Discreditable Incidents - Civilian or Military

JLC - Homosexuality

JLF - Drug use

JLG - Financial Irresponsibility

JLH - Lack of Dependent Support

JLJ - Shirking

JLK - Unsanitary Habits

JLL - Sexual Perversion

JMB - Character or Behavior Disorder

JMC - Enuresis

JMD - Inaptitude

JMF - Sexual Perversion

JMG - Alcoholism

JMH - Financial Irresponsibility

JMJ - Motivational problems

JML - Homosexuality

JMM - Drug use

JMN - Navy, USMC, USAF Unsuitability (Reason Unknown)

JMP - Unsanitary Habits

JNC - Misconduct, moral or professional dereliction

JND - Other, Concealment of arrest record

JNF - Army Trainee Discharge

JNF - Navy, USMC, USAF Other

JNG - Unfitness (Reason Unknown)

JPB - Drug use

JPC - Drug abuse rehabilitative failure

JPD - Alcohol abuse rehabilitative failure

JRA - Engaged, attempted to engage or solicit another to engage in a homosexual act

JRB - Admission of Homosexuality or bisexuality

JRC - Marriage or attempted marriage to a person known to be of the same biological sex

KAK - Expiration of Term of Service

KBD - Retirement - 20 - 30 Years Service

KBH - Other

KBJ - Other

KBK - Normal expiration of Service

KBM - Early Release - Precluded from attaining eligibility for retirement with pay

KCC - Early Release - Other

KCE - Early Release - To attend school

KCF - Early Release - To attend school

KCK - Early Release - In the national interest

KCM - Conscientious Objector

KCO - Sole surviving son

KCP - Other

KCQ - See MCQ

KDB - Dependency or Hardship

KDF - Pregnancy

KDG - Parenthood

KDH - Dependency or Hardship

KDJ - Early Release - In the national interest

KDK - Security program

KDM - Early Release - Other

KDM1- Marine Corps order applicable to all members of a class, USMC

KDN - Other

KDP - Breach of Contract

KDQ - Breach of Contract

KDR - Early Release - Other

KDS - Breach of Contract

KEA - Expiration of Term of Service

KEB - Early Release - Other -

KEC - Expiration of Term of Service

KFB - Minority

KFF - Secretarial Authority, to be discharged or retire as an officer

KFG - Other

KFN - Released for Physical disability Existing Prior to Service

KFS - Good of the Service, in lieu of court martial

KFT - Failure to qualify medically for flight training, no disability

KFV - Unqualified for Active Duty - Other

KGF - Failure to meet minimum qualifications for Retention

KGH - No information on this code at this time.

KGL - Officer or Warrant Officer Commission program

KGM - Officer Commission program

KGN - Officer Warrant Officer Commission program in another service

KGS - Officer Commission program

KGT - Warrant Officer program

KGU - Service Academy

KGX - Officer Commission program

KHC – Immediate reenlistment

KHD - Other

KHF - Other

KHK - Substandard performance

KLG - Financial Irresponsibility

KLM - Unfitness (Reason Unknown)

KMN - Army Expeditious Discharge

KNC - See BNC

KND - No definition on this code at this time

KNF - Other

KNL - Good of the Service

KOG - Early Release - Police Duty

KOJ - Early Release - Seasonal Employment

L68 - Involuntary release: non-selection for Indefinite Reserve status, USAF

LBB - Involuntary release maximum age, USN - Officers

LBB - Maximum age

LBC - Involuntary release completion of maximum period service according to grade, USN - Officers

LBC - Maximum service

LBH - Early Release - Insufficient Retainability

LBK - Expiration of Term of Service

LBK - Involuntary discharge at end active obligated service, USN - Enlisted

LBM - Navy, USMC, USAF Short length of time remaining after return from overseas or other duty

LBM - Within 3 months of end active obligated service, USN - Enlisted

LCC - Early Release - Reduction in authorized strength

LCC - General demobilization, reduction in force, USN - Enlisted

LDG - Inability to perform prescribed duties due to parenthood

LDK - Security reason

LDL - See JDL

LDM - Strength adjustment, USN - Officers

LDN - Early Release - Lack of jurisdiction (other than void enlistment)

LDP - Breach of Contract

LDP6 - Non-fulfillment of service contract, convenience of the government, with breach of contract payment, USAF

LDP7- Non-fulfillment of service contract, with breach of contract and readjustment payment, USAF

LDP8- Non-fulfillment of service contract, failure of selection for promotion, with breach of contract payment, USAF

LDP9- Non-fulfillment of service contract, request for extension of active duty disapproved, with breach of contract and readjustment payment, USAF

LDPA- Non-fulfillment of service contract, failure of selection for promotion, with breach of contract and readjustment payment, USAF

LDPB- Non-fulfillment of service contract, convenience of the government, with readjustment payment, USAF

LDPC- Non-fulfillment of service contract, with readjustment payment, USAF

LDPD- Non-fulfillment of service contract, termination of extended active duty, with breach of contract payment, USAF

LDR - Early Release - Other

LED - CONUS based airman lacks retainability for assignment, USAF

LED - Early Release - Insufficient Retainability

LET - Entry level status performance and conduct or pregnancy

LFC - Erroneous entry

LFF - Directed by service authority

LFG - Other

LFN- Physical disability existing prior to service as established by medical board, not entitled to severance pay., USN - Officers

LFR - Revert to inactive status. Retire age 60. No disability severance pay, USAF

LFT - Erroneous Enlistment or Induction or Unqualified for Active Duty - Medical

LGA - See LET

LGB - Failure of selection for permanent promotion

LGB - Failure of selection for permanent reserve promotion, USN - Officers

LGB - Involuntary release. Failed permanent promotion or removed from list, USAF

LGC - Failure of selection for temporary promotion

LGC - Involuntary release: twice failed temporary promotion, USAF

LGH - Failure to meet minimum standards of service

LGJ - Early Release - Disapproval of request for extension of service

LGJ – Involuntary release: disapproved request for extension of tour, USAF

LGJ -   Request for extension of active duty denied (USNR), USN - Officers

LGJ1- Request for extension of service denied upon initial EAS without readjustment pay/not selected for retention, USAF

LGJ2- Request for extension of service denied upon extended EAS without readjustment pay/not selected for retention, USAF

LHD - Other

LHF - Navy, USMC, USAF Other

LHH - Service under sentence to dismissal awaiting appellate review

LHJ - Unsatisfactory performance

LIF - Secretarial Authority

LLM - Army Trainee Discharge

LMJ - See LHJ

LND- Miscellaneous reasons (medical service personnel who receive unfavorable background investigation or National Agency check

LNF - Army Trainee Discharge

MBD - Hardship

MBH - Early Release - Insufficient Retainability

MBK - Completion of active duty service commitment or expiration of term of service, USAF

MBK - Expiration of Term of Service

MBN- (ANGUS) (USAFR) Release from active duty completion of required service, USAF

MBN - Expiration of Term of Service

MCF - To attend educational facility

MCK - Early Release - In the national interest

MCQ - Sole surviving son, daughter or family member

MDB - Hardship

MDF - Pregnancy

MDG - Parenthood

MDH - Dependency or Hardship

MDJ - National interest

MDL - Early Release - To attend school

MDM- Early Release - Other

MDN - Other

MDP - Breach of Contract

MDR - Early Release - Other

MDS - Breach of Contract

MEB - Early Release - Other

MEC - Completed extended enlistment, USAF

MEC - Erroneous Enlistment or Induction

MEC - Expiration of Term of Service

MFA - Expiration of Term of Service

MFF – Secretarial Authority

MFG - Other

MGC - Early Release - Other

MGH - Warrant Officer program

MGJ - Early Release - Other

MGM - To accept commission

MGO - Early Release - Police Duty or Seasonal Employment

MGP - Interdepartmental transfer

MGR - Revert to Regular Army warrant officer status

MGU - To enter Service Academy

MGX - Officer Commission program

MHC - Immediate enlistment

MND- Miscellaneous reasons (in lieu of serving in lower grade than Reserve grade or by request - includes MC and DC officers) or in lieu of unqualified resignation

MNF - Other

MOD - Sole surviving son

MOJ - Early Release - In the national interest

NBD - Retirement - 20 - 30 Years Service

NDB - Dependency or Hardship

NDH - Early Release - To teach

NEF - Secretarial Authority

NET - Unqualified for Active Duty - Other

NVC - Erroneous Enlistment or Induction

PGU - Service Academy

RB - Retirement - Over 30 Years Service

RBB - Retirement - Other

RBD - Retirement - 20 - 30 Years Service

RFJ - Permanent Disability - Retired

RFJ1 - Permanent disability retired list, USAF

RFK - Temporary Disability - Retired

RFK1 - Temporary disability retired list, USAF

SBB - Attain maximum age. mandatory retirement, USN - Officers

SBB - Mandatory retirement on established date, maximum age, USAF

SBC - Attain maximum time in grade/service. mandatory retirement, USN - Officers

SBC - Mandatory retirement on established date. maximum years of service, USAF

SBD - Retirement - 20 - 30 Years Service

SFE - Placed on temporary disability retired list, USN - Officers

SFJ - Permanent Disability - Retired

SFJ - Permanent disability retirement, USAF

SFJ - Permanent disability, USN - Enlisted

SFJ - Permanent disability, USN - Officers

SFK - Place on temporary disability retired list, USAF

SFK - Placed on temporary disability retired list, USN - Enlisted

SFK - Temporary Disability - Retired

SGB - Failure of selection for promotion, permanent, USN - Officers

SGB - Retired on established date non-selection permanent promotion or retained for retirement non-selection permanent promotion, USAF

SGC - Failure of selection for promotion, temporary, USN - Officers

SKU - No definition at this time

TCC - See LCC

VFJ - Permanent Disability - Retired

VFJ - Revert to retired list with permanent disability, USAF

VFK - Revert to retired list and placed on temporary disability retired list, USAF

VFK - Temporary Disability - Retired

VNF - Other

WFK - Temporary Disability - Retired

XBK - Retirement - Other

XDM - Early Release - Other

XET - Unqualified for Active Duty - Other

XND - Other

XOH - Dependency or Hardship

XOP - Breach of Contract

XOS - Retirement - Other

YBK - Retirement - Other

YCP - Other

YDN - Other

YFB - Minority

YKG - Fraudulent Entry

YND - Other

The above alphabetical designations are not the only separation codes in use. There is also a series of numerical codes that can also be used by the military to reveal confidential information. These codes are contained in your military records and may be annotated on various military separation documents. These codes are also subject to change, and the Department of Defense will no longer allow the military services to release the meanings of these codes to the general public. The below definitions were obtained before this prohibition went into effect.

201 - Enlisted Personnel - Expiration of term of service (includes personnel on ADT as initial trainees).

21L - Enlisted Personnel - Separation for good & sufficient reason when determined by secretarial authority.

21T - Enlisted Personnel - Release of REP 63 trainees due to emergency conditions. (Does not apply to active duty.)

21U - Separation for failure to demonstrate adequate potential for promotion.

202 - Expiration of term of enlistment.

203 - Expiration of term of active obligation service

205 - Release from active & transferred to reserve.

209 - Release from Active Duty within 3 mos of expiration of USN service.

212 - Honorable wartime service subsequent to desertion.

213 - Discharge for retirement as an officer.

214 - To accept commission as an officer in the Army, or to accept recall to active duty as an Army Reserve officer.

215 - To accept appointment as warrant officer in the Army or to accept recall to active duty as Army Reserve warrant officer.

217 - To accept commission or appointment in the Armed Forces of the United States (other than Army).

219 - Erroneous induction.

220 - Marriage, female only.

221 - Pregnancy.

222 - Parenthood

225 - Minority.

226 - Dependency.

227 - Hardship.

239 - Surviving family members

230 - Retirement after 20 years but less than 30 years active federal service

231 - Retirement after 30 years active federal service.

238 - Service retirement in lieu of other administrative action.

240 - Unconditional resignation of enlisted personnel serving on unspecified enlistment

241 - Resignation of enlisted personnel on unspecified enlistment in lieu of resignation for misconduct or inefficiency.

242 - Resignation of enlisted personnel on unspecified enlistment for the good of the service.

243 - Resignation of enlisted personnel on unspecified enlistment in lieu of board of action when based on unfitness.

241 - Resignation of enlisted personnel on unspecified enlistment in lieu of board action when based on unsuitability.

245 - Resignation of enlisted personnel on unspecified enlistment in lieu of separation for disloyalty or subversion.

246 - Discharge for the good of the service.

247 - Unsuitability, multiple reasons.

248 - Unsuitability.

258 - Unfitness, multiple reasons

251 - Punitive discharge. Class I homosexual - general court martial

252 - Punitive discharge. Class I homosexual - general court martial

253 - Homosexual - board action

255 - Punitive discharge. Class II homosexual - general court martial

256 - Homosexual, acceptance of discharge in lieu of board action

257 - Unfitness, homosexual acts

258 - Unfitness, ineptitude

260 - Unsuitability, ineptitude

261 – Psychiatric or psychoneurotic disorder.

262 - Behavioral disorder, Bed wetter

263 – Bed wetter

264 -   Unsuitability, character and behavioral disorders

265 -   Unsuitability, character disorder

270 -   Placed on temporary disability retired list

271 -   Permanently retired by reason of physical disability

273 -   Physical disability with entitlement to receive severance pay.

274 -   Physical disability resulting from international misconduct or willful neglect or incurred during period of unauthorized absence. Not entitled to severance pay.

276 -   Released from EAD & revert to retired list prior to ETS.

277 -   Physical disability, EPTS, established by medical board. Discharged by reason of physical disability upon application by individual. Not entitled to severance pay.

278 -   Physical disability, EPTS, established by physical evaluation board proceedings. Not entitled to severance pay

279 -   Release from EAD & revert to retired list at ETS

28B -   Unfitness, frequent involvement in incidents of a discreditable nature with civil or military authorities.

28G -   Unfitness, an established pattern for showing dishonorable failure to contribute adequate support to dependents or failure to comply with order, decrees, or judgment of a civil court concerning support of dependents

280 -   Misconduct/fraudulent entry into the Army.

282 -   Misconduct/prolonged unauthorized absence for more than 1 year desertion.

283 -   Misconduct/AWOL trial waived or deemed inadvisable.

284 -   Misconduct/convicted or adjudged a juvenile offender by a civil court during current term of active military service.

285 -   Initially adjudged a juvenile offender by a civil court during current term of active military service. Rescinded.

290 -   Desertion (court martial).

293 - Other than desertion (court martial)

293 - General court martial.

294 - Special court martial.

311 - Alien without legal residence in the United States.

312 - Separation of members of Reserve components on active duty who, due to age, would be precluded from attaining eligibility pay as provided by 10 USC 1331.1337.

313 - To immediately enlist or reenlist

314 - Importance to national health, safety or interest

316 - Release, lack of jurisdiction.

318 - Conscientious objection.

319 - Erroneous enlistment

320 - To accept employment law enforcement agency.

333 - Discharge of Cuban volunteers upon completion of specified training. Rescinded.

344 - Release of Cuban volunteers upon completion of specified training. Rescinded.

367 - Aggressive reaction.

370 - Released from EAD by reason of physical disability & revert to inactive status for the purpose of retirement under Title 10. USC Sections 1331 - 1337, in lieu of discharge with entitlement to receive severance pay.

375 - Discharge because of not meeting medical fitness standards at time of enlistment

376 - Release from military Control (void Inductions) because of not meeting medical fitness standards at time of induction.

377 - Non - fulfillment of enlistment commitment.

38A - Desertion/trial deemed inadvisable (WW2) Rescinded.

38B - Desertion/trial deemed inadvisable (peacetime desertion) Rescinded.

38C - Desertion/trial deemed inadvisable (Korean War). Rescinded

380 - Desertion/trial barred by 10 USC Section 834 (Art 34 UCMJ). Rescinded.

351 - Desertion/trial deemed inadvisable (Spanish - American War/ WWII>. Rescinded.

383 - Criminalism.

41A - Apathy, lack of interest

41C - To accept a teaching position.

41D - Discharge of enlisted personnel on unspecified enlistment who completed 20 years active federal service, do not submit application for retirement: commander determines discharge will be in best interest of the government

41E - Obesity.

411 - Early separation of overseas returnee

412 - Enlisted members of medical holding detachments or units who, upon completion of hospitalization, do not intend to immediately enlist or reenlistment in the regular Army

413 - To enter or return to college, university, or equivalent institution.

414 - To accept or return to employment of a seasonal nature

415 - Early release of inductees who have served on active duty prior their present tour of duty

416 - Physical disqualification for duty in MOS

418 - Discharge of enlisted personnel bn unspecified enlistment who complete 30 years active federal service & do not submit application for retirement.

419 - Discharge of enlisted personnel on unspecified enlistment over 55 years of rage who have completed 20 years active federal service & do not submit application for retirement

420 - Discharge or release of individuals with less than 3 months remaining to serve who fail to continue as students (academic failure) at service academies.

421 - Early release at Christmas will be issued as appropriate by Army & has been Included in separation edit table. Rescinded.

422 - Early release at original ETS of enlisted personnel who have executed a voluntary extension. Rescinded.

423 - Early release after original ETS of personnel serving on voluntary extension. Rescinded.

424 - Separation at ETS after completing a period of voluntary extension. Rescinded

425 - Discharge (Inductees) to enlist in Warrant Officer Flight Training.

426 - Discharge (inductees) to enlist to attend critical MOS school.

427 - Discharge (inductees) to enlist for Officer Candidate School.

420 - Discharge for failure to complete Officer Candidate. School

429 - Discharged because of not meeting medical fitness standards for Flight training.

430 - Early separation of personnel denied reenlistment under Qualitative Management Program.

431 - Reduction in authorized strength.

432 - Early release to serve 1 year in an ARNG or USAR unit

433 - Involuntary release of personnel on compassionate assignment

434 - Early release of AUS & first team RA Personnel - phase down release programs (Early - out from Vietnam.)

436 - Reduction In strength a USASA option/First Team.

437 - AUS, RA First Team, exempted from 90 day suspension of Early Release Program for reasons for intolerable personal problems.

440 - Separation for concealment of serious arrest record.

46A - Unsuitability, apathy, defective attitudes & inability to extend effort constructively 46B Sexual deviate

46C - Apathy/obesity

460 - Emotional instability reaction.

461 - Inadequate personality

463 -   Paranoid personality

464 -   Schizoid personality

469 -   Unsuitability.

480 -   Personality disorder.

482 -   Desertion/trial barred by 10, USC, Sec. 843 (Art 43 UCMJ) Rescinded.

488 -   Unsuitability (general discharge separation).

489 -   Military Personnel Security Program (disloyal or subversive)

500 -   Resignation - hardship.

501 -   Resignation - national health, safety, or interest

502 -   Resignation - completion of required service.

503 -   Resignation - enlistment in the regular Army - regular officer.

504 -   Resignation - withdrawal of ecclesiastical endorsement

505 -   Resignation - serving under a suspended sentence or dismissal.

508 -   Resignation - to attend school.

510 -   Resignation - Interest of national security (in lieu of elimination).

51B -   Resignation - In lieu of elimination because of unfitness or unacceptable conduct

522 -   Resignation in lieu of elimination because of conduct triable by court martial or in lieu thereof.

524 -   Resignation - unqualified other miscellaneous reasons

528 -   Resignation - marriage.

529 -   Resignation - pregnancy.

530 -   Resignation - parenthood (minor children)

536 -   Voluntary discharge substandard performance of duty.

539 -   Voluntary discharge - termination of RA or AUS warrant to retire commissioned status

545 -   Voluntary discharge - failure of selection for permanent promotion (commissioned officers)

546 -   Involuntary discharge a failure of selection for permanent promotion (warrant officer).

550 -   Involuntary discharge - reasons as specified by HDQA

551 -   Involuntary discharge - administrative discharge GCM

554 -   Dismissal - General court martial.

555 -   Involuntary discharge - failure to complete basic, Company officer or associate company officer course - USAR officers.

556 -   Failure to complete basic, company officer or associate company officer course - ARNGUS officers.

558 -   Voluntary discharge - conscientious objection.

586 -   Involuntary discharge - for reasons involving board action or in lieu thereof (homosexuality),

588 -   Involuntary discharge - reasons involving board action, or in lieu thereof - unfitness or unacceptable conduct

589 -   Voluntary discharge - reasons involving board action or in lieu thereof, due to substandard performance of duty.

590 -   Involuntary discharge - interest of national security.

595 -   Involuntary discharge pregnancy

596 -   Involuntary discharge - parenthood (minor children).

597 -   Voluntary discharge - administrative

599 -   Voluntary REFRAD - lack of jurisdiction.

600 -   Voluntary REFRAD - to enlist an regular Army.

601 -   Voluntary REFRAD - to enlist in regular Army for purpose of retirement

602 -   Voluntary REFRAD - national health, safety, or interest

603 -   Involuntary REFRAD - due to disapproval of request for extension of service.

604 -   Voluntary REFRAD - hardship

606 -   Voluntary REFRAD - dual status officer to revert to regular Warrant Officer

609 -   Voluntary REFRAD - to attend school or accept a teaching position.

610 -   Voluntary REFRAD - marriage.

611 -   Voluntary REFRAD - expiration of the duty commitment voluntarily serving on active duty.

612 -   Voluntary REFRAD - expiration active duty commitment involuntary serving on active duty.

616 -   Voluntary REFRAD - selection for entrance to a service academy.

618 -   Voluntary REFRAD - In lieu of serving in lower grade than reserve grade.

619 -   Voluntary REFRAD - by request includes MC & DC officers

620 -   Voluntary REFRAD - interdepartmental transfer of other than medical officers

621 -   Voluntary REFRAD - in lieu of unqualified resignation.

623 -   Voluntary REFRAD - interdepartmental transfer of medical officers

624 -   Voluntary REFRAD - release from ADT to enter on 24 months active duty.

625 -   Voluntary REFRAD - annual screening, voluntary release prior to 90th day subsequent to receipt of notification.

627 -   Involuntary REFRAD - maximum age.

631 -   Involuntary REFRAD - failure of selector for permanent reserve promotion (discharged).

632 -   Involuntary REFRAD - failure of selection for permanent reserve promotion (commission retained).

633 -   Involuntary REFRAD - failures of selection for promotion, temporary

640 -   Involuntary REFRAD - commissioned officer under sentence of dismissal & warrant officer discharge awaiting appellate review.

644 -   Voluntary & Involuntary REFRAD - convenience of government or as specified by Secretary of the Army

645 -   Involuntary REFRAD - annual screening, release on 90th day subsequent to receipt of notification.

646 -   Involuntary REFRAD - maximum service, warrant officers.

647 -   Involuntary REFRAD - maximum service, commissioned officers

648 - Involuntary REFRAD - completion of prescribed years of service.

649 - Involuntary REFRAD - withdrawal of ecclesiastical endorsement

650 - Involuntary REFRAD - physically disqualified upon order to active duty.

651 - Involuntary REFRAD - release of reserve unit & return to reserve status.

652 - Involuntary REFRAD a release of unit of NG or NG(US) & return to state control.

655 - Involuntary REFRAD - revert to retired list, not by reason of physical disability

657 - Involuntary REFRAD - physical disability. Revert to inactive status for purpose of retirement under Chapter 67. 10 USC in lieu of discharge with entitlement to receive disability severance pay.

660 - Physical disability discharge - entitlement to severance pay.

661 - Physical disability discharge - disability resulting from intentional misconduct or willful neglect or incurred during a period of unauthorized absence. Not entitled to receive disability severance pay.

662 - Physical disability discharge - EPTS, established by physical evaluation board. Not entitled to disability severance pay.

668 - Dropped from rolls - AWOL conviction & confinement by civil authorities.

669 - Dropped from rolls - AWOL desertion.

672 - Involuntary REFRAD - medical service personnel who receive unfavorable background investigation and/or National Agency Check

681 - Voluntary REFRAD - to accept employment with a legally established law enforcement agency

685 - Resignation - failure to meet medical fitness standards at time of appointment

686 - Involuntary discharge - failure to resign under Chapter 16 - AR 535 - 120 when determined to be in the best interest of the government and the individual

689 -   Voluntary REFRAD - reduction in strength, voluntary release prior to 90th day subsequent to receipt of notification

690 -   Involuntary REFRAD - reduction in strength. release on 90th day subsequent to receipt of notification.

70A -   mandatory retirement - 35 years service/five years In grade. Regular army major general.

70B -   Mandatory retirement - age 62, regular army major general.

70C -   Mandatory retirement 60, regular Army mayor general whose retirement has been deferred.

70D -   Mandatory retirement - age 64, regular Army major general whose retirement has been deferred & each permanent professor and the registrar of the US Military Academy.

70E -   Mandatory retirement - 30 years service/five years in grade, regular army brigadier general.

70F -   Mandatory retirement 30 years of service/five years In grade, regular colonels.

70G -   Mandatory retirement - 28 years service. Regular Lt. Colonels.

70J -   Mandatory retirement - age 60, regular commissioned officer below major general.

70K -   Mandatory retirement - more than 30 years active service, professors US military Academy.

70L -   Mandatory retirement - 30 years of more active service, regular warrant officers.

70M -   Mandatory retirement - age 62 regular warrant officers

701 -   Enlisted separation - early release of personnel assigned to installations or units scheduled for inactivation, permanent change of station, or demobilization.

741 -   Mandatory retirement - failure of selection for promotion, established retirement date, commissioned officer.

742 - Mandatory retirement - failure of selection for promotion, estab'd retirement date. warrant officer.

743 - Enlisted separation - early release of personnel from release of unit of the ARNG or the ARNGUS from active federal service & return to state control

744 - Mandatory retirement - failure of selection for promotion, early retirement date, commissioned officer

745 - Mandatory retirement - failure of selection for promotion. early retirement date, warrant officers.

747 - Mandatory retirement - failure of selection for promotion, retained for retirement, commissioned officers.

748 - Mandatory retirement - failure of selection for promotion, retained for retirement, warrant officer

749 - Enlisted separation - early release of Puerto Rican personnel who will to qualify for training.

753 - Enlisted separation - early release of reserve personnel upon release of reserve units

764 - Enlisted separation - release of REP 63 trainees upon completion of MOS training.

77E - Mandatory retirement - surplus In grade after 30 years service. Removal from acting list (regular Army).

77J - Voluntary retirement - placement on retired list at age 60.

77M - Mandatory retirement - permanent retirement by reason by physical disability

77N - Mandatory retirement - paced on temporary mandatory solemnity retired list

77P - Voluntary retirement in lieu of or as a result of elimination board proceedings. Regular Army & reserve commissioned officers and Warrant officers.

77C -   Mandatory retirement - temporary disability retirement in lieu of or as a result of elimination proceedings.

77R -   Mandatory retirement - permanent disability retirement in lieu of or as a result or elimination proceedings.

77S -   Voluntary retirement a regular Army & reserve commissioned officers

77T -   Voluntary retirement - regular Army and reserve warrant officer.

77U -   Voluntary retirement - regular Army commissioned officers with 30 or more years of service.

77V-   Voluntary retirement - enlisted personnel, voluntarily retired as commissioned officer.

77W -   Voluntary retirement - enlisted personnel, voluntarily retired as a warrant officer.

77X -   Voluntary retirement a warrant officer voluntarily retired as a commissioned officer.

77Y -   Mandatory retirement - retirement a director of music, USMA, as the President may direct

77Z -   Mandatory retirement - regular Army commissioned officers with World War 1 service.

771 -   Mandatory retirement - commissioned officers, unfitness or substandard performance of duty.

772 -   Mandatory retirement - warrant officers, unfitness or sub - standard performance of duty.

78A -   Mandatory retirement - formerly retired other than for disability who while on active duty incurred a disability of at least 30%.

78B -   Mandatory retirement a formerly retired for disability who where on active duty suffered aggravation of disability for which he was formerly retired.

79A -   Voluntary REFRAD - as USAR warrant officer (aviator) to accept USAR commission (aviator) with concurrent active duty.

79B - Resignation - as RA a WO (aviator) to accept USAR commission (aviator) with concurrent active duty.

941 - Dropped from rolls (as deserter).

942 - Dropped from rolls (as military prisoner).

943 - Dropped From rolls (as missing or captured).

944 - Battle casualty.

945 - Death (non-battle - resulting from disease).

940 - Death (non-battle - resulting from other than disease).

947 - (Current term of service voided as fraudulent enlisted, while AWOL from prior service.

94B - To enter US military Academy.

949 - To enter any area of the service academies (other than USMA).

971 - Erroneously reported as returned from dropped from rolls as a deserter (previously reports under transaction GA).

972 - Erroneously reported as restored to duty from dropped from rolls of military prisoner previously reported under transaction code GB).

973 - Erroneously reported as returned from dropped from rolls or missing or captured (previously reported under transaction code GC).

976 - Minority. Void enlistment or induction - enlisted personnel.

Now that you have the most up to date list of these separation codes, check your DD214 to find out what the service is telling the world about you. Mistakes can happen even in the best of organizations.

CHAPTER TEN

ENTITLEMENTS

As every member of the military knows, prior preparation can be your greatest assistance when going into an operation. Though the military has a tremendous bureaucracy, it is nothing compared to the one that the newly minted veteran will have to deal with once the military uniform is taken off for the last time. The interesting fact is that the one that has the easiest time navigating the maze of the VA is someone who was generally a less than stellar soldier.

I am not being insulting to anyone, but it is a fact that the soldier (or sailor or marine) who spent a large amount of time on sick call or getting his complaints made a part of his or her military medical record was not generally considered an outstanding soldier. In fact, quite often, this individual was a source of amusement to the officers of the command. However, this individual usually has the last laugh upon entry into the civilian world.

At least in my battalion, if a limb was not falling off, a bone was not poking out of the skin or blood was not gushing, then it was felt that there was plenty of time to get the problem treated by the medics. However, I quickly discovered that for an NCO or a junior officer to ask to go to a real doctor was considered an admission to being less than a man by my superiors. However, if the injury in question was not documented in the medical record, then the VA refuses to grant service for the problem. This can result in a grave disservice to the veteran.

Then there are the soldiers who themselves consider a minor injury as not something important enough to waste the time of the physicians and in and of itself, the immediate problem may well be minor. These individuals were generally the hard charging completely dependable member of every command that take up the slack when others give a less than stellar performance. These are also the soldiers who neglect themselves for the good of the organization.

However, these overlooked minor injuries can well lead to more serious problems down the line. For example, arthritis is not normally service connected, however, if there was an injury to a joint while on active duty arthritis can well be the result. In this case, it would now become a service connected disability secondary to the joint injury. The more serious problem may be the basis of a disability rating, but only because it stemmed, or was secondary to, the minor injury. However, the failure to have every injury fully documented at the time of injury, or illness, can be a potentially insurmountable stumbling block to a successful disability claim for such a condition. So a soldier's dedication to the organization can become a serious problem in the future.

The pathway to successfully establishing your entitlement to veterans' benefits is well marked, but it can also be confusing. However, just as important as establishing your entitlement to veterans' benefits is ensuring that you make sure that you receive everything you are entitled to while preparing to leave the service. This can make the transition to the world of the veteran a somewhat less bumpy ride.

SERVICE BONUSES

Until recently, the last military paycheck that a soldier received was considered the only service bonus that he or she was going to get, along with any accrued leave or other entitlements not yet collected. However, over the years some other programs have been put in place that might well make other funds available to the soon to be veteran.

In the 1990s peace broke out unexpectedly with the collapse of the Soviet Union. The Democratically controlled Congress apparently thought that the need for a large standing military was a thing of the past[12] and it was decided to reduce the size of our military. However, it was readily apparent that they could not just send people home; that would be the same as just firing them after years of dedicated service. Therefore, it was decided to create a bonus that could be offered to people to voluntarily leave the service. Other bonuses were created to soften the blow when career soldiers were also involuntarily separated or RIFTED. However, unlike the disability payments that will be discussed later, each of these separation bonus programs is fully taxable as income.

As with every government program, the idea has grown far beyond he original concept. Now, there is a series of bonuses that someone leaving the

---

[12] Urging on the Congress in these efforts to reduce the military was President William Jefferson Clinton, the first President who had never served in the armed forces. He was also said not to be a fan of the military, even though he used military force in more locations than any other peacetime president in history.

military may be entitled to as an incentive to just go. The primary bonus programs are:

- Voluntary Separation Incentive (VSI),

- Special Separation Benefit (SSB),

- Separation Pay, and

- Fifteen year retirement.

While each of the programs has an eligibility criterion that a recipient must meet, there is one eligibility rule that all of the programs have in common. The recipient must be officially notified that he or she is eligible. While this might seem like a common sense rule, it should be remembered that these programs were created in order to weed out those with unneeded skills and retain those with skills that were deemed important to keep in the service. Therefore, there was absolutely no intention to give bonuses to those with important needed skills who were leaving the service.

There has been some question raised as to the legality and the terms of the various bonus programs. Therefore, I am including some of the background of these programs.

PUSPOSE

The purpose of the bonus payments was to provide special incentives for members of the armed forces to voluntarily agree to separate from active duty components.

BACKGROUND

In the aftermath of the Cold War, and in light of the expected consequent drawdown in active duty strength levels, the National Defense Authorization Act for Fiscal Years 1992 and 1993, Public Law 102-190, 105 Stat. 1290 (1991), established two programs to encourage members of the active duty forces--both regular and reserve components--to voluntarily separate from active duty. One of the programs--adopted by Section 662(a) of the National Defense Authorization Act for Fiscal Years 1992 and 1993, Public Law 102-190, id., §662(a), 105 Stat. at 1396-1398, codified at 10 U.S.C. §1175, and generally referred to the "voluntary separation incentive" program, or "VSI"--provides a temporary, variable-length annuity to members separating from the active duty forces and affiliating with reserve components.

The second program--adopted by Section 661(a) of the National Defense Authorization Act for Fiscal Years 1992 and 1993, Public Law 102-190, id., §661(a), 105 Stat. at 1394-1395, codified at 10 U.S.C. §1174a, and generally referred to as the "special separation benefit" program, or "SSB"--provides enhanced separation pay benefits for members of the active duty services voluntarily agreeing to terminate all connection with the armed forces. The National Defense Authorization Act for Fiscal Year 1993, Public Law 102-484, §4403, 106 Stat. 2315, 2702-2704 (1992), as amended, established a third program of separation incentives that authorizes early retirement for members of the armed forces with at least 15 but less than 20 years of service who agree to retire before October 1, 1999.

Voluntary Separation Incentive Program(VSI)

Under the voluntary separation incentive program or VSI--the program aimed at providing incentives to members of the active duty services to separate from active duty and affiliate with reserve components--the National Defense Authorization Act for Fiscal Years 1992 and 1993, Public Law 102-190, id., §662(a), 105 Stat. at 1396-1398, authorized the Secretary of Defense to "provide a financial incentive to members of the armed forces ... for voluntary appointment, enlistment, or transfer to a Reserve component ... for the period of time the member serves in a reserve component."

As originally enacted, the amount of the annual VSI payment authorized was to be computed by multiplying the product of the member's terminal monthly basic pay and 12 by the product of the member's number of years of service at separation and 2.5 percent, and subtracting from that amount the sum of any basic pay the member subsequently received for active or reserve service as a member of a reserve component and any compensation the member received for inactive duty training during the year. A member entitled to an annual VSI payment computed as above was to be paid that amount for twice the member's years of service at separation so as long as the member maintained membership in a reserve component. A member of the active duty force was eligible to participate in the VSI program if the member had served on active duty for at least six but less than 20 years, had served at least five years of continuous active duty immediately before the date of separation, and met such other requirements as the Secretary of Defense might provide. A member participating in the VSI program who subsequently became entitled to retired or retainer pay was to have his retired or retainer pay entitlement reduced by an amount based on the service for which he received the VSI until the total amount deducted equaled the total VSI the member received.

Special Separation Benefit Program (SSB)

Under the special separation benefit program, or SSB--the program aimed at providing incentives to members of the active duty services to terminate all connection with the armed forces--the National Defense Authorization Act for Fiscal Years 1992 and 1993, Public Law 102-190, id., §661(a), 105 Stat. at 1394-

1395, directed the Secretaries of each of the military departments to develop "special separation benefits program[s]" under which an "eligible member" could request separation and, upon approval of the request, be "released from active duty or discharged". For the purpose of each departmental "special separation benefit program", a member of that department's armed force on active duty was eligible for the program only if the member had served on active duty for more than six but less than 20 years as of the date of enactment of the 1992/1993 Authorization Act, had served on continuous active duty for at least five years immediately before the member's separation from active duty under the program, had not been approved for "payment of a voluntary separation incentive", and met such other requirements as the Secretary of Defense might provide.[2] In addition, an enlisted member of a regular component was required to enter into a written agreement not to request reenlistment in a regular component any time in the future. An eligible member whose request for separation under the SSB program was approved was entitled to a SSB payment computed by multiplying the product of the member's terminal monthly basic pay and 12 by the product of the member's years of active service and 15 percent. Various non-monetary benefits were also extended to members separated under the SSB program.

Fifteen Year Retirement Benefit

With respect to the third of the voluntary separation incentive programs, the National Defense Authorization Act for Fiscal Year 1993, Public Law 102-484, §4403, 106 Stat. 2315, 2702-2704 (1992), adopted early retirement authority--for members with between 15 and 20 years of service--as a "temporary additional force management tool with which to effect the drawdown of military forces through 1995." National Defense Authorization Act for Fiscal Year 1993, Public Law 102-484, id., §4403(a), 106 Stat. at 2702. Under the subject authority, the Secretaries of the military departments are authorized to accept applications of members of the Army, the Navy, the Marine Corps, and the Air Force having at least 15 but less than 20 years of service for voluntary early retirement. This early retirement authority is applicable during the "active force drawdown period", which as originally enacted, was defined to be the period beginning on the date of enactment of the National Defense Authorization Act for Fiscal Year 1993, Public Law 102-484, id., i.e., October 23, 1992, and ending on October 1, 1995. The National Defense Authorization Act for Fiscal Year 1994, Public Law 103-160, §561(a), 107 Stat. 1547, 1667 (1993), subsequently extended the termination date for the "active force drawdown period" to October 1, 1999.

A member whose application for early retirement is accepted is entitled to retired or retainer pay effectively computed by multiplying the member's "retired or retainer pay base" by an adjusted "retired or retainer pay multiplier." The member's adjusted "retired or retainer pay multiplier" is determined by multiplying 2.5 percent times the member's years and months of creditable service (counting 1/12th of a year for each month of creditable service in excess of the number of whole years of service) and then subtracting from that result, stated as a percentage, 1/12th of one percent for each full month by which the member's total months of active service at retirement are less than 240.

In support of the early retirement authority granted by the National Defense Authorization Act for Fiscal Year 1993, Public Law 102-484, §4403, 106 Stat. 2315, 2702-2704 (1992), the Senate Armed Services Committee, which sponsored the proposal, noted:

The committee anticipates that the active component strength levels of some of the military services in the current DOD Base Force Plan, which total to an active duty strength level of 1,626,300 by the end of fiscal year 1997, are likely to be reduced substantially. The committee expects such a reduction will result from the Defense Department's own revisions to its current Base Force Plan as a result of budget decisions, a more efficient allocation of roles and missions among the military services, a more efficient active/reserve force mix, and other economies and efficiencies that are discussed elsewhere in this report.

In order to cope with the active duty strength reductions that are currently planned by the DOD, the Congress provided authorities to the military services to assist them in implementing the planned reductions prudently. These authorities included separation benefits that the military services could offer to career personnel to induce them to voluntarily separate from active duty.

The committee notes that these authorities have been effective in helping the military services reduce strength in the six to 15-years-of-service element of the career inventory. At the same time, the committee notes that the military services do not have an effective tool to reduce active duty strength in the 15 to 20-year element of the career inventory.

In view of the committee's expectation that the active duty strengths in the current Base Force Plan will be reduced substantially, and in view of the absence of an effective tool that the military services can use to reduce the 15 to 20-year element of the personnel inventory, the committee believes that existing transition provisions should be augmented....

Therefore the committee recommends...

Section 534 [of the Senate bill, S. 3114, 102d Congress, 2d Session (1992)] would authorize active duty personnel who have 15 but less than 20 years of service to apply for and be approved for early retirement. The committee expects the military services to use this authority selectively to trim surpluses in the 15 to 20-year element of the personnel inventory.[13]

Current rates of special voluntary separation incentives authorized:

* VSI: Varies depending on pay grade and length of service.

* SSB: Varies depending on pay grade and length of service.

* Early retirement: Varies depending on pay grade and length of service.

As initially enacted, the early retirement authority did not extend to members of the Coast Guard or to the commissioned officer corps of the National Oceanic and Atmospheric Administration or the Public Health Service. Early retirement authority was, however, subsequently extended to members of the Coast Guard with at least 15 but less than 20 years of service by the National Defense Authorization Act for Fiscal Year 1995, Public Law 103-337, §542(d), 108 Stat. 2663, 2769 (1994), and to members of the commissioned officer corps of the National Oceanic and Atmospheric Administration by the National Defense Authorization Act for Fiscal Year 1996, Public Law 104-106, §566(c), 110 Stat. 186, 328 (1996).

CHAPTER ELEVEN

DD214

The most important paper for a U.S. veteran is his or her DD-214 (Separation Paper). The Defense Department form 214 is a condensed version of the vet's service record, including length of service, overseas service, training, medals, commendations and character of service. This is also the primary document the "secret" codes can be found that will follow your throughout your life. Make sure those codes are accurate.

The DD-214s are required proof of service for VA benefits and are also useful in obtaining non-VA services such as jobs, Social Security benefits, burial benefits and military funeral honors. If your discharge papers have been destroyed or lost, your local County Veterans' Service Officer can help you replace it using one or more of the following sources:

1. If you recorded your DD-214 at a county courthouse, it can be easily retrieved. The county recorder will give you a certified copy and there is no charge for vets to record or retrieve 214s. Recording your DD-214 is a good idea, however it does become a public record, which should not be a problem unless you have exaggerated your war record and your discharge does not square with that story. A fear lately among many veterans is the threat of identity theft, and the act of recording your DD-214 makes the information accessible to anyone. If your county does not have good control over access to these public records, or is making the records accessible over the internet, you may not want to record your military discharge and may want to leave a copy with your County Veterans Service Officer instead. Otherwise, you should record your discharge and keep a copy in a safe place.

2. Copies of some DD-214s can be located at your State Department of Veterans Affairs (SDVA) or in the State Archives. If the state has the DD-214, your Service Office can usually receive copies of these in about two weeks.

3. If you ever filed a claim with the VA or ever applied for a VA Home Loan or for educational benefits from the VA, a copy of your DD-214 should be

on file at the VA Regional Office in the state where you applied. Your Veterans' Service Officer can help you locate it.

4. Some County Veteran' Service Offices are now scanning military discharges into their computers for your convenience and can print you out a copy whenever you need it. If you ever filed a VA claim through a County Veterans' Service Office, there should be a copy of your discharge on file. Your Service Officer can call any county in any state to help your replace your DD-214.

5. Last resort is the National Personnel Records Center (NPRC), in St. Louis. (See the article below.) To retrieve a copy from this source, a Standard Form (SF) 180 must be filled out. The SF180 can be obtained at any County Veterans Service Office. We now have an on-line application that seems to be speeding up the process, but it can still take 2-6 weeks. A DD-214 cannot be found without a Social Security number, correct name spelling, date of birth, and month and year of separation from service. The NPRC has 55 million files in their archives, but these are paper files in cardboard boxes and it takes time to retrieve them.

6. National Guard separation papers, NGB-22s, may be obtained through your State National Guard headquarters. It is advisable that you not wait until you have an immediate need for your DD-214. If you don't have a copy, contact your nearest County Veterans' Service Office.

NATIONAL INFORMATION

Getting a Copy of Your Military Records

The National Personnel Records Center, Military Personnel Records (NPRC-MPR), in St. Louis, MO, is the repository of millions of military personnel, health, and medical records of discharged and deceased veterans of all services during the 20th century.

The NPRC (MPR) and other Centers also store medical treatment records of retirees from all services, as well as records for dependent and other persons treated at naval medical facilities. Copies of most military and medical records, including the DD Form 214, Report of Separation (or equivalent), can be made available upon request.

Veterans and "Next of Kin":

Veterans and next-of-kin of deceased veterans have the same rights to full access to the record. Next-of-kin are the un-remarried widow or widower, son or daughter, father or mother, brother or sister of the deceased veteran. See below for the appropriate address.

<u>Authorized Representatives</u>: Authorized third party requesters, e.g., lawyers, doctors, historians, etc., may submit requests for information from individual records with the veteran's (or next of kin's, for deceased veterans) signed and dated authorization. If you use a signed authorization, it should include exactly what you are authorizing to be released to the third party. Authorizations are valid one year from date of signature.

<u>General Public</u>: The general public can also request some parts of a veteran's military record without the authorization of the veteran or next of kin. The Freedom of Information Act (FOIA) and the Privacy Act provide balance between the right of the public to obtain information from military service records, and the right of the former military service member to protect his/her privacy. In general, information available from military service records which can be released without violation of the Privacy Act are:

- Name,

- Service Number (not Social Security Number),

- Rank,

- Dates of Service,

- Awards and Decorations, and

- Place of Entrance and Separation.

If the veteran is deceased:
- The Place of Birth,

- Date of Death,

- Geographical Location of Death, and

- Place of Burial can also be released.

<u>Court Order:</u> Access to military personnel and medical records on file at the National Personnel Records Center and other Centers, may also be gained pursuant "to the order of a court of competent jurisdiction." Subpoenas qualify as orders of a court of competent jurisdiction only if they have been signed by a judge. To be valid, court orders must also be signed by a judge.

Authority for these requirements is 5 U.S.C. 552a(b) (11), as interpreted by Doe vs. DiGenova, 779 F. 2d 74 (D.C. Cir. 1985), and Stiles vs. Atlanta Gas and Light Company, 453 F. Supp. 798 (N.D. Ga.1978).

The records stored at the National Personnel Records Center cover military personnel who were discharged between the below-listed dates:

- Air Force Officers and Enlisted -- after September 25, 1947

- Army Officers separated between July 1, 1917 and October 2002 (see below)
- Army Enlisted separated between November 1, 1912 and October 2002 (see below)
- Navy Officers separated between January 1, 1903 and the end of 1994 (see below)
- Navy Enlisted separated between January 1, 1886 and the end of 1994 (see below)
- Marine Corps Officers and Enlisted separated between January 1, 1905 and Jan. 2002 (see below)
- Coast Guard Officers and Enlisted separated after January 1, 1898

Military personnel records for individuals separated before these dates are on file at the:

National Archives and Records Administration,
Old Military and Civil Records Branch (NWCTB),
Washington, DC 20408.

E-mail address: inquire@arch2.nara.gov.

Federal law (5 USC 552a(b)) requires that all requests for records and information be submitted in writing. The easiest way to do this is by using Standard Form (SF) 180, Request Pertaining to Military Records.

Requesting Copies of Military Records (Including DD Form 214/215)

Requests must contain enough information to identify the record among the more than 70 million on file at the appropriate Center. The Center needs certain basic information in order to locate military service records. This information includes the veteran's complete name used while in service, service number or social security number, branch of service, and dates of service. Date and place of birth may also be helpful, especially if the service number is not known. If the request pertains to a record that may have been involved in the 1973 fire, also include place of discharge, last unit of assignment, and place of entry into the service, if known.

The SF 180, although not mandatory, is the recommended method to send a request for military service information. This form captures all the necessary information to locate a record. Provide as much information on the form as possible and send copies of any service documents that you may have.

Requests may also be submitted as a letter, containing the basic information listed above. For those records at the National Personnel Records Center, mail the completed SF 180 to:

Records Center
(Military Personnel Records)
9700 Page Avenue
St. Louis, MO 63132-5100

The US Navy stopped retiring personnel records to the National Personnel Records Center (NPRC) approximately in 1995. Navy veterans who received a FINAL discharge or were retired AFTER 1994, any request for personnel related information (i.e. DD 214, copy of personnel record, etc;) should be forwarded to the following address. A final discharge means either being discharged from active duty (not being released from active duty with inactive Naval Reserve service to complete) or being discharged from the US Naval Reserve:

Bureau of Naval Personnel
ATTN: PERS 312-D
5720 Integrity Drive
Millington, TN 38055-3130

The US Marine Corps stopped retiring personnel records to NPRC in January 2002. As in the case of Navy personnel, any Marine Corps personnel discharged or retired AFTER January 2002 should forward requests to the following address:

Headquarters, US Marine Corps
ATTN: MMSB-10
2008 Elliott Road, Suite 225
Quantico, VA 22134-5030

The US Army stopped retiring personnel records to NPRC in October 2002 All Regular Army, Army Reserve, and RETIRED Army National Guard personnel discharged or retired AFTER October 2002 should forward any requests for personnel related information to the following address:

Commander
US Army Human Resources Command-St. Louis
1 Reserve Way
St. Louis, MO 63132-5200

Army National Guard personnel, regardless of when they were discharged, should contact the State Adjutant General's Office of the State in which they served, although the Federal portion of their Army National Guard service should be on file at NPRC.

The US Air Force (to include Air National Guard personnel) and the US Coast Guard continue to retire their personnel records to NPRC.

Military Medical Records:

The military service departments no longer retire service medical records (SMR's-military medical records) to NPRC. Listed below are the dates each service department stopped retiring SMR's to NPRC:

- Army: October 16, 1992

- Navy: January 31, 1994

- Air Force: May 1, 1994

- Marine Corps: May 1, 1994

- Coast Guard: April 1, 1998

SMR's DO NOT include military hospital records. Those types of records are retired to NPRC usually 5 years AFTER the date of last treatment. In order for NPRC to conduct a search of military hospital records (also known as clinical records), NPRC requires the following information:

- date of treatment;

- type of treatment;

- place of treatment;

- whether or not the patient was hospitalized; and

- any other pertinent information that can be provided that will help or assist in finding the information that you are seeking.

Military Dependents Medical Records:

NPRC also maintains military dependent treatment records. In order to search for those records, they require the same information as if the request were for a military member treated at a military hospital. NPRC maintains those dependent treatment records at two separate locations:

For Navy, Marine Corps, Army and Air Force dependents treated at a Naval Hospital, submit request to:

National Personnel Records Center
Military Personnel Records
ATTN: Organizational Records Unit
9700 Page Avenue
St. Louis, MO 63132-5100

For Army, Air Force, Navy or Marine Corps dependents treated at either an Army or Air Force Hospital, submit your request to the following address:

National Personnel Records Center
Civilian Personnel Records
111 Winnebago
St. Louis, MO 63118

Completing a Records Request On-line

Veterans and "Next-of-Kin" can now complete a records request on-line. One must still print out and sign a sign a signature verification, and mail or fax the verification, because Federal Law requires a signature on all records request. However, completing the application online can be easier and faster than completing the SF Form 180.Those who are not veterans or next-of-kin, cannot use the on-line system. They must complete the SF 180.Requesting Copies of Military Medical Records

VA Claims

Veterans who plan to file a claim for medical benefits with the Department of Veterans Affairs (VA) do not need to request a copy of their military health record from the National Personnel Records Center. When you file a VA claim, the Department of Veterans Affairs will request the record automatically, as part of the claims process. Generally there is no charge for military personnel and health record information provided to veterans, next-of-kin, and authorized representatives. If your request involves a service fee, you will be notified as soon as that determination is made.

How Long Does it Take?

It wasn't all that long ago when turnaround time for military records was miserable. It was not unusual for a simple DD Form 214/215 request to take up to 180 days. NPRC has transformed the way it responds to inquiries, to provide dramatically improved customer service. This Business Process Reengineering project has changed structures and systems that in some cases have been in place since the center was formed 40 years ago. However, there is still a heavy backlog.

CHAPTER TWELVE

FILING THE VA CLAIM FORM

As part of your out processing from the military you will be given the opportunity to file a claim with the Department of Veterans Affairs regarding any disabilities that you may have incurred while on active duty. The information you place on the application should be supported by medical records contained in your military medical record and the information on your separation physical. If the VA agrees that you have a service connected disability, then you will be entitled to Disability Compensation and a number of other benefits.

Filing a Claim with the VA

If a veteran believes that he or she has been harmed by anything in his or her military experience, they have the right to file a claim for treatment and compensation with the Department of Veterans Affairs (VA). A claim can be filed at any time and there is never a charge to file a claim. While it is customary for the soldier to be given the opportunity to file a claim during out processing, sometimes, this opportunity is not taken. In this instance, the claim should also be filed as soon as possible after leaving the service.

When you are filling out the claim form, remember to be as concise as possible, but make sure that you list every illness or injury that occurred during your military career. While the initial decision is made upon medical information, the individuals making the decision regarding your disabilities *ARE NOT PHYSICIANS*! Those individuals making these decision, can if they so desire, completely ignore the findings of your actual physicians.

To give an example, I under went one C & P[13] exam where the physician conducting the examination clearly stated in his medical report that my condition was rapidly deteriorating. In spite of this very specific medical finding by a trained physician, the raters refused to increase my disability rating. I had obtained the direct telephone number of the deputy regional director and I called him about this absolutely idiotic decision. He agreed that the examining physician had stated that my condition had worsened, but he said the decision had been made to deny me an increase in my disability rating since in the opinion of the rating board, *"While the physician stated that the condition had worsened, he didn't say it like he meant it."* I am not sure how one determines if someone actually meant what he or she wrote on a report, but apparently the raters in question had access to a crystal ball to be able to read the physician's mind.

This was an interesting exercise in convolutes logic on the part of the raters and shows their freedom of action. These people who were determining the state of my physical condition were not physicians, but in spite of this, they were (and are) charged with making decisions that had a direct impact on my medical treatment. However, no one in the system saw anything wrong with this.

How to File a Claim:

A claim can be filed at any VA office or medical center. Many cities also have storefront "Vet Centers" where a claim may be filed. It can also be done by mail, after requesting the appropriate forms from the VA. Most telephone directories will list the nearest VA facilities under "US Government"

Assistance of a Veterans Service Officer (VSO) may also be sought. All major veterans organizations (American Legion, VFW, DAV, etc) have service officers authorized by the VA to act in behalf of the veteran. In addition, many state and county government agencies have VSO's. Once again, there is never a charge for the assistance of the VSO.

A caution: As with anything else, there are good VSO's and bad VSO's. The veteran must feel comfortable with his VSO, because this person will be handling the veteran's paperwork and (hopefully) advancing the claim. The veteran should be comfortable working with his VSO and feel that progress is being made. If the veteran feels that his claim is not being handled properly, he should not hesitate to find a different VSO to assist him.

---

[13] A C & P exam is a special exam that the VA can require you to undergo in order to establish either the existence of a disability or the extent of a disability. Generally, the raters accept the findings of the examining physician, however, the raters can completely ignore the findings of the exam.

VA Compensation Application Process

You apply for VA Disability Compensation by completing the *Application for Disability Compensation or Pension Benefits*, VA form 21-526. The application form should be given to you during out processing from the military. However, if for some reason it is not, then the same form can be obtained by visiting, calling or writing to any VA regional office.

To receive VA compensation, a veteran's disability or disabilities must first be evaluated and determined by VA to be service-connected to a certain degree that is compensable. For more information, you can call toll-free 1-800-827-1000 or access the form on the Internet at http://vabenefits.vba.va.gov/vonapp.

When you apply for Veterans benefits, you should have copies of:

- Dependency records (marriage and children's birth certificates, and divorce,
- decree, if any)
- Medical evidence (treatment records and hospital reports)
- His/her Report of Separation from Active Military Service (DD Form 214) or
- discharge certificate
- Dependent(s) Social Security number(s)

If you are submitting an application after leaving the service then the best way to submit an application is by U.S. mail. VA forms and applications can be downloaded from the Internet www.va.gov/forms/.

If you do not have the information required by VA then you should call 1-800-827-1000 and explain the situation. A VA representative should be able to determine if there is alternative documentation that can be used. To locate the nearest VA regional office, visit www.va.gov/sta/guide/home.asp.

Application Approval

An *Application for Disability Compensation or Pension Benefits*[14] should be processed within 30 days of submission. However, in actuality, the waiting time can actually be as long as a year. As a part of the application review process, VA may request additional medical records and documentation, or require a

---

[14] VA Form 21-256

physical examination of the person applying. If VA does not receive the medical records or other requested evidence timely, then the application review process will be held up until the information is received.

If benefits are granted and the disability is determined by VA to be non-permanent, then the case may be periodically reviewed to see whether or not the veteran is still disabled. An examination will be occasionally scheduled to review any non-permanent disabilities. If your disability is determined by VA to be permanent, an examination to review his/her disability will not be scheduled.

Well Grounded Claims

During the application review process, a VA rater will try to determine if your case is well grounded. During your time with the VA you will hear the phrase "well grounded claim" until you become sick of it. However, unless your claim is found to be well grounded, it will be denied. For a claim for disability benefits to be considered well grounded, there must be three elements present:

(1) a medical showing of a current medical condition;

(2) lay or in certain circumstances, medical evidence of disease or injury in service; and

(3) medical evidence showing a nexus[15] between the asserted injury in service and the current disability.

Where medical evidence is required, medical journal articles alone will generally not suffice unless they are enhanced by a physician's opinion stating that the current disability was related, is likely to be related, could be related, or even possibly was related to service. A physician's opinion need not be conclusive to establish a well-grounded claim.

Alternatively, both the second and third elements above can be satisfied by the submission of minimum evidence:

(a) that the condition was "noted[16]" during service or during an applicable presumption period;

(b) that there has been post service continuity of symptomatology[17] (as to which lay opinion can suffice; and

---

[15] Connection

[16] Technically speaking, you do not have to have ever been treated for the condition in question while in the military, but it must be at least mentioned in your medical records as existing during your military service.

(c) medical, or in some rare circumstances, lay evidence of a nexus between the present disability between the present disability and the post service symptomatology.

Agent Orange Claims:

Agent Orange was a defoliant used widely during the Vietnam War (and also a few other places) that has shown to have caused serious medical problems in service people exposed to these chemicals over long periods of time. Having recognized the serious side effects of this agent, the VA has begun to recognize some of these medical problems as service connected injuries.

An Agent Orange claim is filed the same as any other claim; essentially it is a claim for injury during service in the military.

It is not necessary to discuss Agent Orange in the filing of the claim, and in fact, it can be detrimental. As the veteran, all you must do is describe, to the best of your ability, the injury or disease. This should be done in layman's terms; you are not a physician and should not attempt self-diagnosis. The VA will accept the claim, and schedule the veteran for a medical examination. At that time, the veteran should inform the physician that he was in Vietnam. A "Agent Orange " tag should then be affixed to the veterans file.

If you have seen a private physician, medical reports can and should be included with the claim. There is no value, however, in a physician's opinion that the disease was caused by Agent Orange. Quite simply put, most physicians are not qualified to make this assessment unless they are a researcher. Many veterans think that a letter from their doctor stating that the physician thinks this was caused by Agent Orange will help --- the truth is that it does not. Currently the VA offers compensation for only certain diseases as related to Agent Orange. This does not mean, however, that your condition may not be awarded. The VA may award for a condition as related to some other cause.

Regardless of what you might believe to be the potential disposition of your claim, if you have a health problem and you believe that it might have begun or worsened during your time in the military: **File the Claim!!**

Laws change, and a condition that may not be compensable today, may well be compensable tomorrow. The only way you can protect your rights is to file the claim. VA claims are usually awarded back to date of filing. If you do not file, you forfeit your rights.

---

[17] Symptomatology simply means a showing that the condition has or is having some effect on your physical well being.

PART III

WORKING WITH THE DEPARTMENT OF VETERANS AFFAIRS

CHAPTER THIRTEEN

THE DEPARTMENT OF VETERANS AFFAIRS

It is an almost universal belief that the military is the largest and most bureaucratic organization in the world. Well I am here to tell you that this is not true. For paper shuffling, administrative mazes and administrative roadblocks, the Department of Veterans Affairs wins hands down.

The Department of Veterans Affairs (VA) was established on March 15, 1989, succeeding the Veterans Administration. It is responsible for providing federal benefits to veterans and their dependents and is headed by the Secretary of Veterans Affairs. The VA is the second largest of the 15 Cabinet departments and operates nationwide programs for health care, financial assistance and burial benefits.

Of the 26 million veterans currently alive, nearly three-quarters served during a war or an official period of conflict. About a quarter of the nation's population, approximately 70 million people, are potentially eligible for VA benefits and services because they are veterans, family members or survivors of veterans.

The responsibility to care for veterans, spouses, survivors and dependents can last a long time. The last dependent of a Revolutionary War veteran died in 1911. About 439 children and widows of Spanish-American War veterans still receive VA compensation or pensions. Six children of Civil War veterans still draw VA benefits.

VA's fiscal year 2003 projected spending is $59.6 billion -- $25.9 billion for health care, $32.8 billion for benefits, $132 million for national cemetery operations, $455 million for all VA construction and $322 million for departmental administration.

Compensation and Pension

In fiscal year 2002, VA spent $25 billion in disability compensation, death compensation and pension to 3.3 million people. About 2.7 million veterans receive disability compensation or pensions from VA. Also receiving VA benefits are 568,852 spouses, children and parents of deceased veterans. Among them are 143,437 survivors of Vietnam era veterans and 273,680 survivors of World War II veterans.

Education and Training

Since 1944, when the first GI Bill began, more than 21 million veterans, service members and family members have received $75 billion in GI Bill benefits for education and training.

The number of GI Bill recipients includes 7.8 million veterans from World War II, 2.4 million from the Korean War and 8.2 million post-Korean and Vietnam era veterans and active duty personnel. VA also has assisted in the education of more than 750,000 dependents of veterans whose deaths or total disabilities were service-connected.

In 2002, VA helped pay for the education or training of 324,505 veterans and active-duty personnel, 85,766 reservists and National Guardsmen and 53,888 survivors.

Medical Care

Perhaps the most visible of all VA benefits and services is health care. From 54 hospitals in 1930, VA's health care system has grown to 163 hospitals, with at least one in each of the 48 contiguous states, Puerto Rico and the District of Columbia. VA operates more than 850 ambulatory care and community-based outpatient clinics, 137 nursing homes, 43 domiciliaries and 73 comprehensive home-care programs. VA health care facilities provide a broad spectrum of medical, surgical and rehabilitative care.

More than 4.5 million people received care in VA health care facilities in 2002. VA is used annually by approximately 75 percent of all disabled and low-income veterans. In 2002, VA treated 564,700 patients in VA hospitals and contract hospitals, 50,267 in nursing homes and 22,541 in domiciliaries. VA's outpatient clinics registered approximately 46.5 million visits.

VA manages the largest medical education and health professions training program in the United States. VA facilities are affiliated with 107 medical schools, 55 dental schools and more than 1,200 other schools across the country. Each year, about 81,000 health professionals are trained in VA medical centers. More than half of the physicians practicing in the United States have had part of their professional education in the VA health care system.

VA's medical system serves as a backup to the Defense Department during national emergencies and as a federal support organization during major disasters.

During the last five years, VA has put its health care facilities under 21 networks, which provide more medical services to more veterans and family members than at any time during VA's long history.

VA has experienced unprecedented growth in the medical system workload over the past few years. The number of patients treated increased by over 9.5 percent from 2001 to 2002.

To receive VA health care benefits most veterans must enroll. More than 6.8 million veterans are enrolled in the VA health care system as of October 2002. When they enroll, they are placed in priority groups or categories that help VA manage health care services within budgetary constraints and ensure quality care for those enrolled.

Some veterans are exempted from having to enroll. People who do not have to enroll include veterans with a service-connected disability of 50 percent or more, veterans who were discharged from the military within one year but have not yet been rated for a VA disability benefit and veterans seeking care for only a service-connected disability.

Severely disabled veterans receive priority access to care. Veterans with service-connected disabilities rated 50 percent or greater receive priority for hospitalization and outpatient care for both service-connected and non-service-connected treatment.

Since 1979, VA's Readjustment Counseling Service has operated Vet Centers, which provide psychological counseling for war-related trauma, community outreach, case management and referral activities, plus supportive social services to veterans and family members. There are 206 Vet Centers.

Since the first Vet Center opened, approximately 1.6 million veterans have been helped. Every year, the Vet Centers serve over 126,000 veterans and handle at least 900,000 visits from veterans and family members.

Vet Centers are open to any veteran who served in the military in a combat theater during wartime or anywhere during a period of armed hostilities. Vet Centers also provide trauma counseling to veterans who were sexually assaulted or harassed while on active duty.

VA provides health care and benefits to more than 100,000 homeless veterans each year. While the proportion of veterans among the homeless is declining, VA actively engages veterans in outreach, medical care, benefits assistance and transitional housing. VA has made more than 300 grants for transitional housing, service centers and vans for outreach and transportation to state and local governments, tribal governments, non-profit community and faith-based service providers.

Programs for alcoholism, drug addiction and post-traumatic stress disorder have been expanded in recent years, along with attention to environmental hazards.

Indispensable to providing America's veterans with quality medical care are more than 118,000 volunteers in VA's Voluntary Service who donate more than 13 million hours each year to bring companionship and care to hospitalized veterans.

Research

In 2002, funding for VA research was $371 million. Another $377 million from VA's medical care account supports research efforts. Funding from the National Institutes of Health and other foundations, combined with supporting funds from pharmaceutical companies, contributed another $624 million to VA research. VA currently conducts more than 15,000 research projects at 115 VA medical centers.

While providing high quality health care to the nation's veterans, VA also conducts an array of research on some of the most difficult challenges facing medical science today. VA has become a world leader in such research areas as aging, women's health, AIDS, post-traumatic stress disorder and other mental health issues. VA research has improved medical care for veterans and the nation.

VA researchers played key roles in developing the cardiac pacemaker, the CT scan, radioimmunoassay and improvements in artificial limbs. The first liver transplant in the world was performed by a VA surgeon-researcher. VA clinical trials established the effectiveness of new treatments for tuberculosis, schizophrenia and high blood pressure. The "Seattle Foot," developed in VA, allows people with amputations to run and jump. VA contributions to medical knowledge have won VA scientists many prestigious awards, including the Nobel Prize.

Seventy-five percent of VA researchers are practicing physicians. Because of their dual roles, VA research often immediately benefits patients. Functional electrical stimulation, a technology using controlled electrical currents to activate paralyzed muscles, is being developed at VA clinical facilities and laboratories throughout the country. Through this technology, paraplegic patients have been able to grasp objects, stand, and even walk short distances.

Special VA "centers of excellence" throughout the nation conduct research in rehabilitation, health services and medical conditions including AIDS, alcoholism, schizophrenia, stroke and Parkinson's disease. Multi-center clinical trials investigate the best therapy for various diseases. Current projects include testing aspirin therapy for heart patients, surgical treatment to reduce the risk of stroke and treatment options for prostate cancer.

VA investigators continue to make major contributions to the understanding of post-traumatic stress disorder and Agent Orange exposure, both research areas resulting from the Vietnam War. More recently, VA has conducted a number of Gulf War-related research projects and has two environmental hazards research centers focusing on the possible health effects of environmental exposures among Gulf War veterans.

Home Loan Assistance

Since 1944, when VA began helping veterans purchase homes under the original GI Bill, through September 2002, about 16.9 million VA home loan guarantees have been issued, with a total value of $748 billion. VA began fiscal year 2003 with 2.8 million active home loans reflecting an amortized loan amount totaling $218.5 billion.

In fiscal year 2002, VA guaranteed 320,000 loans valued at $40.5 billion. VA's programs for specially adapted housing helped about 575 disabled veterans with grants totaling more than $23 million last year.

Insurance

VA operates one of the largest life insurance programs in the world and the seventh largest one in the United States. VA directly administers six life insurance programs with 4.3 million policies in force having a face value of $710 billion.

In 2002, VA returned $625 million in dividends to 4.8 million veterans and service members holding some of these VA life insurance policies. In addition, VA supervises the Service Members' Group Life Insurance and the Veterans' Group Life Insurance programs, which provide $728 billion in insurance coverage to veterans, active-duty members, reservists and Guardsmen, plus 3.1 million spouses and children.

The high customer satisfaction with VA's Insurance Center is marked by a score of 90 in the American Customer Satisfaction Index, an independent survey that measures the performance of private sector and government agencies. Private-sector insurance companies scored an average 75.

VA's National Cemeteries

In 1973, most Army-administered national cemeteries were transferred to VA, which now manages them through its National Cemetery Administration. Currently, VA maintains 120 national cemeteries in 39 states and Puerto Rico.

Interments in VA national cemeteries in 2002 increased by 5.3 percent over 2001, for a total of 89,329. That number is likely to increase to 109,000 in 2008. In 2002, VA provided more than 348,000 headstones or markers for veterans' graves. Since taking over the veterans cemetery program in 1973, VA has provided more than 8.1 million headstones and markers.

Between 1999 and 2002, VA opened five new national cemeteries: the Gerald B. H. Solomon Saratoga National Cemetery near Albany, N.Y.; the Abraham Lincoln National Cemetery near Chicago; the Dallas-Fort Worth

National Cemetery; the Ohio Western Reserve National Cemetery near Cleveland; and the Fort Sill National Cemetery near Oklahoma City. Within the next five years, VA plans to open five more national cemeteries. Those areas are: Atlanta, Detroit, South Florida, Sacramento (Calif.) and Pittsburgh. Achieving this objective will advance VA's goal of serving 85 percent of veterans with a national cemetery or state veterans cemetery within 75 miles of their homes by 2008.

VA administers the Presidential Memorial Certificate program, which provides engraved certificates signed by the president to commemorate honorably discharged, deceased veterans. They are sent to the veteran's next of kin and loved ones. VA provided 290,000 certificates in 2002.

VA also administers the State Cemetery Grants Program, which encourages development of state veterans cemeteries. VA provides up to 100 percent of the funds to develop, expand or improve veterans cemeteries operated and maintained by the states. More than $149 million has been awarded for 49 operational veterans cemeteries in 29 states and Guam. Six state cemeteries are under construction. In 2002, state cemeteries that received VA grants buried more than 17,177 eligible veterans and family members. This figure represented an 11.5 percent increase over the previous year.

VA Employees

On VA's rolls as of February 28, 2003 were 224,724 employees. Among all departments and agencies of the federal government, only the Department of Defense has a larger work force. Of the total number of VA employees, 202,709 were in the Veterans Health Administration, 13,479 in the Veterans Benefits Administration, 1,432 in the National Cemetery System, 3,166 in the Veterans Canteen Service and 409 in the Revolving Supply Fund. The rest - 3,477 employees - are in various staff offices VA is a leader in hiring veterans.

About *53 percent*[18] of all male employees are *veterans*. As of September 30, 2002, VA had 8,508 women employees who served in the U.S. armed forces. About 61 percent of male and 33 percent of female veteran employees served during the Vietnam War. More than 7 percent of all VA employees are disabled veterans and five hold the Medal of Honor.

Chronological History of the Department of Veterans Affairs

1930   The Veterans Administration created by Executive Order 5398, signed by President Herbert Hoover on July 21. At that time, there were 54 hospitals, 4.7 million living veterans and 31,600 employees.

---

[18] Unfortunately many of the 47% who are not veterans are in management and supervisory position.

1933   The Board of Veterans Appeals established.

1944   On June 22, President Franklin Roosevelt signed the "Servicemen's Readjustment Act of 1944" (Public Law 346, passed unanimously by the 78th Congress), more commonly known as "The GI Bill of Rights," offering home loan and education benefits to veterans.

1946   The Department of Medicine & Surgery established, succeeded in 1989 by the Veterans Health Services and Research Administration, renamed the Veterans Health Administration in 1991.

1953   The Department of Veterans Benefits established, succeeded in 1989 by the Veterans Benefits Administration.

1973   The National Cemetery System – renamed the National Cemetery Administration in 1998 – created when Congress transferred 82 national cemeteries from the Army to VA. The Army kept Arlington National Cemetery and the U.S. Soldiers' and Airmen's Home National Cemetery in Washington, D.C.

1988   Legislation to elevate VA to Cabinet status signed by President Reagan.

1989   On March 15, VA became the 14th Department in the President's Cabinet.

Secretaries of Veterans Affairs

Anthony J. Principi	2001 – 2005
Togo D. West, Jr.	1998 – 2000
Jesse Brown	1993 – 1997
Edward J. Derwinski	1989 – 1992
Thomas K. Turnage	1986 – 1989
Harry N. Walters	1982 – 1986
Robert P. Nimmo	1981 – 1982
Max Cleland	1977 – 1981
Richard L. Roudebush	1974 – 1977
Donald E. Johnson	1969 – 1974
William J. Driver	1965 – 1969
John S. Gleason	1961 – 1964
Sumner G. Whittier	1957 – 1961
Harvey V. Higley	1953 – 1957
Carl R. Gray	1948 – 1953
Omar Bradley	1945 – 1948
Frank T. Hines	1930 – 1945

CHAPTER FOURTEEN

VA DEPARTMENTS

Next we will look at the major departments that exist within the Department of Veterans Affairs that are charged with meeting the goals discussed above. Since most veterans only see the medical clinic where they receive treatment, few really understand just how large the Department of Veterans Affairs actually is.

I might also make note that while I am giving the information below that is contained on the Department of Veterans Affairs website about each agency, there is much that is not said on the website that will be discussed later in this book.

Veterans Health Administration

With 158 VA medical centers (VAMCs) nationwide, VHA manages one of the largest health care systems in the United States. The VA medical Centers within a Veterans Integrated Service Network (VISN) work together to provide efficient, accessible health care to veterans in their areas. The Veterans Health Administration also conducts research and education, and provides emergency medical preparedness.

Veterans Benefits Administration

The Veterans Benefit Administration (VBA) provides benefits and services to the veteran population through 58 VA regional offices. Some of the benefits and services provided by VBA to veterans and their dependents include compensation and pension, education, loan guaranty, and insurance.

National Cemetery Administration

The National Cemetery Administration is responsible for providing burial benefits to veterans and eligible dependents. The delivery of these benefits involves managing 120 National Cemeteries nationwide, providing grave markers worldwide, administering the State Cemetery Grants Program that complements the National Cemeteries network, and providing Presidential Memorial Certificates to next of kin of deceased veterans.

Board of Contract Appeals

The Department of Veterans Affairs Board of Contract Appeals considers and determines appeals from decisions of contracting officers pursuant to the Contract Disputes Act of 1978.

Board of Veterans' Appeals

The Board reviews benefit claims determinations made by local VA offices and issues decision on appeals. The Board members, attorneys experienced in veterans law and in reviewing benefit claims, are the only ones who can issue Board decisions.

Center for Women Veterans

The mission of the Center for Women Veterans is to ensure women veterans have access to VA benefits and services, to ensure that VA health care and benefits programs are responsive to the gender-specific needs of women veterans, to perform outreach to improve women veterans awareness of VA services, benefits and eligibility, and to act as the primary advisor to the Secretary for Veterans Affairs on all matters related to programs, issues, and initiatives for and affecting women veterans.

Office of Acquisition & Materiel Management

The Office of Acquisition & Material Management is responsible for overseeing the acquisition, storage, and distribution of supplies, services, and equipment used by VA facilities and other Government agencies. OA&MM manages pharmaceuticals, medical supplies and equipment, and nonperishable subsistence through its procurement system.

Office of Alternate Dispute Resolution (ADR) and Mediation

This office provides effective training and consulting in conflict resolution and ADR (emphasizing mediation) to VA organizations and employees.

Office of Budget

The Office of Budget is the focal point for the Departmental Budget Formulation and Execution, the Capital Investment Board and Performance Reporting.

Office of Public Affairs & Intergovernmental Affairs

The Office of Public Affairs & Intergovernmental Affairs has two major offices, Public Affairs and Intergovernmental Affairs. The primary mission of Public Affairs is to provide information to the Nation's veterans and their eligible dependents and survivors through news media concerning available Department benefits and programs. Intergovernmental Affairs interacts with Federal, state, and local government agencies and officials in developing and maintaining a positive and productive relationship.

Office of Congressional Affairs

The Office of Congressional Affairs is the principal point of contact between the Department and Congress and is the oversight and coordinating body for the Department's Congressional relations. The office serves in an advisory capacity to the Secretary and Deputy Secretary as well as other VA managers concerning policies, programs, and legislative matters in which Congressional committees or individual members of Congress have expressed an interest.

Office of Employment Discrimination Complaint Adjudication

The Office of Employment Discrimination Complaint Adjudication maintains a high quality and high performing workforce and ensures fairness, integrity, and trust throughout the complaint adjudication phase of the Equal Employment Opportunity complaint resolution process..

Office of Financial Management

The Office of Financial Management continually improves the quality of the VA's financial services through the development of sound financial policies and the promotion of efficient financial management systems, operations, policies, and practices.

Office of the General Counsel

The Office of the General Counsel identifies and meets the legal needs of the VA.

Office of Human Resources & Administration

The Office of Human Resources &Administration's functional areas include human resources management, administrative policies and functions, equal opportunity policies and functions, and security and law enforcement.

Office of Information & Technology

The Office of Information & Technology activities include integrated business and information technology (IT) planning; security and contingency planning to protect information and privacy across VA systems and networks; reviews to evaluate the performance of IT programs; review and approval of IT acquisitions; facilitation of intra- and intergovernmental partnerships; educating and informing the Department of IT, initiatives and legislation; and sharing lessons learned.

Office of the Inspector General

The Office of the Inspector General provides service to veterans, VA employees, and citizens concerned with good Government.

Office of Occupational Safety & Health

The staff of the Office of Occupational Safety & Health ensures that the VA complies with requirements of Federal, Occupational Safety and Health Administration (OSHA), Joint Commission for Accreditation of Healthcare Organizations (JCAHO), and VA standards.

Office of Policy, Planning and Preparedness

The Office of Policy, Planning and Preparedness facilitates, coordinates and validates the Department's policy development and formulation processes; coordinates VA's strategic planning process and implementation of the Government Performance and Results Act requirements; supports the identification, development, analysis, and review of issues affecting veterans' programs; links and supplements the actuarial and quantitative analysis capabilities of VA in support of major policy inquiries; serves as VA's focal point for access to and availability of official data; coordinates the independent evaluation of VA program performance; and fosters quality management techniques and procedures throughout VA.

Office of Small & Disadvantaged Business Utilization

The Office of Small & Disadvantaged Business Utilization advocates for the maximum practicable participation of small, small disadvantaged, veteran-owned, women-owned, and empowerment zone businesses in contracts awarded by the VA and in subcontracts, which are awarded by VA's prime contractors.

As I said before, most veterans only see the clinic or other facility to which they have submitted their paperwork. While I am sure that every veteran knows that the VA is part of the great mass of government agencies, this chapter can give some idea of just how large the Department of Veterans Affairs actually is and how many areas in which it operates.

The individual veteran is not applying to an organization where he or she is or can become known as an individual. Rather the veteran is a faceless file folder, which must tell the entire story to the rating board in order for the veteran to receive the benefits requested. This is the key to making the system work.

PART FOUR

ESTABLISHING ELIGIBILITY
FOR VETERAN'S BENEFITS

CHAPTER FIFTEEN

THE IMPORTANCE OF ESTABLISHING ELIGIBILITY

As has been touched upon above, there is a broad range of benefits available to the veteran as a result of completion of military service, but each one is based upon establishing eligibility. Someone can serve in the military for fifty years and be 100% disabled by civilian medical standards, but if he or she cannot establish eligibility based upon VA standards then there are no benefits forthcoming. This is the first confusing aspect of dealing with the VA or any federal agency for that matter, each one uses its own standards for eligibility and does now have to accept determinations from other government agencies.

It must be remembered that when a veteran establishes eligibility for benefits from the Department of Veterans Affairs (VA), he or she is actually establishing that he or she has some medical problems that are service connected and as a result, he or she is eligible to receive medical treatment from the VA. This all important eligibility for most veterans' health care benefits is based solely on active military service in the Army, Navy, Air Force, Marines, or Coast Guard (or Merchant Marines during WW II), and the veteran being discharged under other than dishonorable conditions.

Reservists and National Guard members who were called to active duty by a Federal Executive Order may also qualify for VA health care benefits. Returning service members, including Reservists and National Guard members who served on active duty in a theater of combat operations have special eligibility for hospital care, medical services, and nursing home care for two years following discharge from active duty.

Unlike some programs, Health Care eligibility is not just for those who served in combat and other groups[19] may be eligible for some health benefits.

Most importantly, veteran's health care is not just for service-connected injuries or medical conditions and the veteran's health care facilities are not just for men only. VA offers full-service health care to women veterans.

Medical Coverage

Similar to civilian insurance, the VA provides a Medical Benefits Package, which is a standard enhanced health benefit plan available to all enrolled veterans. This plan emphasizes preventive and primary care, and offers a full range of outpatient and inpatient services within VA health care system.

VA maintains an annual enrollment system to manage the provision of quality hospital and outpatient medical care and treatment to all enrolled veterans. A priority system ensures that veterans with service-connected disabilities and those below the low-income threshold are able to be enrolled in VA's health care system.

Just like civilian medical insurance coverage, the VA enrollment allows health care benefits to become portable throughout the entire VA system. Enrolled veterans who are traveling or who spend time away from their primary treatment facility may obtain care at any VA health care facility across the country without the worry of having to reapply.

There is no question that the standard benefits included in the VA's Medical Benefits Package are outstanding. VA's medical benefits package provides the following health care services to all enrolled veterans.

- Preventive Care Services
    1. Immunizations
    2. Physical Examinations
    3. Health Care Assessments
    4. Screening Tests
    5. Health Education Programs

- Ambulatory (Outpatient) Diagnostic and Treatment Services
    1. Emergency outpatient care in VA facilities
    2. Medical
    3. Surgical (including reconstructive/plastic surgery as a result of disease or trauma)
    4. Chiropractic Care
    5. Mental Health
    6. Bereavement Counseling
    7. Substance Abuse

---

[19] See Appendix A for a list of "other groups".

- Hospital (Inpatient) Diagnostic and Treatment
    1. Emergency inpatient care in VA facilities
    2. Medical
    3. Surgical (including reconstructive/plastic surgery as a result of disease or trauma)
    4. Mental Health
    5. Substance Abuse

- Medications and Supplies
    1. Prescription medications
    2. Over-the counter medications
    3. Medical and surgical supplies - Generally, they must be prescribed by a VA provider and be available under VA's national formulary system

Additionally, in some instances, the VA will pay for medications prescribed by a non-VA physician. Though generally this applies only to veterans with special eligibility, such as veterans receiving Aid and Attendance or Housebound benefits, or who are approved by a VA health care facility for Fee Basis are eligible to receive medications at VA expense.

There are also special benefit and limited benefit programs available to eligible veterans that are reviewed in the next chapter.

Establishing Eligibility

As I have stated, every single benefit hinges on the veteran establishing basic eligibility for health care. Determining eligibility for health care through the VA is a two-step process:

First, the VA must determine your eligibility status as a veteran by reviewing your Character of Discharge from active military service, and your length of active military service

Then the VA must determine whether you qualify for one of the eight enrollment priority groups.

Qualifying military service

The character of discharge you received from the military can be a factor in determining a veteran's eligibility for VA benefits. It is not an issue if you received:

- An honorable discharge

- A general discharge

- A discharge under honorable conditions

If you have a different character of discharge, you may still be eligible for care. However, there may have to be a formal ruling by the VA on a case to case basis depending on the type of discharge. In such circumstances, you should contact your Enrollment Coordinator at your local VA health care facility to see if you qualify.

Qualifying length of military Service

Once the character or type of discharge received has been established, then there is the question of the length of your service. Length of service may be a factor in some situations as well as when you served.

There's no length of service requirement for:

- Former enlisted persons who started active duty before September 8, 1980, or

- Former officers who first entered active duty before October 17, 1981

- All other veterans must have 24 months of continuous active duty military service or meet one of the exceptions described below.

Minimum Service Requirement

Even though one of the specific requirements of eligibility for those enlisted who entered service after September 8, 1980 or former officers who entered service after October 17, 1981 is 24 months of continuous service, you do not have to meet the 24 continuous months of active duty service requirement if you:

- Were discharged with an "early out"; or

- Were discharged or released from active duty for a disability that began in the service or got worse because of the service; or

- Have been determined by VA to have compensable service-connected conditions; or

- Were discharged for a reason other than disability, but you had a medical condition at the time that
  1. was disabling, and

2. In the opinion of a doctor, would have justified a discharge for disability (in this last case, the disability must be documented in service records)

Enrollment

Generally, a veteran must be enrolled in the VA health care system to receive benefits offered in the Medical Benefits Package; however, some veterans do not need to be enrolled in the system in order to receive medical benefits.

Enrollment is not required if the veteran:

* Have been determined by VA to be 50% or more disabled from service-connected (SC) conditions,

* Are seeking care for a VA rated service-connected disability only,

* It is less than one year since you were discharged for a disability that the military determined was incurred or aggravated by your service, but that VA has not yet rated

However, enrolling for medical care will assist VA in planning and budgeting resources to insure that all qualified veterans receive medical care.

CHAPTER SIXTEEN

OTHER BENEFITS AND SERVICES

Establishing eligibility is the minimum requirement that must be achieved to qualify for any veterans' benefits. I have heard a number of veterans say that it is such a hassle to deal with the VA that there is no point in them going through the paper work. Their rationale for not applying for benefits usually boils down to the fact that they have medical coverage with their employer's group policy and they do not need the little bit of money that they would get from VA.

That may be true today, but as they get older, their medical conditions may change drastically. Corporate benefit packages are changing to cover less and less of the needs of the employees. As we have seen with many of the largest corporations in this country, the compensation packages of the senior officers get richer and the benefits of the rank and file are reduced. There have even been instances of entire retirement packages already earned by workers being terminated due to the excessive cost to the corporation.

High positions are also no safeguard to being told that you are no longer needed. In my own case, I was Vice President/General Counsel of a major defense contractor. When I became ill as a result of my service connected injuries, I was told I was no longer needed. Without the VA benefits to which I am entitled, I would have had some serious problems getting medical care.

In addition to the medical benefits package available to an eligible veteran there is also a number of other benefits available to eligible veterans including financial compensation. This compensation is in most cases tax free, and based upon wither the veteran has either a service connected disability or ill health and low income.

These additional VA benefits and services fall into the following major categories:

- Disability Benefits

- Education & Training Benefits

- Vocational Rehabilitation & Employment

- Home Loans

- Burial Benefits

- Dependents' and Survivors' Benefits

- Life Insurance

Disability Benefits

Within the VA system there are two separate disability programs available to eligible veterans. Both pay monthly benefits to disabled veterans and most importantly, these monthly benefits are tax free.

1. Disability Compensation: A veteran may be eligible for disability compensation if he or she is found to be at least 10% disabled as a result of military service.

2. Disability Pension: A veteran may be eligible for a pension if he or she was a limited income and is no longer able to work.

Time Limits: There is no deadline for applying for disability benefits.

Education and Training

The VA has several programs that pay benefits to eligible veterans, dependents, reservists, and service members while they are in an approved training program. These major programs are:

1. Montgomery GI Bill: Persons who first entered active duty after June 30, 1985, are generally eligible. Some Vietnam Era veterans and certain veterans separated under special programs are also eligible. The bill also includes a program for certain reservists and National Guard members.

2. <u>Veterans Educational Assistance Program</u> (VEAP): This program is for veterans who entered active duty for the first time after December 31, 1976, and before July 1, 1985, and contributed funds to this program.

3. <u>Survivors' & Dependents' Educational Assistance</u>: Some family members of disabled or deceased veterans are eligible for education benefits.

Time Limits: Generally, veterans have 10 years from the date they were last released from active duty to use their education benefits. Reservists generally have 10 years from the date they became eligible for the program unless they leave the Selected Reserves before completing their obligation. Spouses generally have 10 years from the date we first find them eligible. Children are generally eligible from age 18 until age 26. These time limits can sometimes be extended.

Vocational Rehabilitation & Employment

The VA can help veterans with service-connected disabilities prepare for, find and keep suitable employment. For veterans with serious service-connected disabilities, VA also offers services to improve their ability to live as independently as possible. Some of the services provided by the VA are:

1. <u>Job Search</u>: Assistance in finding and maintaining suitable employment

2. <u>Vocational Evaluation</u>: An evaluation of abilities, skills, interests, and needs

3. <u>Career Exploration</u>: Vocational counseling and planning

4. <u>Vocational Training</u>: If needed, training such as on-the-job and non-paid work experience.

5. <u>Education Training</u>: If needed, education training to accomplish the rehabilitation goal.

6. <u>Rehabilitation Service</u>: S... ...bilitation and counseling services.

Time Limits: An eligible vete... generally has 12 years from the date the VA notifies the veteran in writing that he or she has at least a 10 percent rating for a service-connected disability.

Re-entry – Under the law, an eligible veteran who has completed a vocational rehabilitation program but whose disabilities have become so severe that they can no longer perform the duties of their chosen profession may re-enter the vocational rehabilitation program for training for a new career.

Home Loans

The VA offers a number of home loan services to eligible veterans, some military personnel, and certain spouses.

1. Guaranteed Loans: The VA can guarantee part of a loan from a private lender to help an eligible individual buy a home, a manufactured home, a lot for a manufactured home, or certain types of condominiums. The VA also guarantees loans for building, repairing, and improving homes.

2. Refinancing Loans: If you have a VA mortgage, the VA can help an eligible individual refinance the mortgage loan at a lower interest rate. Eligible individuals may also refinance a non-VA loan.

3. Special Grants: Certain disabled veterans and military personnel can receive grants to adapt or acquire housing suitable for their needs.

Time Limits: There is no time limit for a VA home loan, except for eligible reservists. Their eligibility expires September 30, 2009.

Burial Benefits

The VA offers certain benefits and services to honor our Nation's deceased veterans.

1. Headstones and Markers: The VA can furnish a monument to mark the unmarked grave of an eligible veteran.

2. Presidential Memorial Certificate (PMC): The VA can provide a PMC for eligible recipients.

3. Burial Flag: The VA can provide an American flag to drape an eligible veteran's casket.

4. Reimbursement of Burial Expenses: Generally, the VA can pay a burial allowance of $2,000 for veterans who die of service-related causes. For certain other veterans, the VA can only pay $300 for burial and funeral expenses and $300 for a plot.

5. Burial in a VA National Cemetery: Most veterans and some dependents can be buried in a VA national cemetery.

Time Limits: There is no time limit for claiming reimbursement of burial expenses for a service-related death. In other cases, claims must be filed within 2 years of the veteran's burial.

Dependents' and Survivors' Benefits

Dependency and Indemnity Compensation (DIC) is payable to certain survivors of:

1. Service members who died on active duty.

2. Veterans who died from service-related disabilities.

3. Certain veterans who were being paid 100% VA disability compensation at time of death.

4. Death Pension is payable to some surviving spouses and children of deceased wartime veterans. The benefit is based on financial need.

VA Civilian Health and Medical Program (CHAMPVA) shares the cost of medical services for eligible dependents and survivors of certain veterans.

Time Limits: There are no time limits for applying for the benefits described above.

Life Insurance

Service members Group Life Insurance (SGLI) is low-cost term life insurance for service members and reservists. Generally, coverage begins when you enter the service. It is available in amounts up to $250,000. Generally, it expires 120 days after you get out of the service.

Veterans Group Life Insurance (VGLI) is renewable five-year term life insurance for veterans. It is available in amounts up to $250,000. You may apply any time within 1 year from the date your SGLI expires.

Service-Disabled Veterans Insurance, also called "RH" Insurance, is life insurance for service-disabled veterans. The basic coverage is $10,000. If your premium payments for the basic policy are waived, due to total disability, you may be eligible for a supplemental policy of to $20,000. Generally, you have 2 years after being notified of your ser cted disability to apply for basic coverage.

Toll-Free Service
Benefits Information and Assistance

Each VA benefit has its own eligibility requirements. For more information about specific benefits, you may visit the nearest VA office or call:

1-800-827-1000

Special Toll-Free Numbers

- Health Benefits   877-222-8387
- Education Benefits   888-442-4551
- VA Life Insurance   800-669-8477
- Office of SGLI   800-419-1473
- CHAMPVA   800-733-8387
- Gulf War   800-749-8387
- Headstones (status
of claims only)   800-697-6947

- Telecommunication
Device for Deaf (TDD)   800-829-4833
- Direct Deposit   877-838-2778

Apply for Compensation, Pension or Vocational Rehabilitation benefits on line: http://vabenefits.vba.va.gov.

For more information and links to the VA regional offices, visit the VA's web-site at: www.va.gov

Within the main website there are a number of specialty pages:

- Compensation and Pension Benefits Education

- Environmental Exposure Health Care

- Home Loans

- Insurance

- Minority Veterans

- Women Veterans

- Vocational Rehabilitation & Employment

PART FIVE

THE CLAIMS PROCESS

CHAPTER SEVENTEEN

SUBMITTING YOUR CLAIM

There are many veterans who seem to believe that establishing eligibility for VA benefits results in automatically obtaining the desired benefit. This could not be further from the truth. Your initial eligibility for VA benefits is actually established through your military service and the meeting of the requirements of the two step process outlined in the previous chapter.

However, even though you may have met the requirements of the two step process for establishing eligibility, there are still other hurdles to overcome. This initial eligibility only allows you to apply for a particular benefit, but then you must also meet the requirements for the specific benefit for which you are applying.

If you left the military with a discharge that was under other than dishonorable conditions you are eligible to apply for certain benefits automatically, such as some medical care and perhaps a VA pension when you retire. However, there are other benefits that are available as a result of a determination that you incurred a disabling problem while on active duty.

The first hurdle that must be cleared in order to gain access to these benefits is the establishment of a disability to VA standards. This process begins with the filing of a claim.

FILING THE CLAIM

This step should have been accomplished during your out processing from the active military. The VA claim form that I discussed in Section II[20] is actually designed to let the soon to be veteran file a claim at the earliest possible

---

[20] The form is VAForm 21-526, Veterans Application for Compensation and/or Pension.

point in the process. Remember, the date of application for benefits is the effective date of your disability.

> HINT: *When filing out VA Form 21-526, Part B, "Tell Us About Your Disability"* **list every single accident, injury or disease you have incurred during your active duty period.** *Do not assume that the VA is going to search your records to see if you missed anything that should have been on the form. The rating specialist will address only those items that you put on this form. Remember, the effective date of your disability will be the date you fill out the form, so if you do not list something and it becomes a problem later, you will not automatically be service connected for that later condition. You must file another claim and show service connection for the new condition.*
>
> *Even if the VA gives you a zero disability rating[21] for a condition, you have established service connection for the condition.*

To every rule there is an exception. I have talked to many veterans who assure me that they were never given the opportunity to fill out the VA Form 21-256 during out processing. Others were told that they could not claim a disability until VA confirmed that they had a disability or they did not know that they had a disability and so they did not submit the 21-256. Whatever may have been the reason, there are many who left the service without filing for benefits. For these people, the VA has VSOs (Veterans Service Officers) on staff at each facility to assist the veteran in filing a claim.

At the first appointment with your VSO make sure you get the appropriate forms and be careful in completing them. Do not wait until you are very ill to file your claim. It is important to get your claim in as soon as you can in order to establish the earliest possible effective date if you are granted benefits.

RECORDS

I have always encouraged every one to keep their own set of their military service and medical records during their time on active duty. Many have told me that they did not keep their own set since the military had their records on file at the records depot in St. Louis. However, since because the military has a set of records does not mean that these records are permanently available. Due to fires and other problems, the service records of many veterans from past years have been lost. Unless you kept your own copy, the military would then have no record of your service. This can be a serious problem when it comes to establishing military service.

---

[21] We will discuss ratings in a later chapter.

However, even keeping your own set of records is no safeguard. Due to moves, fires, accidents or carelessness, sometimes your personal copy of your service records are lost. If you service during Vietnam or later, you should be able to get a replacement set of records from the military.

With this in mind, one benefit that the Federal Government offers to every veteran is a free set of all military service and medical records in the government's possession. In fact, a free set can be requested once a year.

To obtain these records, you, the veteran, must file a Request Pertaining to Military Records, Standard Form 180, with the appropriate military agency. Compile your own records of civilian medical treatment and give a copy to the VA for placement in your VA medical file. Civilian doctors and hospitals have procedures for allowing you to get your records. Many people are surprised to know that you can use examinations and treatment records from your private physicians to establish your service connected disability with the VA.

Records of treatment in VA medical facilities are available for free by filing a VA Form 70-3288 with the VA medical facility. If you have in your possession copies of any military medical records, protect them. No one knows exactly how many records have been lost or destroyed, but some veterans groups estimate as many of 50% of Gulf veterans medical records are missing and a larger percentage are incomplete. Be aware that some psychiatric medical records may be released only to a doctor or counselor.

RESOURCES

It is certainly true that most veterans have no idea how to file a proper claim. Many also are not aware that Congress has passed laws that make it very clear that VA employees have a duty to help you "work up", or develop evidence for, your case. However, they are obligated to do this only after you have presented a "well-grounded claim" to the VA. It is important for you to work with your VSO to put together a well-grounded claim.

Even after you do so, however, the VA employees who will review your claim work with many hundreds of veterans' cases. Consequently, your ongoing participation with your VSO may be critical in the proper development of your claim. Help your VSO and yourself by writing out a list (with dates) of your health problems in the order they have occurred. Submit that list with copies of the medical records that document the problem.

WHAT IS A WELL GROUNDED CLAIM?

Though I talked about this earlier, I cannot stress the importance of giving the VA sufficient information to establish that your claim is well grounded. Like every organization, the VA has its own language. The phrase "well grounded claim" is one that is very important for the veteran who would apply for benefits to understand since it is important for the veteran to submit information that meets the requirement.

During the application review process, a VA rater will try to determine if your case is well grounded. For a claim for disability benefits to be considered a well grounded claim there must be three elements present:

(1) a medical showing of a current medical condition;

(2) lay[22] or in certain circumstances, medical evidence of disease or injury in service; and

(3) medical evidence showing a nexus[23] between the asserted injury in service and the current disability.

Where medical evidence is required, medical journal articles alone will generally not suffice unless they are enhanced by a physician's opinion stating that the current disability *was related, is likely to be related, could be related, or even possibly was related* to the veteran's service. A physician's opinion need not be conclusive to establish a well-grounded claim.

Alternatively, both the second and third elements above can be satisfied by the submission of minimum evidence:

(a) that the condition was "noted" during service or during an applicable presumption period;

The term "noted" means that while the condition may not have been disabling while the applicant was on active duty, there was some mention that the condition did exist during the period of active duty.

(b) that there has been post service continuity of symptomatology (as to which lay opinion can suffice; and

This means did the condition continue to cause the applicant significant problems? The word symptomatology simply means subjective evidence

---

[22] Lay evidence would be someone that you served with writing you a sworn statement that he, or she, has personal knowledge that you were injured during your military service. In the absence of official documentation, sometimes VA will accept such "lay" evidence.

[23] A nexus between the injury and the current disability would be a showing that that there is a causal or logical relation between the injury and the disability such as a written opinion from a specialist that the disability is one that is commonly caused by the type of injury.

of a disease or physical disturbance or something that indicates the presence of bodily disorder.

(c) medical, or in some rare circumstances, lay evidence of a nexus between the present disability between the present disability and the post service symptomatology.

COOPERATE WITH THE VA

Once you file your claim, the VA may make an appointment for you to see one of its doctors for a disability evaluation. If you do not go to this special examination, the VA may reject your claim. If the VA asks for additional information, be very careful to respond within the deadlines in its letter. If you do not have the information requested, or you have already provided it, do not simply ignore the letter -- doing so may let the VA deny your claim.

CHAPTER EIGHTEEN

CLAIMS FOR
UNKNOWN ILLNESSES

How about those veterans who have illnesses that simply cannot be diagnosed by medical science? After Desert Storm, many veterans began to have serious medical problems that defied diagnosis. Initially, the military and the VA took the position that these were just stress related problems or imaginary illnesses. Now it is fairly well accepted that these medical problems are real and were contracted by the soldiers serving in that campaign in the line of duty.

The VA rater is by no stretch of the imagination a physician, but he or she is trained to review files based upon known illnesses and injuries, supported by documentation, so how does one convince the rater that he or she has an unknown illness? The majority of the physicians that work for the VA as well as the rating specialists are fairly well trained in "normal" medicine. However, there are a number of diseases that are rarely seen in the United States and as a result, those physicians who have never practiced outside the continental United States may now be familiar with every problem that plagues a soldier.

The issue of unknown mysterious diseases has become a major issue as a result of some of the mysterious diseases that have affected Gulf War veterans. Not only are their problems caused by manmade toxins such as are found in chemical, biological or radiological weapons, but there are a number of heretofore unknown natural diseases coming from some of the more isolated parts of the world. As a partial answer to this unusual situation, the VA has issued a regulation to compensate veterans of the Gulf War for illnesses they have contracted that have not yet been diagnosed by medical science.

Congress has never before directed the VA to pay compensation benefits for illnesses that cannot be diagnosed and for which a specific cause has not yet been identified. This regulation is called "Compensation for Certain Disabilities Due to Undiagnosed Illnesses." This regulation applies only to illnesses that cannot be diagnosed. If your condition has been completely and adequately diagnosed, the rules explained below do not apply to you.

The new regulation permits the VA to pay compensation benefits for a disability caused by chronic illnesses or symptoms (that exist for at least six months) and that cannot be diagnosed (identified). Before the VA will grant you compensation benefits as a Gulf veteran with undiagnosed illnesses, you must:

- Show that you served in the Southwest Asia theater of operations during the Gulf War (8/2/90 -11/30/95);

- Show you have a chronic, undiagnosed illness;

- Show your undiagnosed illness can be documented by a doctor or by statements from friends or family members; and

- Show the signs and symptoms of your illness revealed themselves during your service in the Gulf War or;

- Show the signs and symptoms of your illness revealed themselves within two years after the date you last served in the Persian Gulf and they were severe enough to warrant at least a 10% VA disability evaluation within those two years.

You need not have suffered from symptoms every day for six months; you may have suffered from symptoms that have come, gone, and then reappeared over a six-month period. And your symptoms do not have to be objective - that is, you do not have to be able to see or touch the symptoms or signs for your illness to qualify. However, you must be able to document the symptoms. New VA regulations have extended the presumptive period from two to ten years. See your service officer immediately for the new regulations and/or to re-open a claim denied on the basis that the undiagnosed symptoms were not documented to occur within the two year presumptive period.

CHAPTER NINETEEN

LAWS AND REGULATIONS REGARDING CLAIMS

When a veteran submits a claim to the VA, he/she should understand there are several prerequisites for a successful disability claim. Among them are:

1.   The evidence of record must show the claimed condition was incurred in (first occurred or diagnosed) during military service. That means the medical evidence provided by the veteran and/or the service department (usually the Fed. Records Center in St. Louis) must show the claimed disability.

If the disability pre-existed service, such as a knee condition, the evidence must show that the condition became worse during military service. That is one reason it is important to insist on a discharge physical examination. It is your last chance to make certain disabilities are in your record. REMEMBER, AS FAR AS THE VA IS CONCERNED, if the claimed disability is not shown in your service medical records it DIDN'T happen. Exceptions to this rule are conditions, which may not manifest until after military service is complete.

One example of a condition that might not manifest until after the completion of military service would be Post Traumatic Stress Disorder. In such cases, the veteran's service record is requested to determine if his/her service was under such conditions, that the present diagnosis can clearly be associated with military service. The fact that your drill sergeant was mean to you or that the other soldiers didn't treat you nice would not qualify.

2.   Assuming service medical records show the claimed disability exists then it must be determined how disabling the condition is at the present time. Usually the claimant is scheduled for an examination at the

nearest VA Medical Center. The examining physician completes a report showing his/her diagnoses and clinical findings. Keeping with the knee example, the doctor will check for range of motion, looseness of the joint, pain, etc. For sake of our discussion, we will assume the knee was initially injured during military service.

3.   The report is sent to the Regional Office for review. The rating specialist reviews all the medical evidence, with special consideration to the examining physician's report. The rating specialist then consults a rating schedule. The diagnosis tells him/her under which disability to rate the knee. For example, chronic knee strain, torn ACL, traumatic arthritis, etc. The clinical findings will be compared to descriptions given to various percentages. The percentage, which closest agrees with the physician's findings, will be given as the evaluation of the disability.

4.   If the veteran has more than one disability, each of which is considered at least 10% disabling, they will be applied to a combined rating schedule to yield a combined evaluation. The individual disabilities are not added to give a final percentage. For example: Assume our hypothetical veteran has 3 disabilities: knee, heart, and psychological. Each disability is considered 50% disabling. The veteran is not considered 150% disabled. What happens is each % is applied to the remaining healthy person. With no disabilities the veteran is considered 100% healthy. When the knee condition is considered, the veteran is now 50% disabled and 50% healthy. The 50% evaluation of his heart is applied to the remaining healthy 50% and he/she is considered 75% disabled and 25% healthy. Since evaluations are only in even 10%, the evaluation is rounded off to 80% disabled and 20% healthy. The final 50% psychological condition is applied to the remaining 25% healthy person. Remember the actual combined evaluation was 75%. It was just rounded to 80%. He/she is now 88% disabled. The evaluation is rounded to 90% disabled and 10% healthy.

5.   The veteran would automatically be considered for individual unemployability. The rating specialist would determine that if based on the veteran's education, skills, etc. are his/her disabilities so severe as to render him/her individually unemployable. If the answer is yes, he/she is paid at the 100% rate although his/her disabilities only warrant a 90% evaluation. Although the monetary benefit is the same, there is an important distinction between a combined scheduler 100% and 100% due to individual unemployability. If the 100% is by the schedule, the veteran may, if able, hold a regular job. If the 100% is due to being unemployable, he/she may not engage in anything other than marginal employment. The VA checks annually through the individual states for

veterans, who are considered unemployable and are holding a regular job. It can become very ugly financially for the veteran, if he/she is caught. It could result in anything from a reduced evaluation, to full repayment, to jail time. Contrary to popular belief, the mind set in the VA is to resolve all doubt in favor of the veteran. Consider, if the claimed benefit can be granted, there is a happy veteran and one less file someone must review.

RESULTS OF A WELL GROUNDED CLAIM

If the VA rater determined that your claim is well grounded, then service connection will be granted for the disability and you will receive disability compensation. If it is determined that your claim is not well grounded and your disability is not caused by your service, but you are now totally disabled, you could receive a VA pension. Disability compensation and pension are VA entitlements that make up for your loss of income when you become disabled.

Service connected compensation is available for disabilities that were incurred during, or aggravated by, military service. Compensation is payable based on the degree to which you are disabled by the service connected condition. Effective 12/1/95, the benefit rate for a 10% disability is $91; for a 100%, or total, disability, it is $1870. Veterans who are rated at 30% or greater for service connected disabilities may receive additional compensation for dependants.

Non service connected pensions are available to veterans with very low income who served during war time and are totally disabled. The disabilities do not have to be service connected, and combat service is not required. Additional pension benefits for dependants are also available.

Benefit payments are also available to eligible survivors of deceased veterans.

SERVICE CONNECTED CLAIMS

Service connected compensation is available to veterans with physical or mental disabilities that were incurred during or aggravated by service. It is not income dependant; that is, your income and assets are not considered when determining compensation. The disability does not have to be related to combat; it just has to be connected in some way to your time in service. In general, you have to prove three things to establish service connection:

- You currently have a physical or mental disability;

- Something happened in service: for example, you contracted a disease that began in service; you suffered an injury in service; something happened to you that affected your health while in service; you were treated for a chronic condition shortly after service; or a condition you had before service worsened due to service.

- There is a link between your current disability and what occurred in service. Primarily, this must be proved with an experts' opinion, such as a doctor.

GETTING HELP

Most people try to fill out the VA form 21-256 by themselves and do not submit sufficient supporting documentation. As a result, the claim is denied. For most people, the best thing you can do for yourself is to get help from a well-trained Veterans Service Officer (VSO) in your area as early as possible in the claims process. The claims process is confusing, technical, and frustrating - so be prepared for the long haul. VSOs are trained by the various veterans' service organizations (VFW, DAV, etc.) and provide free representation. They are often located at the VA's regional offices, although they do not work for the VA.

On occasion you will get letters from the VA asking for more information. Quite often, the letter will indicate if more information is not forthcoming then the VA will deny your claim. Write back and state the evidence was previously provided or that you do not have the required information. Emphasize to the VA that you think the evidence already provided is enough to allow your claim -- if you and your VSO believe that to be the case. When writing to the VA, be sure to use your claim # and the VA's reply # on all correspondence.

THE HARDEST PART

Once you have submitted all of the information in your possession that supports your claim, then you must simply wait for the VA to make a determination. Most of us are somewhat impatient and try to follow up on matters. However, unlike most federal agencies, in most instances, the only telephone numbers available for the VA is 1-800-827-1000, all other numbers are unlisted. Many of the members of senior management and rating staff refuse to even speak to the veteran, which can be very frustrating and is frankly insulting.

Currently the backlog of claims waiting for adjudication is enormous. Gulf war claims have been sent back from one of four major regional centers to the local regional centers for adjudication -- and there is a big backlog of claims. Your claim may take up to a year or more to adjudicate -- especially if you have not done good work up-front providing the necessary documentation.

IF THE ANSWER IS NO

If your claim is denied, be prepared to appeal. While it is no excuse, the VA is under tremendous pressure to decide claims quickly. As a result, claims that are not clearly supported may be turned down in order to allow the raters to show a higher percentage of decided claims[24]. Their theory seems to be what else does the veteran have to do but submit documentation for claims. Additionally, as was discovered in California regarding claims for various state benefits, over 50% of those denied the first time will not reapply. This lightens the workload.

As of March 1996, only 12% of environmental exposure claims and 5% of undiagnosed illnesses claims of Persian Gulf veterans had been granted compensation. Frankly, the odds are that your claim will be denied. When the VA denies your claim, they must notify you and tell you what additional rights you have for appeal. Don't be discouraged - request a reconsideration, or appeal, within the deadline. Often the appeals are denied as well, but don't despair and whatever your do, don't give up.

At this point you get to go to a Medical Review Board - in person if you desire. This is where you may well have success, and you can bring in expert medical and technical testimony to bolster your case.

NON SERVICE CONNECTED PENSIONS

Disabled veterans who lose their claims for compensation should consider applying for pension. Pension benefits are available to veterans with war-time service, who have limited incomes and assets and who are totally and permanently disabled for reasons primarily not related to their military service. VA Form 21-526 can be used to apply for a pension. A pension usually provides much less money than compensation, but for many veterans it is a necessary means of support.

---

[24] Remember the old CYA (Cover Your Ass) defense.

CHAPTER TWENTY

LAWS AND REGULATIONS TO CONSIDER
WHEN PREPARING YOUR CLAIM

There are a number of other important points to consider in regard to your claim. It is not well known, but the VA has an obligation to help you obtain the supporting documentation you need to file your claim. This responsibility quite often falls under the classification of *"If you don't ask, we won't tell!"*

There are also a number of very specific definitions that very clearly lay out what you may and may not submit in the way of evidence to support your claim. The various distinctions must be clearly understood in order to increase your chances of your claim for benefits being granted. Most of these definitions can be found in Title 38 of the United States Code, Section 3.159. Making you aware of these definitions is part of the VA's responsibility to assist you in the development of your claim. However, quite often, this responsibility is discharged by the VA only *after* your claim has been denied. I think that you need to know these important definitions prior to preparing and submitting your claim.

Some very important definitions and duties that the claimant needs to understand are:

Competent Medical Evidence means evidence provided by a person who is qualified through education, training or experience to offer medical diagnosis, statements or opinions. Competent medical evidence may also mean statements conveying sound medical principles found in medical treatises. It would also include statements contained in authoritative writings such as medical and scientific articles and research reports or analyses. In other words, it is not just your physician's medical reports and in fact, under the laws, the person making the statement does not even have to be a practicing physician. He or she may well be a researcher.

Competent lay evidence means any evidence not requiring that the proponent have specialized education, training or experience. Lay evidence is competent if is provided by a person who has knowledge of facts or circumstances and conveys matters that can be observed and described by a lay person.

Substantially complete application means an application containing the claimant's name; his or her relationship to the veteran, if applicable; sufficient service information for VA to verify the claimed service, if applicable; the benefit claimed and any medical condition(s) on which it is based; the claimant's signature, and in claims for non-service connected disability or death pension and parents' dependency and indemnity compensation, a statement of income.

Information means non-evidentiary facts, such as the claimant's Social Security number or address; the name and military unit of a person who served with the veteran; or the name and address of a medical care provider who may have evidence pertinent to the claim.

VA's duty to notify claimants of necessary information or evidence begins when the VA receives a complete or substantially complete application for benefits. At that time, the VA will notify the claimant of any information and medical or lay evidence that is necessary to substantiate the claim. VA will inform the claimant which information and evidence, if any, that the claimant is to provide to the VA and which information and evidence, if any, the VA will attempt to obtain on behalf of the claimant. The VA will also request that the claimant provide any evidence in the claimant's possession that pertains to the claim. If the VA does not receive the necessary information and evidence requested from the claimant within one year of the date of the notice, VA cannot pay or provide any benefits based upon the application. If the claimant has not responded to the request within 30 days, the VA may decide the claim prior to the expiration of the one year period based upon all the information and evidence contained in the file, including information and evidence it has obtained on behalf of the claimant and any VA medical examinations or medical opinions. If the VA does so, however, and the claimant subsequently provides the information and evidence within one year of the date of the request, the VA must re-adjudicate the claim[25].

---

[25] 38 U.S.C., Section 5103.

If the VA receives an incomplete application for benefits, it will notify the claimant of the information necessary to complete the applicant and will defer assistance until the claimant submits the information[26].

VA's duty to assist claimants in obtaining evidence begins upon receipt of a substantially complete application for benefits. VA will make reasonable efforts to help a claimant obtain evidence necessary to substantiate the claim. In addition, the VA will give the assistants described in paragraphs a, b and c below to an individual attempting to reopen a finally decided claim. Provided, however, that the VA will not pay any fees charged by a custodian to provide the records requested.

1. *Obtaining records not in the custody of a Federal Department or Agency.* VA will make reasonable efforts to obtain records not in the custody of a Federal department of agency. This would include records from State or local governments, private medical care providers, current or former employers, and other non-Federal governmental sources. Such reasonable efforts will generally consist of an initial request for the records and if the records are not received, at least one follow-up request. A follow-up request is not required if a response to the initial request indicates that the records sought do not exist or that a follow up request for the records would be futile. If the VA receives information showing that subsequent requests to this or another custodian cold result in obtaining the records sought, then reasonable efforts will include an initial request, and, if the records are not received, at least one follow-up request to the new source or an additional request to the original source.

   a. The claimant must cooperate fully with VA's reasonable efforts to obtain relevant records from non-Federal agency or department custodians. The claimant must provide enough information to identify and locate the existing records, including the person, company, agency, or other custodian holdings the records, the approximate time frame covered by the records, and in the case of medical treatment records, the condition for which treatment was provided.

   b. If necessary, the claimant must authorize the release of existing records in a form acceptable

---

[26] 38 U.S.C., Section 5102(b) and 5103A(3)

to the person, company, agency or other custodian holding the records[27].

2. *Obtaining records in the custody of a Federal Department or Agency.*

The VA will make as many requests as are necessary to obtain relevant records from a Federal Department or agency. These records include but are not limited to military records, including service medical records; medical and other records from VA medical facilities; records from non-VA facilities providing examination or treatment at VA expense; and records from other Federal agencies such as the Social Security Administration. VA will end its efforts to obtain records from a Federal Department or agency only if the VA concludes that the records sought do not exist or that further efforts to obtain those records would be futile. Cases in which the VA may conclude that no further efforts are required include those in which the Federal Department or agency advises VA that the requested records do not exist or the custodian does not have them.

    a.   The claimant must cooperate fully with VA's reasonable efforts to obtain relevant records from Federal agency or department custodians. If requested by the VA, the claimant must provide enough information to identify and locate the existing records, including the custodian or agency holding the records; the approximate time frame covered by the records; and in the case of medical treatment records, the condition for which treatment was provided. In the case of records requested to corroborate a claimed stressful event in service, the claimant must provide information sufficient for the records custodian to conduct a search of the corroborative records.

    b.   If necessary, the claimant must authorize the release of existing records in a form acceptable to the custodian of agency holding the records[28].

3. *Obtaining records in compensation claims:* In a claim for disability compensation, VA will make efforts to obtain the claimant's service medical records, if relevant to the claim; other relevant records pertaining to the claimant's active military,

---

[27] 38 U.S.C., Section 5103A(b)
[28] 38 U.S.C., Section 5103A(b)

naval or air service that are held or maintained by a governmental entity, VA medical records or records of examination or treatment at non-VA facilities authorized by VA; and any other relevant records held by any Federal department or agency. The claimant must provide enough information to identify and locate the existing records including the custodian or agency holding the records, the approximate time frame covered by the records, and in the case of medical treatment records, the condition for which treatment was provided[29].

4. *Providing medical examinations or obtaining medical opinions:* (i) In a claim for disability compensation, the VA will provide a medical examination or obtain a medical opinion based upon a review of the evidence of record if VA determines it is necessary to decide the claim. A medical examination or medical opinion is necessary if the information and evidence of record does not contain sufficient competent medical evidence to decide the claim, but:

  a. Contains competent lay or medical evidence of a current diagnosed disability or persistent or recurrent symptoms of disability.

  b. Establishes that the veteran suffered an event, injury or disease in service, or has a disease or symptoms of a disease listed in Section 3.309, Section 3.313, Section 3.316 or Section 3.317 (of 38 U.S.C.) manifesting during an applicable presumptive period provided the claimant has the required service or triggering event to qualify for that presumption; and

  c. Indicates that the claimed disability or symptoms may be associated with the established event, injury, or disease in service or with another service connected disability[30].

REASONABLE DOUBT DOCTRINE

It is the defined and consistently applied policy of the Department of Veteran Affairs to administer the law under a broad interpretation, consistent,

---

[29] 38 U.S.C., Section 5103A(c)

[30] This section could be satisfied by competent evidence showing post service treatment for a condition or other possible association with military service.

however, with the facts shown in every case. When after careful consideration of all procurable and assembled data, a reasonable doubt arises regarding service origin, the degree of disability, or any other point, such doubt will be resolved in favor of the veteran. The term reasonable doubt is defined as a doubt which exists because of an approximate balance of positive and negative evidence, which does not satisfactorily prove or disprove the claim[31]. It is a substantial doubt and one within the range of probability as distinguished from pure speculation or remote possibility.

It is not a means of reconciling actual conflict or a contradiction of the evidence. Mere suspicion or doubt as to the truth of any statements submitted, as distinguished from impeachment or contradiction by evidence or known facts, is not a justifiable basis for denying the application of the reasonable doubt doctrine if the entire complete record otherwise warrants invoking this doctrine.

The reasonable doubt doctrine is also applicable even in the absence of official records, particularly if the basic incident allegedly arose under combat, or similarly strenuous conditions, and is consistent with the probably results of such known hardships[32].

This would apply to those situations were it would be impossible for the normal medical reports to have been prepared. As an example, there were several situations during Vietnam where headquarters and supporting medical units were overrun and the records destroyed. Since the field medical file is the basis for substantiating claims, it would not be fair or proper to penalize those soldiers whose records were destroyed. Claims by these individuals would therefore have to be substantiated by secondary evidence such as lay evidence or the existence of injuries that "could" have been caused by military service.

Those who have a severe problem establishing service connection are those who operated in areas where US troops were not supposed to enter such as Laos and Cambodia during Vietnam. It would not be politically correct to pay benefits or recognize medical problems caused by being present in such areas. It would also require an admission by higher authorities that in fact they had illegally sent troops into neutral areas. Such honesty would be almost a miracle.

---

[31] I call this the "flip a coin" doctrine.
[32] 38 U.S.C., Section 501(a)

CHAPTER TWENTY-ONE

EFFECTIVE DATE OF AWARDS

Even after the awarding of benefits, there are sometimes still questions that arise. One of the most important questions to veterans is when does the date of the award become effective? The answer to this question can have some serious consequences for the veteran, sometimes meanings a substantial retroactive pay increase. Remember though it can sometimes take years to get a decision, disability compensation will normally start on the date of the application. This can result in substantial back pay situations. There can actually be a number of answers to this question regarding the effective date of an award depending on certain factors that can vary in almost every case.

The general rule regarding effective dates of awards is that except as otherwise provided, the effective date of an evaluation and award of pension, compensation or dependency and indemnity compensation based on an original claim, a claim reopened after final disallowance, or a claim for increase will be the date of receipt of the claim or the date entitlement arise, whichever is later[33]. However, as can be seen below, there can be some variance to this rule depending on certain factors.

(a) Unless specifically provided. On basis of facts found.

(b) Disability benefits:

---

[33] 38 U.S.C., Section 5110(a)

1. The award of a <u>disability pension</u> may not be effective prior to the date entitlement arose.

   (i) Claims received prior to October 1, 1984 – The award will be effective either on the date of receipt of the claim or the date on which the veteran became permanently and totally disabled, if claim is filed within one year from such date, whichever is to the advantage of the veteran.

   (ii) Claims received on or after October 1, 1984.

      a. Except as provided below, on the date of receipt of the claim.

      b. If, within, one year from the date on which the veteran becomes permanently and totally disabled, the veteran files a claim for retroactive award and establishes that a physical or mental disability, which was not the result of the veteran's own willful misconduct, was so incapacitating that it prevented him or her from filing a disability pension claim for at least thirty days immediately following the date on which the veteran became permanently and totally disabled, the disability pension award may be effective from the date of receipt of the claim or the date on which the veteran became permanently and totally disabled, whichever is to the advantage of the veteran. While rating board judgment must be applied to the facts and circumstances of each case, extensive hospitalization will generally qualify as sufficiently incapacitating to have prevented the filing of a claim. For purposes of this subparagraph, the presumptive provisions of Section 3.342(a) do not apply.

2. Disability Compensation

   (i) <u>Direct service connection</u> – Effective date if the day following separation from active service or date entitlement arise if claim is received within 1 year after separation from service; otherwise, date of receipt of claim, or date entitlement arose, whichever is later. Separation from service means separation under conditions other than dishonorable from continuous active service which extended form the date disability was incurred or aggravated.

(ii) <u>Presumptive service connection</u> – Date entitlement arose, if claim is received within 1 year after separation from active duty; otherwise date of receipt of claim, or date entitlement arose, whichever is later. Where the requirement for service connection are met during service, the effective date will be the day following separation from service if there was continuous active service following the period of service on which the presumption is based and a claim is received within 1 year after separation from active duty.

c. Death Benefits

1. **Death in Service** – the effective date of the death benefits will be the first day of the month fixed by the Secretary concerned as the date of actual or presumed death, if the claim is received within 1 year after the date of the initial report of actual death or finding of presumed death was made; however, benefits based on a report of actual death are not payable for any period for which the claimant has received, or is entitled to received an allowance, allotment or service pay of th4e veteran[34] .

2. **Service-connected death after separation from service** – the effective date of the death benefits will be the first day of the month in which the veteran's death occurred if the claim is received within 1 year after the date of death, otherwise, the date of receipt of the claim.

3. **Non-service-connected death after separation from service**

(i) For awards based on claims received prior to October 1, 1984, the effective date is the first day of the month in which the veteran's death occurred if the claim is received within 1 year after the date of death, otherwise, the effective date is the date of the receipt of the claim.

---

[34] 38 U.S.C., Section 5110(j), Public Law 87-825.

(ii) For awards based on claims received

PART SIX

THE APPEALS PROCESS

CHAPTER TWENTY-TWO

IF YOUR CLAIM IS DENIED

If your claim is denied, you and/or your advocate should promptly do two things:

- file a notice of disagreement (NOD) and
- request a copy of the rating decision.

An NOD can be as simple as a letter to the VA Regional office saying that you disagree with its decision. The notice should include the date of the adverse decision and the claim number (C-number). The NOD must be postmarked within one year of the date on the denial letter or you will lose your right to appeal. There are no extensions. In this letter state specifically what you decisions you are disagreeing with.

Once you file a NOD, two important things happen. First, the VA will either grant your claim or respond to your NOD with a statement of the case (SOC). The SOC should describe the facts, laws, regulations and reasons that the VA used to make the decision. With the State of the Case will also be a VA form 9 "Appeal to the Board of Veterans' Appeals." You must complete the VA form 9 and return it within the allotted time if you want to continue you appeal.

You and/or your advocate must complete and return this form to the VA if the Board of Veterans' Appeals in Washington, DC is to consider your case. You have 60 days from the date on the SOC or you have the remainder of one year from the date the VA first denied you claim, whichever deadline is later, to file the VA Form 9. The Form 9 asks if you wish to appear at a hearing before the BVA in Washington, DC or before a traveling BVA member at the regional office. At a hearing, a BVA member will listen to arguments and permit you to submit evidence about your appeal. In most cases, if you are at all able to appear in person at a hearing before the BVA, you should do so. Even if you do not request a hearing, however, the members of the BVA will review the evidence in you case and make another decision about your claim.

Second, once you file an NOD you can also request a hearing in front of a VA hearing officer at the regional office. If the hearing officer determines that you have presented new and relevant evidence, he or she can make a new decision. If the decision of the hearing officer is unfavorable, you can still appeal to the Board of Veterans' Appeals.

If you disagree with a BVA decision, you might appeal to the US Court of Veterans Appeals in Washington, DC. You could also file a motion for reconsideration with the BVA or, if you have new and material evidence about your claim, you can reopen your claim at a regional office.

LATE APPEALS

If you fail to appeal within the allotted time, the decision of the VA will become final. Once the decision becomes final, you are permanently prohibited from obtaining the denied benefit unless you can:

- Show that the VA was clearly wrong to deny the benefit, or

- Send the VA new evidence that related to the reason that they denied the claim.

To be perfectly frank, once a decision is made by a rater or a rating board, it almost takes an act of Congress to get the VA to change the decision and if you miss an appeal deadline the VA will rarely find that you have met the burden of proof to have the deadline set aside. So even if you are not sure that you want to appeal, send the Notice of Disagreement letter within the specified time limit.

CHAPTER TWENTY-THREE

BOARD OF VETERANS APPEALS

Once you have exhausted your possibilities within the VA claims process, then it is time to look at the possibility of appealing to a higher authority. This appeal would be to The Board of Veterans' Appeals (also known as "the BVA" or "the Board"). The Board of Veterans Appeals is a part of the Department of Veterans Affairs (VA), located in Washington, D.C. "Members of the Board" review benefit claims determinations made by local VA offices and issue decisions on appeals. These Board members, attorneys experienced in veterans' law and in reviewing benefit claims, are the only ones who can issue Board decisions. Staff attorneys, referred to as Counsel or Associate Counsel, are also trained in veterans' law. They review the facts of each appeal and assist Board members.

THE APPEAL

An appeal is a request for a review of a VA determination on a claim for benefits issued by a local VA office. The appeal can be filed by anyone who has filed a claim for benefits with VA and has received a determination from a local VA office.

The appeal can be filed up to one year from the date the local VA office mails you its initial determination on your claim. After that, the determination is considered final and cannot be appealed unless it involved clear and unmistakable error by VA[35].

---

[35] 38 U.S.C. § 7101(a)and 38 U.S.C. § 7104 (This legalese translates as Title 38 of the United States Code, Section 7101a and Section 7104).

WHAT MAY BE APPEALED?

You may appeal any determination issued by a VA regional office (RO) on a claim for benefits. Some determinations by VA medical facilities, such as eligibility for medical treatment, may also be appealed to the Board. You may appeal a complete or partial denial of your claim or you may appeal the level of benefit granted. For example, if you filed a claim for disability and the local office awarded you a 10% disability, but you feel you deserve more than 10%, you may appeal that determination to the Board.

WHAT MAY NOT BE APPEALED?

You may not appeal decisions concerning the need for medical care or the type of medical treatment needed, such as a physician's decision to prescribe (or not to prescribe) a particular drug or order a specific type of treatment, are not within the Board's jurisdiction. (Occasionally, the Board receives an appeal of this nature, but since it doesn't have the legal authority to decide this type of case, the Board must dismiss it.)

FILING THE APPEAL

There is no special form is required to begin the appeal[36] process. All that's needed is a written statement that:
(1) you disagree with your local VA office's claim determination and

(2) you want to appeal it.

This statement is known as the Notice of Disagreement, or NOD. If you received notice of determinations on more than one claim issue, your NOD needs to be specific about which issue or issues you wish to appeal. For example, if you were notified about local VA office determinations on a knee disability and a heart condition, but you only want to appeal the heart condition determination, say that. Being specific helps VA concentrate on what is most important to you and moves your case along more quickly.

While the NOD is all that's needed to begin the appeal process, you will eventually need to complete and file a VA Form 9 to finish your appeal.

---

[36] 38 U.S.C. § 511(a), 38 U.S.C. § 7104(a), 38 C.F.R. § 20.101 and 38 C.F.R. § 20.101(b)

WHERE TO FILE THE APPEAL

Normally, you file your appeal with the same local VA office that issued the decision you are appealing, because that is where your claims file (also called a claims folder) is kept. However, if you have moved and your claims file is now maintained at a local VA office other than the one where you previously filed your claim, you should file your appeal at the new location.

THE PROCESS

When the local VA office receives and reviews your NOD, it is possible (But not likely) that it will change its original determination and allow your claim. If it doesn't, it will prepare and mail to you a Statement of the Case (SOC) and a blank VA Form 9. (The VA Form 9 is discussed in the next section.) This SOC summarizes the evidence and applicable laws and regulations used in deciding your case and gives you the local VA office's reasons for making the determination you appealed.

Within 60 days of the date when the local VA office mails you the SOC, you need to submit a Substantive Appeal. However, if the one-year period from the date the local VA office mailed you its original determination is later than this 60-day period, you have until that later date to file the Substantive Appeal.

To file a Substantive Appeal, simply fill out and submit the VA Form 9 that the local VA office sent you. The form comes with detailed instructions that the VA has tried to write in easy-to-understand language. On one portion of the VA Form 9 there is a specific section used to request a BVA hearing.

On the VA Form 9, you should make sure that you clearly state the benefit you want and that you point out any mistakes you think VA made when it issued its determination. You should also identify anything in the SOC that you disagree with. If you submit new information or evidence with your VA Form 9, the local VA office will prepare a Supplemental Statement of the Case (SSOC).

A SSOC is similar to the SOC, but addresses the new information or evidence you submitted. If you are not satisfied with the SSOC, you have 60 days from date the SSOC was mailed to you to submit, in writing, what you disagree with.

If, for some reason, you don't want BVA to examine an issue listed in the Statement of the Case or the Supplemental Statement of the Case, simply state (on the VA Form 9) that you are withdrawing that specific issue (or issues) from the appeal. Withdrawing issues you don't really want to appeal will help VA move your case along more quickly.

Remember, you should not delay submitting the VA Form 9 to the local VA office. If you don't file the VA Form 9 on time, you could lose your right to appeal. Use the following formulas to figure out when the VA Form 9 is due.

EXTENSIONS OF TIME TO FILE

While the filing deadline is very specific and almost set in stone, it is possible to ask for an extension of the sixty day period in which you are required to file your substantive appeal or to respond to a Supplemental Statement of the Case. You request this extension to the deadline for filing your appeal by writing to the local VA office that is handling you appeal. You should explain why you need the extra time to file (this explanation is called "showing good cause").

The time limits we have given you are good in most cases, but there is one kind of case, called a simultaneously contested claim, where the filing times are a lot shorter. A simultaneously contested claim is a claim where more than one person is trying to get a VA benefit or status that only one of them can have. An example would be a case where two different people claim that they are entitled to all of the same life insurance policy proceeds[37].

If you are appealing a determination in a simultaneously contested claim, your NOD must be filed within 60 days from the date the local VA office mailed you its determination, not one year from that date. The VA Form 9 has to be filed within 30 days of the date when the local VA office mailed you the Statement of the Case, not 60 days. The alternative period for filing the VA Form 9 (one year from the date the Regional Office mailed you its original determination) does not apply to simultaneously contested claims. Also, if there is a SSOC that you want to respond to in a simultaneously contested claim, you only have 30 days to file your response, not 60 days.

These kinds of appeals are fairly rare, but I wanted you to know about them because the filing deadlines inn these cases are different and yet filing deadlines in general are so important. If you are not sure whether these shorter filing deadlines apply to your appeal, ask your local VA office or your representative.

REPRESENTATION

As with most procedures conducted by the Department of Veterans Affairs, you are at liberty to represent yourself during the appeals process and if you are well versed in the appropriate regulations this might be the way to go for you. However, about 90 percent of all people who appeal to the Board do obtain representation. Most appellants (about 85 percent) choose to be represented by a Veterans' Service Organization (VSO) or their state's veterans department.

Many VSOs have trained personnel who specialize in providing help with claims and appeals. VSOs do not charge for this service and do not require you to be a member of their organizations. Many state and county governments

---

[37] 38 U.S.C. § 7105(d)(3), 38 C.F.R. § 20.303, 38 U.S.C. § 7105A, 38 C.F.R. part 20, subpart F

also have trained personnel in their veterans departments who can help. Your local VA office can provide a list of approved veterans' appeal representatives in your area.

While an appeal representative may be able to help you, bear in mind that your case is only one of the many that they will be handling at any point in time. In my own case, I went to Washington DC to appear before the BVA. It was strongly recommended that I use an appeal representative from one of the Service Organizations. His presentation was a verbatim reading of the Executive Summary that I had prepared to be presented to the Board. However, his delivery was so confusing that I finally had to take over the presentation of my case since he was clearly not well versed in the issues in my case.

I was able to take over and make my case to the BVA since early in my career I had practiced law. As a result of my training and subsequent practice, I had spent many hours presenting cases before various courts. However, most people will not be able to make their case in a logical cohesive manner.

For some, another option will be to hire a lawyer to represent you. A private lawyer should be extremely well versed in the issues of your case. However, most lawyers will charge you for their services, although there are strict guidelines about what a lawyer may charge[38]. In most cases, no fees can be charged for work performed before BVA issues its final decision.

In addition to the service organization representatives and attorneys discussed above, there are also a few non-attorney "agents" recognized by VA to represent appellants.

If you desire representation, you should fill out a VA Form 21-22 to authorize a VSO to represent you, or a VA Form 22a to authorize an attorney or recognized agent to represent you. Your local VA office can provide these forms.

THE APPEAL

The purpose of an appeal is for the applicant to be able to show the VA that it made the wrong decision. Therefore, it is important that you send VA any evidence that supports your argument that its determination on your claim was wrong. If you have additional evidence, such as records from recent medical treatments or evaluations that you feel make your case stronger, you can submit the evidence to the office holding your claims folder. An appeal representative can also submit additional written information in support of your claim.

If you have new or additional evidence, and your file is still at the local VA office you can send your new evidence there and ask for reconsideration. The VA will review this new or additional evidence and will either grant your request or, if it stands by the original decision send you a SSOC if it still does not allow your claim after reviewing the new or additional evidence. The new evidence you

---

[38] 38 U.S.C. § 5904, 38 C.F.R. part 20, subpart G

submitted will be included in your claims folder and considered when the Board reviews your appeal.

If your file is at the Board and you plan to send your new evidence there, be sure to read "What is the 90-day Rule" for some important information about time deadlines. Also, if you want the Board to consider your new evidence without sending your case back to the local VA office, include a written statement saying that you waive local VA office consideration of your new evidence and that you want the Board to review the evidence even though the local VA office hasn't seen it. Otherwise, there could be a considerable delay while the Board sends your new evidence back to the local VA office to consider.

OTHER CONSIDERATIONS

In most cases, you are not required to submit any more paperwork to finish your appeal once you've filed a completed VA Form 9. There is one important exception that you should know about. If you have received a SSOC that covers a new issue, you will need to complete and file a supplemental VA Form 9 covering the new issue if you want to appeal it.

For example, let's say that you appealed a local VA office determination on your knee disability, it sent you a SOC on that issue, and you filed your VA Form 9 on that issue. Later, before the Board decided the appeal on your knee disability, you also appealed a decision about a heart disability and you local VA office sent you a SSOC on that. If you wanted the Board to consider your appeal on the heart issue, you'd have to send you local VA office a VA Form 9 on that issue too. Your VA Form 9 becomes part of your claims folder and is the basis for adding your appeal to BVA's docket. The Board will review it when it considers your appeal.

BOARD PROCEDURES

The law requires the Board to decide cases on a "first come, first served" basis. To do that, the Board needs to know when each case was received in relationship to every other case. To keep the cases in order, the Board creates a list of all of the cases that it must decide. This list is called the Board's "docket." Your case is added to this list when VA receives your substantive appeal (VA Form 9).

The Board keeps track of where your case is in the pipeline by assigning it a "docket number" when it's added to the list. The first 2 digits show the year the case was added to the list and the rest of the numbers show in what order the case was added to the list that year. For example, if your appeal was the very first appeal added to the list in 1999, it would have docket number 99-00001.

The older the year and the lower the number for that year, the sooner your case will come up for review. The later the year and the higher the number, the longer it will take[39]. (This is another reason it's important to file your VA Form 9 promptly.)

THE APPEAL PROCESS

It is important that the veteran understands that the appeals process is not a quick fix for a denial by the VA. It is difficult to say just how long it will take from the time you file your appeal until you receive the Board's decision. As of the Fall of 1999, it took an average of about two years from the time a NOD was filed until a final decision was issued. Complex cases can take longer, particularly if the Board must remand the case.

If you believe your appeal should be decided sooner than the appeals of others who filed before you did, you can write directly to the Board explaining why the Board should hear your cases earlier than it is scheduled to be heard based upon its docket number. This procedure of asking that a case be heard early is called filing a motion to advance on the docket.

Over the years, BVA has granted fewer than 3 out of every 20 requests for advancement on the docket. That's because most appeals involve some type of hardship and the Board wishes to treat everyone fairly. You need to show convincing proof of exceptional circumstances before your case can be advanced. Some examples of exceptional circumstances are terminal illness, danger of bankruptcy or foreclosure, or an error by VA that caused a significant delay in the docketing of your appeal. Be sure to send the BVA proof of your exceptional circumstances with your motion to advance on the docket. For example, if you are about to lose your home due to foreclosure, send the BVA a copy of the notice you received telling you that[40]. If you have a terminal illness, include a statement about that from your doctor. To file a motion to advance on the docket, send your request to:

Board of Veterans' Appeals (014)
Department of Veterans Affairs
810 Vermont Avenue, NW
Washington, DC 20420

THE HEARING

As with most VA and BVA procedures there are a number of options available to the applicant. One of these procedures is a personal hearing between you (and your representative, if you have one) and an official from VA who will decide your case. During this meeting, you present testimony and other evidence supporting your case. There are two types of personal hearings: local office

---

[39] 38 U.S.C. § 7107(a), 38 C.F.R. § 20.900
[40] 38 U.S.C. § 7107(a)(2), 38 C.F.R. § 20.900(c)

hearings (also called Regional Office hearings, RO hearings, or hearing officer hearings) and BVA hearings.

As its name implies, a "local office hearing" is a meeting held at a local VA office between you and a "hearing officer" from the local office's staff. To arrange a local office hearing, you should contact your local VA office or your appeal representative as early in the appeal process as possible. If your issue can be satisfied to your satisfaction at the local office level, then you will conclude your appeal much quicker than if you are forced to go to the BVA.

In addition to a local office hearing, you also have the right to present your case in person to a member of the Board. Appellants in most areas of the country can choose whether to hold this "BVA hearing" at the local RO, commonly called a Travel Board hearing, or at the BVA office in Washington, D.C. (but not both)[41]. Some Regional Offices are also equipped to hold BVA hearings by videoconference. With this kind of hearing, you would be located at the RO and the Board member conducting the hearing would be in Washington, D.C. You would communicate with each other by closed circuit television. Sometimes, VA can offer videoconference hearings more quickly than Travel Board hearings.

If you are interested in this kind of hearing, check with your RO to see if a videoconference hearing is a possibility in your area. When deciding where to hold a BVA hearing, please keep in mind that VA cannot pay for any of your expenses — such as lodging or travel — in connection with a hearing.

The usual way to request a BVA hearing is to check a box on the VA Form 9 telling us what kind of hearing you want. However, if you didn't ask for a BVA hearing on the VA Form 9, you can still request one by writing directly to the Board. (This is subject to the "90-Day Rule," which is explained later.) If you want a BVA hearing, be sure you clearly state whether you want it held at the RO or at the Board's office in Washington, D.C. (You cannot have a BVA hearing in both places.) Please do not use the VA Form 9 to request a local office hearing. Write directly to that office instead.

SCHEDULING OF THE HEARING

The speed with which your hearing will be held depends on what type of hearing you requested and where you requested that it be held. Local VA office hearings are generally held as soon as they can be scheduled on the hearing officer's calendar.

The scheduling of Travel Board hearings — BVA hearings held at regional offices — is more complicated, because Board members must travel from Washington, D.C., to the Regional Office to conduct the hearings. (Travel Board hearings may not be available at Regional Offices located near

---

[41] 38 U.S.C. § 7105(a), 38 U.S.C. § 7107(d)(e), 38 C.F.R. part 20, subpart H

Washington, D.C.) Factors that affect when Travel Board hearings can be scheduled include the docket number (a guide to how old cases awaiting hearings are), the total number of requests for hearings in your area, how soon the Board will be able to review the cases associated with the hearings, and the resources, such as travel funds, available to the Board. Because video conferenced hearings do not involve travel by Board members, they are less complicated to arrange and can usually be scheduled more quickly than Travel Board hearings.

Hearings held at the Board's offices in Washington, D.C., will be scheduled for a time close to when BVA will consider the case — usually about three months before the case is reviewed[42].

THE CLAIMS FOLDER

If you do not request a BVA hearing, your claims folder will stay at the local VA office until it is transferred to BVA shortly before the Board begins its review of your appeal. If you request a Travel Board hearing, your claims folder will stay at the local VA office until the hearing is completed and will then be transferred to the Board.

If you request a video conferenced BVA hearing or a hearing held at the Board's office in Washington, D.C., your claims folder will stay at the local VA office until shortly before the hearing is held. It will be transferred to BVA in time for your hearing and the Board's review.

THE 90-DAY RULE

Your local VA office will send you a letter when it transfers your claims folder to Washington, D.C. That letter will let you know that you have 90 days (from the date of that letter) or until the Board decides your case, whichever comes first, during which you can add more evidence to your file, request a hearing, or select (or change) your representative.

For the Board to accept any of these items after this 90-day period is up, you must submit a written request (called a "motion") with the item asking the Board to accept the item even though it is late. The request must include an explanation of why the item is late and show why the Board should accept it (called "showing good cause")[43]. A motion to accept items after the 90-day period will be reviewed by a Board member who will issue a ruling either allowing or denying the motion.

---

[42] 38 U.S.C. § 7107, 38 C.F.R. § 20.702, 38 C.F.R. § 20.704

[43] 38 C.F.R. § 20.1304

KEEPING TRACK OF YOUR APPEAL'S STATUS

Until your file is transferred to the Board, your local VA office is the best place to get information about your appeal. VA will notify you in writing when your file is transferred to the Board in Washington, D.C. You will also be notified in writing when the Board receives your file.

After your file is transferred to the Board, you can call (202) 565-5436 to check on its status. Please bear in mind that Board employees cannot discuss the legal merits of a case or predict the outcome of an appeal. Also, because every case is different, it is impossible to give you a precise estimate of when your appeal will be decided.

Remember that it is important to act as early as possible if you want to send new evidence, appoint or change a representative, or request a hearing for two reasons.

(1)   By acting before the 90 days are up, you avoid having to file a motion and the risk that your motion will be denied.

(2)   (2) You might not have the full 90 days because the Board could decide your case before the 90 days are up.

AT THE BOARD

The Board will notify you in writing when it receives your appeal from the local VA office. The Board examines the claims folder for completeness and provides your representative (if you have one) with an opportunity to submit additional written arguments on your behalf. Your case is then assigned to a Board member for review. (If you requested a "BVA hearing," the Board member assigned to your case will conduct the hearing before reaching a decision.)

When the docket number for your appeal is reached, your file will be examined by a Board member and a staff attorney (Counsel or Associate Counsel) who will check it for completeness, review all the evidence and your arguments, as well as the transcript of your hearing (if you had one), the statement of your representative (if you have one), and any other information included in the claims folder. The staff attorney, at the direction of the Board member, may also conduct additional research and

To learn the current status of your appeal after it is transferred to Washington, D.C., call: (202) 565-5436. Be sure to have your claim number handy since this is how cases are tracked at the BVA. If the Board has "remanded" your case to your local VA office for any reconsideration, call that office.

Your case is first reviewed by a BVA staff attorney who prepares an executive summary as well as recommendations for disposition of the case for the Board member's review. The recommendations are based upon the applicable laws and the evidence. Before a decision is reached, however, the Board member will thoroughly examine all of the material in the claims folder along with the recommendations prepared by the staff attorney. The Board member will then issue a decision.

THE DECISION

The Board will give you its decision in writing. BVA tries to make its decisions as understandable as possible. However, because they are legal documents, decisions may contain complex information, such as references to laws and court cases. Many BVA decisions also contain detailed medical discussions.

Your decision will be mailed to the home address that the Board has on file for you, so it is extremely important that you keep VA informed of your correct address.

If your appeal is denied, the Board will send you a "Notice of Appellate Rights" that describes additional actions you can take. We'll also tell you more about that later. If you move, or get a new home or work phone number, you should notify the office where your claims folder is located.

IF YOUR CASE IS REMANDED

Sometimes the Board will review an appeal and find that the case isn't ready for a final decision. It will then return the case to the local VA office with instructions to do whatever needs to be done. This action of sending a case back for more work (sometimes described as "additional development") is called a remand.

After performing the additional work, the local VA office will review your case and issue a new determination. If it is unable to allow your claim, it will return the case to the Board for a final decision. The case keeps its original place on BVA's docket, so it is reviewed soon after it is returned to the Board. Depending on what was done after your case was remanded, the local VA office may provide you with a SSOC. If so, you have 60 days from the date the SSOC was mailed to you to comment on it.

Some cases are remanded for reasons neither you nor the Board can control, such as new rulings by the United States Court of Appeals for Veterans Claims or other changes in the law that require the Board to return them for local VA office review or some other action.

However, some remands might be avoided if you do —or don't do— certain things. If the Board doesn't have to remand your case, you will get your decision more quickly.

IF YOU DISAGREE WITH THE DECISION

If you are not satisfied with the Board's decision, you can appeal to the United States Court of Appeals for Veterans Claims (the Court). The Court is an independent court that is not part of the Department of Veterans Affairs. Normally, to appeal a BVA decision, you must file the Notice of Appeal with the Court within 120 days from the date when the Board's decision is mailed. (The date of mailing is stamped on the front of the Board's decision.)

To appeal a Board decision to the Court, you must file an original Notice of Appeal directly with the Court at:

United States Court of Appeals for Veterans Claims
625 Indiana Avenue, NW, Suite 900
Washington, DC 20004

If you filed a motion to reconsider (discussed in the next section of this pamphlet) with the Board within this 120-day time frame and that motion was denied, you have a new 120-day period to file the Notice of Appeal with the Court. This new 120-day period begins on the date the Board mails you a letter notifying you that it has denied your motion to reconsider. A "Notice of Appellate Rights," that discusses this in detail, will be mailed to you if the Board denies your motion to reconsider your appeal.

If you appeal to the Court, you should also file a copy of the Notice of Appeal with the VA General Counsel at the following address:
Office of the General Counsel (027)
Department of Veterans Affairs
810 Vermont Avenue, NW
Washington, DC 20420

To obtain more specific information about the Notice of Appeal, the methods for filing with the Court, Court filing fees, and other matters covered by the Court's rules, you should contact the Court directly at the Indiana Avenue address given above. You may also contact the Court by telephone at 1-800-869-8654. See "Internet Resources for Information," in a later section, for the Court's World Wide Web site address.

Caution! While you should file a copy of your Notice of Appeal to the Court with the VA General Counsel, the original Notice of Appeal you file with the Court is the only document that protects your right to appeal a BVA decision. The copy sent to VA's General Counsel does not protect that right or serve as your official appeal filing.

What else can I do if I disagree with a Board decision?

1. **M o t i o n f o r Reconsideration**

. If you can demonstrate that the Board made an obvious error of fact or law in its decision, you can file a written "motion to reconsider" your appeal. If you are represented, you may wish to consult with your representative for advice about whether you should file a motion (and for assistance in preparing one). If you do file a motion to reconsider, it should be sent directly to the Board, not to your local VA office.

A motion to reconsider should not be submitted simply because you disagree with BVA's decision. You need to show that the Board made a mistake and that the Board's decision would have been different if the mistake had not been made.

2. **Reopening**. If you have "new and material evidence," you can request that your case be re-opened. To be considered "new and material," the evidence you submit must include information related to your case that was not included in the claims folder when the Board decided your case. To re-open your case, you need to submit your new evidence directly to the local VA office and not to the Board[44].

3. **CUE Motion**. The law was amended in 1997 to provide one more way to challenge a Board decision. A Board decision can be reversed or revised if you are able to show that the decision contained "clear and unmistakable error" (CUE). Your written request for the Board to review its decision for CUE is called a "motion." CUE motions should be filed directly with the Board, and not with your local VA office.

Because CUE is a very complicated area of law, we urge you to seek help from your representative if you decide to file a CUE motion. A motion for CUE review of a prior Board decision must meet some very specific requirements, described in the Board's Rules of Practice. If the motion is denied you can't ask for another CUE review of the way the Board decided the issues you raised in your first CUE motion, so it is very important that the motion be prepared properly the first time out.

Not many CUE motions are successful, because CUE is a very rare kind of error, the kind that compels a conclusion that the Board would have decided your case differently but for the error. A difference of opinion is not enough.

When you file your CUE motion, you must tell the Board clearly and specifically, in writing, exactly what the "clear and unmistakable" error, or errors, were. You can file a motion to review a Board decision for CUE at any

---

[44] 38 U.S.C. § 7103, 38 C.F.R. § 20.1000, 38 C.F.R. § 20.1001, 38 U.S.C. § 5108, 38 U.S.C. § 7104(b), 38 C.F.R. § 3.156, 38 C.F.R. § 20.1105

time, but if you file your CUE motion after filing a timely Notice of Appeal with the Court, the Board will not be able to rule on your CUE motion[45].

IF THE APPELLANT DIES BEFORE DECISION

I have heard many veterans make the joking comment that they hope a decision is made before they die. Sadly, due to the long times that are involved in deciding appeals, this is actually a situation that happens quite often. According to the law, the death of an appellant generally ends the appeal. So, if an appellant dies, the Board normally dismisses the appeal without issuing a decision.

The rights of a deceased appellant's survivors are not affected by this action. Survivors may still file a claim at the Regional Officer for any benefits to which they may be entitled[46].

FOR MORE INFORMATION

Need general information about veterans' benefits? Speak to a VA Veterans Benefits Counselor by calling 1-800-827-1000.

Internet Resources for Information Here are just a few of the many helpful resources for information on veterans' benefits and veterans' law on the "World Wide Web."

The Department of Veterans Affairs http://www.va.gov/

The site has a wealth of veterans' information including links to an "on-line" version of this pamphlet and archives of Board of Veterans' Appeals decisions. There is extensive information about veterans programs and benefits. A number of VA forms are available. This site also contains extensive information about veterans' benefits, links to VA forms, copies of many benefits regulations, and more.

United States Court of Appeals for Veterans Claims
http://www.vetapp.uscourts.gov/

This site includes information about how to appeal a Board of Veterans' Appeals decision to the Court, Court filing fees, forms needed for filing an appeal with the Court, copies of the Court's opinions, and more.

National Archives and Records Administration

Code of Federal Regulations http://www.access.gpo.gov/nara/cfr/

---

[45] 38 U.S.C. § 7111, 38 C.F.R. part 20, subpart O
[46] 38 U.S.C. § 7104(a), 38 C.F.R. § 20.1302

Published Federal regulations, including the sections of 38 C.F.R. cited in this pamphlet, may be found here.

The Office of the Law Revision Counsel U.S. House of Representatives
http://uscode.house.gov/usc.htm
This site permits you to search for, read, and print sections of the United States Code, including the 38 U. S. C. sections cited in this pamphlet.

Department of Veterans Affairs
Electronic FOIA Reading Room http://vaww.va.gov/foia/
VA's Electronic FOIA (Freedom of Information Act) Reading Room has links to numerous VA publications, including directives, manuals, and handbooks. The site features VA's "One-Stop Customer Service Inquiry Page," described as "the place to find answers to question about any number of VA issues."

TERMS

NOD
Notice of Disagreement

Not more than a year after it mails you notice of its determination of your VA benefits claim, you tell your local VA office in writing that you disagree with its determination and want to appeal.

Statement of the Case

You local VA office sends you a summary of law, evidence and reasons for VA's denial of benefits called a "Statement of the Case" (SOC).

Substantive Appeal

You file a VA Form 9 with the local VA office not later than 60 days from the date the SOC was mailed to you, or 1 year from the date that office first mailed you notice of its determination, whichever is later.

Docketing and File Transfer
BVA Review
Local VA Office:
- adds your appeal to BVA's docket
- notifies you when 90 days remain for submitting
additional evidence, appointing or changing a
representative, or asking for a hearing
- sends your claims folder to BVA

BVA:
- conducts hearing, if requested

- reviews your appeal
- issues decision (grant/remand/deny)

BVA
Grants Appeal

BVA Remands Appeal
Appeal returned to local VA office for development, decision, and possible return to BVA

BVA Denies Appeal
You have 120 days to file appeal to Court of Appeals for Veterans Claims Filing reconsideration or CUE motion with BVA or reopening at local VA office possible or

Caution! These filing time limits apply in most cases, but don't apply to "simultaneously contested claims."

If you intend to appeal:

- Do consider having an appeal representative assist you.

- Do file your NOD and VA Form 9 as soon as you're sure you want to appeal. (Because so many appeals are filed, delaying could add months to your wait for the Board's decision.)

- Do be as specific as possible when identifying the issue or issues you want the Board to consider.

- Do be specific when identifying sources of evidence you want VA to obtain. For example, provide the full names and addresses of physicians who treated you, when they treated you, and for what they treated you.

- Do keep VA informed of any change to your current address, phone number, or number of dependents.

- Do be aware that copies of your doctor's treatment records are generally more helpful than just a statement from the doctor.

- Do be clear (on your VA Form 9) about whether or not you want a BVA hearing and where you want it held.

- Do provide all the evidence you can that supports your claim, including additional evidence or information requested by VA.

- Do include your claim number on any correspondence you send to VA and have it ready if you call. This helps VA find your records.

DON'TS

- Don't try to "go it alone" unless you are well versed in the VA rules and regulations. Consider getting a representative. A skilled representative can save you a lot of time, help you prepare the best possible appeal, and help you avoid mistakes.

- Don't send in material that doesn't have anything to do with your claim or send duplicates of things you have already sent to VA. This will only slow down the process.

- Don't use the VA Form 9 to raise new claims for the first time. The VA Form 9 is only used to appeal decisions on previously submitted claims.

- Don't use the VA Form 9 to request a local office hearing. Write to that office instead.

- Don't raise additional issues for the Board to consider late in the appeal process, especially after your claims folder has been sent to the Board in Washington, D.C. This could well cause your case to be sent back to your local VA office for additional work and result in a longer wait for a BVA decision.

- Don't submit evidence directly to the Board unless you include a written or typed statement saying that you waive consideration of the new evidence by the local VA office and clearly indicating that you want the Board to review the evidence even though the local VA office has not seen it. If you submit evidence directly to the Board without such a waiver, the case may be remanded for review and could result in delays.

- Don't submit a last minute request for a hearing or a last minute change to the type or location of a hearing unless it is unavoidable. This almost always results in a delay in getting a final decision.

Glossary

Advance on the Docket — A change in the order in which an appeal is reviewed and decided — from the date when it would normally occur to an earlier date.

Agency of Original Jurisdiction — See "Local VA Office."

Appellant — An individual who has appealed a local VA office claim determination.

Associate Counsel — See Counsel.

Abbreviations
The following abbreviations are used in the text. Complete definitions of the terms are given in this Glossary.

BVA	Board of Veterans' Appeals
CUE	Clear and Unmistakable Error
RO	Regional Office
NOD	Notice of Disagreement
SOC	Statement of the Case
SSOC	Supplemental Statement of the Case
VA	The Department of Veterans Affairs
VSO	Veterans' Service Organization

This glossary contains many of the terms commonly used in the appeal process. 38 U.S.C. § 101 also defines many claim and appeal terms.

Board - The Board of Veterans' Appeals.

Board of Veterans' Appeals — The part of VA that reviews benefit claims appeals and that issues decisions on those appeals.

Board Member — See Member of the Board.

BVA Hearing — A personal hearing, held at the BVA office in Washington, D.C., or at a VA regional office, that is conducted by a member of the Board.

These hearings can be held by videoconference from some regional offices. Also see Travel Board Hearing.

Claim — A request for veterans' benefits.

Claim Number — A number assigned by VA that identifies a person who has filed a claim; often called a "C-number." VA now uses the veteran's Social Security number for this purpose, but older files still bear the "C-number."

Claims File — Same as claims folder.

Claims Folder — The file containing all documents concerning a veteran's claim. (Other VA records folders, like education or loan guaranty folders, may also be involved, but "claims folders" are the most common and that term has been used in this pamphlet for convenience.)

Counsel — Counsel, and Associate Counsel, are attorneys skilled in veterans' law who assist Members of the Board in preparing decisions. They are like a law clerk who helps a judge.

Court of Appeals for Veterans Claims — See United States Court of Appeals for Veterans Claims.

Decision — The product of BVA's review of an appeal. A decision might, for example, grant or deny the benefit or benefits claimed, or remand the case back to the local VA office for additional action.

Determination — A decision on a claim made by a local VA office.

Docket — A listing of appeals that have been filed with BVA. Appeals are listed in numerical order, called docket number order, based on when a VA Form 9 is received by VA.

Docket Number — The number assigned to an appeal when a VA Form 9 is received by VA. By law, cases are reviewed by the Board in docket number order.

File — To submit written material, usually by mailing it or delivering it in person.

Hearing — A meeting, similar to an interview, between an appellant and an official from VA who will decide an appellant's case, during which testimony and other evidence supporting the case are presented. There are two types of personal hearings: local office hearings (also called regional office hearings or hearing officer hearings) and BVA hearings.

Hearing Officer Hearing — See Regional Office Hearing
.

Issue — Something specific you want the Board to grant you when it reviews your appeal. For example, if you filed an appeal asking the Board to grant you service connection for a heart disorder, grant you service connection for a knee disability, and grant you a higher disability rating for an already service-connected shoulder disability, the appeal would be said to contain three issues.

Local Office Hearing — See Regional Office Hearing.

Local VA Office — a term used in this pamphlet for any local office of the Department of Veterans Affairs where claims for VA benefits are received and determined. Usually, this is a VA Regional Office or an administrative office at a VA medical center. (The legal term for such an office is "agency of original jurisdiction.")

Member of the Board — An attorney, appointed by the Secretary of Veterans Affairs and approved by the President of the United States, who decides veterans' benefit appeals.

Motion — A legal term used to describe a request that the Board take some specific action in processing your appeal (such as advance your case on the docket), or that it give you permission to do something concerning your appeal (such as send in evidence late in the appeal process). The Board's "Rules of Practice" tell you when a motion is required, what a particular motion should include and where you should file it. Most motions must be in writing.

Motion to Advance on the Docket — A request that BVA review and decide an appeal sooner than it normally would for a specified reason.

Motion to Reconsider — A request for BVA to review (reconsider) its decision on an appeal.

Notice of Disagreement — A written statement saying that you disagree with a local VA office's determination on your claim and that you want to appeal that determination.

Regional Office — One of 58 VA regional offices throughout the U.S. and its territories where most claims for VA benefits are filed and determined.

Regional Office Hearing — A personal hearing conducted by a RO "Hearing Officer." A regional office hearing may be conducted in addition to a BVA hearing.

Remand — The action the Board takes in returning an appeal to the local VA office where the claim originated. This action is taken when something else needs to be done before the Board can make a decision in an appeal.

Representative — Someone familiar with VA's benefit claim process who assists claimants in the preparation and presentation of an appeal. Most representatives are Veterans' Service Organization employees who specialize in veterans' benefit claims. Most states, commonwealths, and territories also have experienced representatives to assist veterans. Other individuals, such as lawyers, may also serve as appeal representatives.

RO Hearing — See Regional Office Hearing.

Rules of Practice — Federal regulations, found at 38 C.F.R. part 20, that set out procedures for appeals to the Board of Veterans' Appeals. The 38 C.F.R. part 20 sections cited in this pamphlet are "Rules of Practice."

Simultaneously Contested Claim — A simultaneously contested claim is a claim where more than one person is trying to get a VA benefit or status that only one of them can have. Examples might be two people each claiming they are entitled to all of the proceeds of the same life insurance policy, or two people each asking to be recognized as a particular veteran's lawful surviving spouse.

Statement of the Case — This is a document prepared by the local VA office processing your appeal. It gives you a summary of the evidence considered in your case, a listing of the laws and regulations used to decide your claim, and an explanation of why the local VA office decided your claim as it did. Reviewing the SOC will help you prepare your substantive appeal.

Substantive Appeal — Normally, a completed VA Form 9
.
Supplemental Statement of the Case — An update to an SOC prepared when VA receives new evidence, or a new Glossary issue is added to an appeal, after the SOC was prepared.

Testimony — Testimony is the legal term used to describe what you and others who know about the facts of your case (witnesses) say at a hearing. Basically, to "testify" at a BVA hearing just means to tell what you know about your case. VA hearings are much more informal than court hearings, so you don't need to worry about technical rules of evidence or being cross examined when you testify.

Travel Board Hearing — A personal hearing conducted at a RO by a member of the Board.

United States Court of Appeals for Veterans Claims — An independent Federal court that reviews appeals of BVA decisions. (The court used to be called the United States Court of Veterans Appeals.)

VA Form 9 — You receive this VA form, titled "Appeal to the Board of Veterans' Appeals," with the SOC. It is the form that you fill out and file with the local VA office to complete your appeal.

Veterans' Service Organization — An organization that represents the interests of veterans. Most Veterans' Service Organizations have specific membership criteria, although membership is not usually required to obtain assistance with benefit claims or appeals. There are many such organizations. The American Legion, the Disabled American Veterans, the Veterans of Foreign Wars, and Vietnam Veterans of America are examples of these organizations. Your RO can provide information about VSOs serving your area.

CHAPTER TWENTY-FOUR

UNITED STATES COURT OF APPEALS FOR VETERANS CLAIMS

There are instances where the decisions made by the raters are not even logical, but once made, the rater rarely reverses themselves. Even more disheartening, many times the Board of Veterans Appeals either agrees with the original decision or refers the matter back to the Regional office for a re-determination. This is an open invitation for the rater that made the original decision that is under appeal to reaffirm his or her decision.

Most veterans think that they can take the VA to court and get some justice, but this is not the case. The system currently isolates the rater from any fear of a trial court reviewing what they have done. Going to a trial court would allow a de novo (new) review of the evidence. The VA is totally opposed to this procedure.

However, in the interests of due process, there is a special court where such cases can be heard. This the United States Court of Appeals for Veterans Claims located at 625 Indiana Avenue, NW, Suite 900, Washington, D.C. 20004-2950. If you think this Court can consider your appeal, you should get advice from an attorney or from a service officer in a veterans organization or a state or county veterans affairs office. You may represent yourself, but VA will be represented by its attorneys. Your case may be better presented if you are represented.

The Public List of Practitioners shown below may help you. It shows people who are allowed to represent appellants in this Court and have said that they are available to do that. Most charge a fee. The Court does not recommend or appoint them, or anyone else, to represent you.

You can also request assistance from The Veterans Consortium Pro Bono Program. The Pro Bono Program offers free representation by a qualified lawyer if you meet their eligibility requirements. To learn more about this Program, go to www.vetsprobono.org or call the Pro Bono Program at their toll free number: (888) 838-7727.

TIME LIMIT

As with every VA procedure, you must meet the following important time limit or the Court cannot consider your appeal. You must file your Notice of Appeal with the Court by mail or fax at the address/number below within 120 days after the date when the Board of Veterans Appeals (BVA) mailed a copy of its final decision to you and/or your representative. The date stamped on the front of the BVA's decision is the date when it was mailed.

FORMS AND FEES

If you decide to appeal, fill in the Notice of Appeal form. The fee for an appeal is $50.00. If you cannot pay this fee, use the Declaration of Financial Hardship form. Follow the instructions on the forms carefully and mail them to:

Clerk, U.S. Court of Appeals for Veterans Claims
625 Indiana Avenue, NW, Suite 900
Washington, D.C. 20004-2950
or fax them to the Court at 202-501-5848. You may not file them by email

INFORMATION ON THE COURT

The Court was created under Article I of the Constitution by the Veterans' Judicial Review Act (Pub.L[47]. No. 100-687) on November 18, 1988. Originally named the United States Court of Veterans Appeals, its name was changed effective March 1, 1999, by the Veterans' Programs Enhancement Act of 1998 (Pub.L. No. 105-368).

The Court's seven judges are appointed by the President, and confirmed by the Senate, for 15 year terms. The law that created the Court is in chapter 72 of Title 38, United States Code. This federal court is not part of the Department of Veterans Affairs (VA). It is not connected to the Board of Veterans' Appeals (BVA), which is an administrative body within VA.

The Court can only review final decisions of the BVA. New issues cannot be raised at this level, only appeals of BA decisions. Only the claimant may seek such review, but in most cases, the veteran is totally lost when it comes

---

[47] Public Law

to dealing with the rules of the court and the framing of a proper brief. Failure to follow the rules can result in your appeal being dismissed.

Most of the cases that come before this court deal with entitlement to disability or survivor benefits, or the amount of those benefits, but a few deal with education benefits, life insurance, home loan foreclosure, or waiver of indebtedness.

COURT PROCEDURES

The Court's *Rules of Practice and Procedure* govern its procedures and are available at this site. The Court does not hold trials, hear witness testimony, or receive new evidence. In deciding a case, it considers only the BVA decision, the briefs submitted by the parties, and the record that was considered by VA and was available to the BVA.

If the issues warrant, the Court holds oral argument where the veteran presents his side of the case and a VA representative presents the VA's side. However, only about 1% of decided cases involve oral argument. When a case does involve oral arguments, the Court holds most arguments in its Washington courtroom, but it will sometimes conduct the oral argument portion of the case by telephone conference call.

Either party may appeal from a decision of the Court to the U.S. Court of Appeals for the Federal Circuit and, thereafter, may seek review in the Supreme Court of the United States. The Court's precedential opinions are published in West's Veterans Appeals Reporter. They are available in WESTLAW, LEXIS, and--without digest--on this web site (under Search Court Decisions & Opinions). They are also sent to the Government Printing Office for microfilm distribution to its nationwide depository library system.

The Public Office of the court is open from 9:00 a.m. to 4:00 p.m., except weekends and holidays. The telephone number for case-related matters is 202-501-5970. FAX for case-related filings, 24 hours per day, 7 days per week: 202-501-5848.

REPRESENTATION

For almost all appellate courts, those who represent cases in front of the court must be registered with the court clerk. As with everything else in the law, there are those who specialize in representing these types of claims. Somewhat uniquely, many of those who hold themselves out as capable of representing the veteran in front of this particular court are not trained attorneys. This may seem unusual, but the level of specialization that such a unique court requires, may well lend itself to non-attorney representation and the court has felt that these people are certainly capable.

Below is the most recent list of attorney practitioners:

Alabama Attorneys

John F. Cameron
P.O. 240666
Montgomery AL 36124-0666
334-502-9500
johncameronlaw@aol.com

Wayne A. Ehlers
P.O. Box 1727
Semmes AL 36575
251-649-4297
wayneaehlers@yahoo.com

Jonathan P. Gardberg
1015 Montlimar Dr., # B-4
Mobile AL 36609
251-343-1111

Marvin C. Hill, Jr.
501 Madison St., # 200-B
Huntsville AL 35801
256-319-4878
cliff@personal-injured.com

James C. Pino
363 Canyon Park Dr.
Pelham AL 35124
205-663-1581
jcpalalaw@aol.com

John M. Poti
696 Silver Hills Dr., # 107
Prattville AL 36066
334\361-3535
john@jmpoti.com

Clarence F. Rhea
930 Forrest Ave.
Gadsden AL 35901
256-547-6801

Richard A. Rhea
930 Forrest Ave.
Gadsden AL 35901
256-547-6801

Ronald C. Sykstus
415 Church St., # 100
Huntsville AL 35801
256-539-9899
rsykstus@bondnbotes.com

Everett M. Urech
P.O. Dwr 70
Daleville AL 36322
334-598-4455
daleatty@snowhill.com

Alaska Attorneys

Paul B. Eaglin
P.O. Box 81910
Fairbanks AK 99708-1910
907-374-4744

Arizona Attorneys

Theodore C. Jarvi
3030 S. Rural Rd., # 114
Tempe AZ 85282-3800
480-838-6566
theodore.jarvi@azbar.org

Matthew B. Meaker
3200 N. Central Ave, # 2300
Phoenix AZ 85012
602-256-0000
mbmeaker@azbar.org

Wendy E. Ravin
28150 N Alma School Pkwy, # 103/104
Scottsdale AZ 85262
949-510-3850
wravin@earthlink.net

198\Getting Your Benefits
Antonio M. Rosacci
3411 N. 32nd St.
Phoeniz AZ 84018
602-954-1300
amrosacci@hotmail.com

Arkansas Attorneys

Robert L. Depper, Jr.
314 East Oak
El Dorado AR 71730
870-862-5505

Clark C. Evans
3719 Lakeshore Drive
N. Little Rock AR 72116
501-758-5738
cevans1@sbcglobal.net

Tammy L. Harris
212 Center Street, Suite 100
Little Rock AR 72201
501-375-5545
tlh@wallacelawfirm.com-BADCKD

Jesse L. Kearney
P.O. Box 6606
Pine Bluff AR 71611
870-536-4057
attyjkearn@aol.com

Vicky B. Lowery
314 E. Oak St.
El Dorado AR 71730
870\862-5505
bdepper@ipa.net

Roy E. Meeks
202 West Broadway
Pocahontas AR 72455
870-892-1444
meekslaw@cox-internet.com

Virginia Y. Middleton
113 East Davidson St
Fayetteville AR 72701
479-443-4675
vymiddleton@juno.com

Nona M. Morris
425 W. Capitol, # 3700
Little Rock AR 72201
501-375-9151
nmorris@ddh-ar.com

Bennie O'Neil
1423 Main St.
North Little Rock AR 72114
501-370-9259

Byron C. Rhodes
221 Hazel St. (SPA Law)
Hot Springs AR 71901-5132
501-321-2734
lawspa@aol.com

Frederick S. Spencer
409 E. 6th St.
Mountain Home AR 72653
870-425-6984
www.spencer-law-firm.com

James W. Stanley, Jr.
301 N. Broadway
North Little Rock AR 72114
501-324-2889
james@jwstanleylaw.com

Tom Stone
425 W. Capitol Ave., # 3700
Little Rock AR 72201
501-375-9151
tstone@ddh-ar.com

200\Getting Your Benefits
David R. Trussell
P.O. Box 34117
Little Rock AR 72203-4117
501-376-9467
davtruss@swbell.net

California Attorneys

William T. Bogue
P.O. Box 1155
Ventura CA 93002-1155
805-643-7292
wbogue3093@aol.com

Gregory Chandler
1255 Post St., # 939
San Francisco CA 94109
415-885-6623

Clement Cheng
17220 Newhope St., # 127
Fountain Valley CA 92708
714-825-0555

Thomas P. Clark, Jr.
660 Newport Center Dr., # 1600
Newport Beach CA 92660
949-725-4140
tclark@sycr.com

Bruce W. Ebert
SBN 151576
775 Sunrise Ave., # 160
Roseville CA 95661
866-320-7233
bpsylaw@aol.com

Fred J. Fleming
3701 Wilshire Blvd., # 410
Los Angeles CA 90010-2898
213-381-1321

John L. Gezelius
1352 Irvine Blvd., # 301
Tustin CA 92780
714-225-5007
elderlawoc@msn.com

George J. Gliaudys, Jr
1532 Maplegrove St.
West Covina CA 91792-1214
626-917-1162
maplgrv78@earthlink.net

Samuel L. Hart
6355 Topanga Canyon Blvd.
Suite 429
Woodland Hills CA 91367
818-992-4225

Rick Hicks
499 North Canon Drive, # 307
Beverly Hills CA 90210
310-887-7027

Thomas P. Higgins
390 Spar Ave., # 101
San Jose CA 95117-1643
408-590-9790
vetlaw@sbcglobal.net

Karen D. Hill
861 Bryant St.
San Francisco CA 94103
415-626-7131

Mark R. Lippman
8070 La Jolla Shores Dr., #437
La Jolla CA 92037
858-456-5840
mark8070@aol.com

Martin J. Martinez
1109 Jefferson St.
Napa CA 94559
707-251-9383
attymar@sbcglobal.net

James H. Miller
P.O. Box 10891
Oakland CA 94610
510-451-2132

Jeffrey D. Moffatt
43625 N. Sierra Hwy, Ste A
Lancaster CA 93534
661-945-6121
jeffreymbajd@hotmail.com

Roger E. Naghash
4400 MacArthur Blvd., # 900
Newport Beach CA 92660-2040
949-955-1000
lawfirm@lawfirm4u.com

Bradley Patterson
1301 Dove St.
Newport Beach CA 92660-2444
714-757-7165

Erin M. Prangley
200 West Santa Ana Blvd., # 1030
Santa Ana CA 92701
714-834-9002
erinp@wedemeyerprangley.com

Jonathan Robbins
Wilson, Sonsini, Goodrich & Rosati
650 Page Mill Road
Palo Alto CA 94304
650-320-4564

Elinor Roberts
Swords to Plowshares
1063 Market St.
San Francisco CA 94103-1605
415-252-4788
elinoroberts@swords-to-plowshares.org

Ann Gabriella Sahlberg
1440 Veteran Ave., # 341
Los Angeles CA 90024-4893
310-473-1323

Cindy B. Smith
P.O. Box 9170
Truckee CA 96162
530-587-8299
jimcin@usamedia.tv

Henry C. Su
801 California Street
Mountain View CA 94041-2008
650-335-7651
hsu@fenwick.com

Thomas W. Turcotte
P.O. Box 31186
San Francisco CA 94131
415-821-6493

Daniel D. Wedemeyer
P.O. Box 4729
West Hills CA 91308-4729
818-710-0053
www.wedemeyerprangley.com

J.Craig Williams
WLF|The Williams Law Firm, PC
4100 MacArthur Bldv., # 100
Newport Beach CA 92660-2070
949-833-3088
jcraigwms@wlf-law.com

<u>Colorado Attorneys</u>

Stephen C. Harkess
191 University Blvd., # 119
Denver CO 80206
720-993-0444
cikisgarj@bigfoot.com

Sean A. Kendall
P.O. Box N
Boulder CO 80306-1876
303-449-4773
seankendall@bsuites.com

William J. La Croix
225 South Boulder Rd., # 201
Louisville CO 80027
303-449-5297

Eileen R. Lerman
50 South Steele St., # 820
Denver CO 80209
303-394-3900
eileen@lermanpc.com

Anthony K. McEahern
1740 Broadway, 49th Fl
Wells Fargo - Private Client Services
Denver CO 80274
720-947-6639
anthony.k.mceahern@wellsfargo.com

Melanie Merritt
P.O. Box 285
Blanca CO 81123
719-379-5238
mel@fone.net

Frederick (Ric) N. Morgan
Box 131
Elbert CO 80106
303-520-6088
morgan@hayday.org

Richard J. Nolan
2275 East Arapahoe Rd., # 210
Littleton CO 80122
303-734-0262

Valeria J. Perea
P.O. Box 773690
Steamboat Springs CO 80477
970-871-1649
vp11@springsips.com

John J. Zodrow
1050 Seventeenth St., # 1940
Denver CO 80265-2077
303-572-0700
jzodrow@zodrow.com

Connecticut Attorneys

Edmond Clark
83 Scotland Ave.
Madison CT 06443-2501
203-245-4602
eclarkmadisonlaw@aol.com

Diane M. Sauer
P.O. Box 165
Willimantic CT 06226
860-456-1202

Paul S. Vayer
50 Hillcrest Ave.
New Britain CT 06053
860-224-4874
paulvayer@aol.com

Winona W. Zimberlin
2 Congress St.
Hartford CT 06114
860--249-5291
wzimberl@aol.com

Delaware Attorneys

Alex J. Mili, Jr
440 Barley Dr.
Newark DE 19702
302-571-4200
amili@aol.com

Rick S. Miller
824 Market St., # 904
P.O. Box 1351
Wilmington DE 19899
302-575-1555
rmiller@ferryjoseph.com

District of Columbia Attorneys

Derek L. Anderson
1735 New York Ave., NW, # 500
Washington DC 20006-5209
202-661-3889
danderson@sandw.com

Gordy N. Anomnachi
P.O. Box 4551
Washington DC 20017
202-529-9472
fairfieldslawofc@aol.com

Valentine C. Anyaibe
P.O. Box 3137
Washington DC 20010
301-408-3880
valibe@juno.com

William S. Bach
717 D St., NW, # 400,
Washington DC 20004
202-737-2930
williambach@aol.com

Bruce J. Barnard
2000 Pennsylvania Ave., NW
Suite 5500
Washington DC 20006-1888
202-778-1661
bbarnard@mofo.com

Merritt Blakeslee
deKieffer & Horgan
729 15th St., NW, #800
Washington DC 20005
202-783-6900
mblakeslee@dhlaw.com

Orva L. Boothby
4545 42nd St., NW, # 201
Washington DC 20016
202-363-1773
leeboothby@aol.com

Curtis A. Boykin
1401 New York Ave., NW, # 600
Washington DC 20005
202-434-9100

Kevin M. Clark
4123 Arkansas Ave., NW
Washington DC 20011
202-549-7867
kevin_m_clark@hotmail.com

Ardelia L. Davis
717 D St., NW, # 300
Washington DC 20004
202-737-6366

Michael W. Dolan(DC)
2021 L St., NW, 2nd Fl
Washington DC 20036
202-293-2776
mwdolan@att.net

Olekanma A. Ekekwe
611 Pennsylvania Ave., SE, # 160
Washington DC 20003
202-584-5450
academylaw@yahoo.com

Jared K. Ellison
Temple Law Offices
1200 G Street, NW, #370
Washington DC 20005
202-628-1101
jared.ellison@verizon.net

Bernard Englander
1717 N St., NW
Washington DC 20036
202-955-6230
bernie.law@verizon.net

Dennis C. Galarowicz
800 7th St., NW, # 201
Washington DC 20001
202-232-3200
vettorney@aol.com

Sergio Gregorio
2121 K St., NW, # 800
Washington DC 20037
202-256-1124
sergio.gregorio@comcast.net

Karen T. Grisez
1001 Pennsylvania Ave. NW #800
Washington DC 20004-2505
(202)639-7043
griseka@ffhsj.com

T.Michael Guiffre
Patton Boggs LLP
2550 M St., NW
Washington DC 20037
202-457-6000
mguiffre@pattonboggs.com

Robert B. Haemer
Pillsbury Winthrop Shaw Pitman
2300 N St., NW
Washington DC 20037-1128
202-663-9086
robert.haemer@pillsburylaw.com

John E. Howell
Sperduto Law Firm
2021 L St., NW, 2d Fl
Washington DC 20036
202-408-8900
jhowell@sperdutolaw.com

Stephen A. Jackson
419 7th St., NW, # 401
Washington DC 20004
202-393-7347
sajdmb@aol.com

Mary E. Keane
1330 New Hampshire Ave., NW
Suite 721
Washington DC 20036
202-223-2069
mekjd@hotmail.com

Joseph B. Kennedy, Jr.
2029 Connecticut Ave., NW
Suite 23
Washington DC 20008-6141
202-462-4519
joebkennedy@erols.com

William J. Kenney
600 Pennsylvania Ave., SE, # 105
Washington DC 20003
202-547-5129
kenneyfex@aol.com

Edith E. Lane
Wright, Robinson, Osthimer & Tatum
5335 Wisconsin Ave., NW, # 920
Washington DC 20015
202-895-7204
elane@wrightrobinson.com

Geralyn B. Lawrence
1250 H St., NE, # 101
Washington DC 20002
202-662-1380
attylawren@aol.com

Kathy A. Lieberman
1050 17th St., NW, #600
Washington DC 20036
202-776-0646
lieberman-mark@erols.com

Kendra A. Loar
5335 Wisconsin Ave., # 920
Washington DC 20015
202-895-7204

George S. Mahaffey, Jr.
5335 Wisconsin Ave., NW, # 920
Washington DC 20015-2030
202-895-7202
gmahaffey@wrightrobinson.com

Jeany C. Mark
1050 17th St., NW, #600
Washington DC 20036
202-776-0646
jeany@lieberman-mark.com

George T. Masson, Jr.
1775 Pennsylvania Ave., NW
Suite 1100
Washington DC 20006-4605
202-463-8282
gtm@hamiltonlaw.com

Joseph L. Mayer
1050 17th St., NW, # 440
Washington DC 20036
202-833-8575
copbrass@aol.com

Jeffrey E. McFadden
Steptoe & Johnson
1330 Connecticut Ave., NW
Washington DC 20036-1795
202-429-3000
jmcfadden@steptoe.com

Jennifer L. McGehee
5335 Wisconsin Ave., NW, # 920
Washington DC 20015-2030
202-244-4668

Michael McGonnigal
Columbus Community Legal Serv.
3602 John McCormack Rd., NE
Washington DC 20064-0001
202-319-6788
mcgonnigal@law.edu

Kerwin E. Miller
3118 Banneker Dr., NE
Washington DC 20018-1645
202-269-6261
vetlaw@worldnet.att.net

Blake J. Nelson
Shaw Pittman, LLP
2300 N St., NW
Washington DC 20037
202-663-9099
blake.nelson@shawpittman.com

Chidi Ambara Ogolo
733 15th St., NW, # 700
Washington DC 20005
202-628-0668
cogolo@aol.com

Victoria A. Phillips
2243 40th St., NW
Washington DC 20007
202-965-9739
vphillips@ioip.com

Kathleen S. Pirri
5335 Wisconsin Ave., # 920
Washington DC 20015-2030
202-895-7210
kpirri@wrightrobinson.com

Aaron E. Price, Sr.
P.O. Box 75910
Washington DC 20013
240-398-8077
aprice1911@aol.com

Sean A. Ravin
2800 Quebec St., NW, # 814
Washington DC 20008
202-607-5731
ravinesq@earthlink.net

Thomas Reed
1001 Pennsylvania Ave. NW #800
Washington DC 20004
(202)639-7023

Rhonda R. Robertson-Chappelle
621 P Street, NW, # 1
Washington DC 20001
202-236-0474

David J. Rose
5335 Wisconsin Ave., NW, # 920
Washington DC 20015-2030
202-244-4668
david.rose@wrightrobinson.com

John M. Simpson
Fulbright & Jaworski L.L.P.
801 Pennsylvania Ave., NW
Washington DC 20004-2615
202-662-4539
jsimpson@fulbright.com

Sherrie A. Smith
10903 K St., NW, # 805
Washington DC 20001
202-347-5991

Todd M. Stein
401 Ninth St., NW, # 1000
Washington DC 20004
202-274-2866
todd.stein@troutmansanders.com

Harold M. Vaught
1320 G St., SE
Washington DC 20003
202-544-4813
hvaught@laborcops.com

Jennifer M. Wagman
1401 Eye St., NW, # 300
Carter, Ledyard & Milburn
Washington DC 20005
202-623-5714
wagman@clm.com

Steven Weisbaum
1850 M St., NW, # 250
Washington DC 20036
202-293-2299

Joseph M. Werner
5505 Connecticut Ave., NW, # 183
Washington DC 20015-2601
202-215-0623
werneresq@yahoo.com

214\Getting Your Benefits

Michael E. Wildhaber
911 U St., NW
Washington DC 20001
202-299-1070
lawyer@wildhaberlaw.com

Nicholas W. Woodfield
888 17th Street, NW Suite 900
Washington DC 20006
202-261-2812
nwoodfield@hughesbentzen.com

Kathleen A. Wynne
5335 Wisconsin Ave., NW, # 920
Washington DC 20015
888-697-5462
kwynne@wrightrobinson.com

Robert E. Young, Jr.
1329 R St., NW
Washington DC 20009-4322
202-236-0170
bobyoung@mindspring.com

Florida Attorneys

Carol Avard-Hicks
P.O. Box 101110
Cape Coral FL 33910-1110
941-945-0808

N. Albert Bacharach, Jr.
115 N.E. 6th Ave.
Gainesville FL 32601
352-378-9859
n.a.bacharach@worldnet.att.net

Lars O. Bodnieks
P.O. Box 61-1154
Miami FL 33261
305-895-0610

David C. Cory
P.O. Box 3975
Brandon FL 33509-3975
813-662-0760
lawcory@gte.net

Edward T. Culbertson
3621 Central Ave
St. Petersburg FL 33713
727-327-7526

E.Audrey G. Dichter
P.O. Box 822437
South Florida FL 33082-2437
954-450-1563
veteranslaw@aol.com

Alice R. Feld
5701 N. Pine Island Rd., # 260
Tamarac FL 33321
954-726-6602

Fennie L. Fiddler
13245 Atlantic Blvd., # 4-145
Jacksonville FL 32225
904-221-2450
fenfiddler@aol.com

Matthew Fornaro
700 South Andrews Ave., # 200
Ft. Lauderdale FL 33316
954-954-9944

Louis A. Frashuer
8810 Goodby's Executive Dr., Suite A
Jacksonville FL 32217
904-737-5930
afrashuer@aol.com

Theodore F. Greene, III
P.O. Box 720157
Orlando FL 32872-0157
407-482-8212
tfgreene3@msn.com

Christine C. Hardin
31 West Garden St., # 204
Pensacola FL 32502
850-432-5981

Brian D. Hill
605 East Robinson St., # 500
Orlando FL 32802
407-422-4665

Franz C. Jobson
18350 NW Second Ave., # 500
Miami FL 33169
305-374-1770
fjobson@aol.com

Benedict P. Kuehne
NationsBank Tower, # 3550
100 S.E. 2d St.
Miami FL 33131-2154
305-789-5989
ben.kuehne@lawyers.com

Richard A. LaPointe
P.O. Box 1520
Marco Island FL 34146
800-940-4557
lapointesr@earthlink.net

David R. Lane
907 Versailles Circle
Maitland FL 32751-4566
407-417-4435
davidrlane@yahoo.com

John M. Lawrence, Jr.
900 Bishop Park Ct., # 1019
Winter Park FL 32792
407-983-6251

Nancy Lehman, J.D., R.N.
2247 Palm Beach Lakes Blvd
#220
West Palm Beach FL 33409
561-689-8281
tlehman1@aol.com

Ronald J. Marzullo
2910 W. Waters Ave.
Tampa FL 33614
813-932-0900

Kenneth B. Mason, Jr.
P.O. Box 2474
Ponte Vedra Beach FL 32004
904-273-8100

Joel M. McTague
120 East Palmetto Pack Rd., # 450
Boca Raton FL 33432-6090
561-347-1700
jmctague@rtllp.com

Peter J. Meadows
1314 East Las Olas Blvd., # 1088
Fort Lauderdale FL 33301
954-462-4323
meadowslaw@comcast.net

David E. Midgett
1521 SE 36th Ave., # 2
Ocala FL 34471
352-369-3333
attorney@atlantic.net

John S. Morse
One Urban Centre, Suite 750
4830 West Kennedy Blvd.
Tampa FL 33609-2522
813-286-4300
jsmorse@flash.net

Donovan L. Parker
838 NW 183rd St., # 206
Miami FL 33169
305-655-0239
donovanparker@yahoo.com

Carol J. Ponton
915 N. Nova Rd.
P.O. Box 2630
Daytona Beach FL 32115
386-257-2100
ponton4@aol.com

Laura S. Rotstein
3800 Inverrary Blvd., # 101-E
Lauderhill FL 33319
954-714-8811

Alan M. Scarnavack
900 8th AVe., So., # 103
Naples FL 34102
773-497-9485
corps57@aol.com

Michael A. Steinberg
1000 N. Ashley Dr., # 520
Tampa FL 33602
813-221-1300
frosty28@aol.com

Steven M. Stepper
2247 Palm Beach Lakes Blvd.
Suite 226
West Palm Beach FL 33409
561-615-0098
stepperlaw@aol.com

Howard C. Tompkins, II
P.O. Box 888
Brandon FL 33509-0888
813-685-7564 Ex
tompkinslaw@earthlink.net

John E. Tuthill
3300 49th St. North
Clearwater FL 33710
727-572-4444
tuthilllaw@aol.com

Harold W. Youmans
4846 Sun City Blvd., # 292
Sun City Center FL 33573-6281
813-671-8852
hal5440@aol.com

Georgia Attorneys

William K. Barber
18 South Main St.
Statesboro GA 30458
912-764-2623
wkbpwb@frontiernet.net

Michael G. Creety, Jr.
1265 Holly Lane, NE
Atlanta GA 30329-3511
404-523-8500
pelican@paddington.org

John P. Cross
1201 Clairmont Rd., # 110
Decatur GA 30030
404-327-4744
crossandrosenzv@mindspring.com

Robert D. Davis
PO. Box 1797
Macon GA 31202-1797
478-745-1651
rd.davis@wpmlegal.com

Thomas P. DeBerry
3781 Presidential Parkway
Suite 103
Atlanta GA 30340
770-457-9082

Michael A. Gabel
2283 Emerald Springs Dr.
Decatur GA 30035
404-288-0693
mike8620@aol.com

Melinda K. Hart
150 E. Ponce de Leon Ave., # 280
Decatur GA 30030
404-373-1649

Michael S. Holcomb
Sutherland Asbill & Brennan
999 Peachtree St., NE
Atlanta GA 30309-3996
404-853-8594
scott.holcomb@sablaw.com

Earle F. Lasseter
P.O. Box 943
Columbus GA 31902-0943
706-324-0050
elasseter@worldnet.att.net

Harold R. Moroz
P.O. Box 5505
St. Marys GA 31558
912-673-9189
moroz@eagnet.com

Nancy L. Presson
P.O. Box 741088
Riverdale GA 30274
770-478-2334
le30306@aol.com

Sharon L. Rowen
225 Peachtree St., # 1410
South Tower
Atlanta GA 30303
404-523-2844
srowen@peachtreelaw.com

Christopher B. Scott
303 Courtyard Sq.
Carrollton GA 30117
770-214-2500
cscottswslaw@aol.com

Howell F. Wright, Jr.
P.O. Box 5489
St. Marys GA 31558
912-729-4788
wildcumberland@eagnet.com

Hawaii Attorneys

David L. Bourgoin
1188 Bishop Street, # 2010
Honolulu HI 96813
808-523-7779
dlbourgoin@juno.com

Idaho Attorneys

Gary W. Haight
P.O. Box 962
Coeur d'Alene ID 83816
208-667-6700

Illinois Attorneys

Clarke C. Barnes
5 Misty Hollow
Geneseo IL 61254-9226
309-944-3674
barnescc@geneseo.net

R. Edward Bates
P.O. Box 894
Naperville IL 60566-0894
630-355-2090
rebateslawfirm@aol.com

Peter C. Drummond
P.O. Box 130
Litchfield IL 62056
217-324-2323

Daniel R. Formeller
233 South Wacker Dr.
Sears Tower, 22nd Fl
Chicago IL 60606
312-627-4000
dformeller@mail.tsmp.com

Maximilian A. Grant
5800 Sears Tower
233 South Wacker Dr.
Chicago IL 60606
312-876-7700
max.grant@lw.com

Robert M. Hodge
36 South Wabash Ave., # 1310
Chicago IL 60603-2906
312-422-1707
bhimgus@ameritech.net

Michael Leonard
123 N. Wacker Dr., # 1800
Chicago IL 60606
312-474-7925
michael.leonard@mbtlaw.com

Matthew Martell
7557 West 63rd St.
Summit IL 60501
708-924-9000
vets-rights@1stcounsel.com

Sheldon B. Nagelberg
53 West Jackson Blvd., # 1657
Chicago IL 60604
312-427-6060
sbnagelberglaw@msn.com

Debra M. Rabin
640 Pearson St., # 300
Des Plaines IL 60016
847-299-0008
debra@rabinsslaw.com

Jeffrey A. Rabin
640 Pearson St., # 300
Des Plaines IL 60016
847-299-0008
jeff@rabinsslaw.com

David M. Short
40520 Bald Eagle Rd.
Antioch IL 60002
847-395-7704
dlshort@ameritech.net

Steven R. Verr
NBC Tower - 18th Floor
455 N. Cityfront Plaza
Chicago IL 60611
312-464-8599

Indiana Attorneys

Georgianne F. Bolinger
1320 Johnson St.
Marion IN 46952
765-668-7531
georgianne@indy.rr.com

Wade R. Bosley
P.O. Box 1223
Marion IN 46952
765-668-7531
wade@indy.rr.com

Charles D. Hankey
434 E. New York St.
Indianapolis IN 46202
317-634-8565

224\Getting Your Benefits

Eric A. Koch
520 North Walnut St.
Bloomington IN 47404
812-337-3120

Kevin P. Podlaski
Carson & Boxberger LLP
1400 One Summit Sq
Fort Wayne IN 46802-3173
260-423-9411
kpp@carsonboxberger.com

C.Robert Rittman
301 S. Adams St.
Marion IN 46952
765-668-3207

Steven K. Robison
P.O. Box 647
308 West 2nd St.
Seymour IN 47274
812-522-4109
sslawyer@hsonline.net

Kansas Attorneys

John C. Betts
5920 Nall Ave., # 117
P.O. Box 117
Overland Park KS 66201
913-362-9700

Derrick C. Carpenter
510 SW 10th St.
Topeka KS 66614
785-232-3104
dcarpen058@aol.com

Kenneth M. Carpenter
P.O. Box 2099
Topeka KS 66601-2099
785-357-5251
carpgh@mindspring.com

Barbara S. Girard
ABS Legal Services, LLC
3301 Clinton Pkwy Ct., # 1
Lawrence KS 66047
785-749-2440
bsgirard@sunflower.com

Ira D. Hawver
6993 Highway 92
Ozawkie KS 66070
785-876-2233
hawverlaw@umacs.net

Teresa M. Meagher
P.O. Box 6851
Leawood KS 66206-0851
913-649-1747
tmameagher@aol.com

John R. Showalter
1122 SW Tenth St.
Topeka KS 66604
785-357-6868
showalter2@aol.com

Curtis E. Watkins
P.O. Box 475
Kingman KS 67068
620-532-3108
gwwlaw@websurf.net

Kentucky Attorneys

R. Michael Kelly
400 Starks Bldg.
455 S. 4th Ave.,
Louisville KY 40202
502-587-0112

Jeffrey J. Kuebler
4064 Pepper Tree Dr.
Lexington KY 40513
859-219-1299
jkuebler@mis.net

226\Getting Your Benefits
D. Sean Ragland
239 South Fifth St., # 2000
Louisville KY 40202
502-584-1210

Saeid Shafizadeh
P.O. Box 21244
Louisville KY 40221-0244
502-363-0000
pars@ntr.net

Michael Stevens
Black & Shaw
115 North Watterson Trail
Louisville KY 40243
502-244-3153
stevens@louisvillelaw.com

Louisiana Attorneys

Naomi E. Farve
3305 Montegut St.
New Orleans LA 70126
504-289-5389

Franklin J. Foil
7904 Wrenwood Blvd., Suite C
P.O. Box 80179
Baton Rouge LA 70898-0179
225-928-4444

Charles A. Riddle
P.O. Box 608
Marksville LA 71351
318-253-4551
criddle777@aol.com

Michael B. Thomas
Capital Area Legal Services
200 N. Third St.
Baton Rouge LA 70801
2225-338-5278
mbthomas@calscla.org

John B. Wells
317 Portsmouth Dr.
Slidell LA 70460
985-641-1855
johnlawesq@msn.com

Maine Attorneys

Daniel C. Cabral
4 Ryan Rd.
Saco ME 04072
207-284-8646
golfers@gwi.net

Edward R. Heath, Sr
P.O. Box 115
Mechanic Falls ME 04256
207-345-0988
edsylheath@aol.com

Francis M. Jackson
P.O. Box 17713
Portland ME 04112-8713
207-772-9000

John F. Zink
28 Marshview Dr.
Freeport ME 04032
207-865-6611
jfrederickzink@aol.com

Maryland Attorneys

Alexander N. Agiliga
6875 New Hampshire Ave., # 200
Takoma Park MD 20912
301-270-2002
agiliga@bellatlantic.net

Milton W. Armiger
3714 Astoria Road
Kensington MD 20895
301-946-6427
miltarmigeresq@aol.com

Veronica G. Awkard
6490 Landover Rd., Suite A
Landover MD 20785
302-773-4724
awkardfelisa@aol.com

Randolph C. Baker
405 E. Joppa Rd.
Towson MD 21286
410-823-2222

William C. Barnes
29 W. Susquehanna Ave., # 600
Towson MD 21204
410-828-1050

John F. Burgan
409 Washington Ave., # 707
Towson MD 21204
410-337-3755
john.burgan@verizon.net

Elmer A. Davis, III
69 Gentry Court
Annapolis MD 21403-1023
410-263-6940
modavis@eadavislaw.com

Michele M. Florack
429 Rosier Rd.
Fort Washington MD 20744
301-567-0704

Elizabeth H. Goldberg
P.O. Box 161
Hyattsville MD 20781
301-779-7464
elizabethgoldbergesq@yahoo.com

Charles D. Hayden
8805 Patricia Ct.
College Park MD 20740
301-935-2798
dhaydenjd@att.net

Morton Hollander
4511 Avamere St.
Bethesda MD 20814
301-530-3333

Eugene C. Holloway, III
1118 Little Magothy View
Annapolis MD 21401-5322
410-349-8352
ech@holloway-law.com

A. Paul Ingrao
2322 Patuxent River Rd.
Gambrills MD 21054-1910
410-721-8561
apingrao@us.com

Charles M. James
P.O. Box 1238
Cheverly MD 20785
301-627-4000
cmj3@lawyer.com

David L. Jamison
The Veterans Law Group
816 Easley St., # 1423
Silver Spring MD 20910
202-271-3226
djlawlaw2001@aol.com

Thomas P. Johnson, III
3904 Montrose Dr.
Chevy Chase MD 20815
301-215-9889

James G. Kolb
414 Hungerford Dr., # 234
Rockville MD 20850-4125
301-340-6850
jimk36@aol.com

230\Getting Your Benefits

Anthony D. Martin
7500 Greenway Center Dr.
1100
Greenbelt MD 20770
301-486-0700
tonymartin@erols.com

Lisa Merchant
16415 Elkhorn Lane
Bowie MD 20716
301-464-0807

Jonathan K. Miller
300 East Joppa Rd., # 303
Towson MD 21286-3004
443-921-1100

Lawal Momodu
4550 Montgomery Ave., # 601N
Bethesda MD 20814
301-961-6464
lawmod@msn.com

Joseph R. Moore
837 Still Creek Lane
Gaithersburg MD 20878
877-838-2889
joe@veteranlaw.com

Michael G. Morin
P.O. Box 778
Severn MD 21144-0778
301-585-6800
mikemorin@email.msn.com

Roxanne D. Neloms
1027 Marton St.
Laurel MD 20707
301-490-9441

Alan J. Nuta
702 Russell Ave., # 300
Gaithersburg MD 20877
301-840-1500

Rosalyn W. Otieno
7029 Palamar Turn
Lanham MD 20706
301-437-2707
rwotieno@hotmail.com

Robert H. Plotkin
785 F Rockville Pike, # 500
Rockville MD 20852
800-813-1445
bobplotkin@aol.com

William O. Sanford
11705 Tradewind Ter
Laurel MD 20708-3527
301-589-1208

Michael J. Sepanik
P.O. Box 1068
Bowie MD 20718-1068
202-215-8447

Florence L. Smith
5225 Pooks Hill Rd., # 1819-S
Bethesda MD 20814
301-564-0666

Keith D. Snyder
P.O. Box 5
Olney MD 20830-0005
301-774-1525
keithsnydr@aol.com

Russell D. Torwelle
9731 Wyman Way
Upper Marlboro MD 20772-4639
301-868-1845

Patrick J. Tracy
4203 Anthony St.
Kensington MD 20895
301-897-8298

232\Getting Your Benefits
Andrew J. Waghorn
P.O. Box 1068
Bowie MD 20718-1068
301-648-0209

Stephen J. Zawacki
8 Sykes St.
Gaithersburg MD 20877
202-465-5448
steve.zawacki@usa.com

Massachusetts Attorneys

Steven M. Autieri
800 South Main St.
Residential Title Services
Mansfield MA 02048
401-337-3363

Michael J. Calabro
88 Black Falcon Ave., # 274
Boston MA 02210-2429
617-737-7123
mjcal@prodigy.net

Donald R. Furman, Jr.
112 Fulton St.
Boston MA 02109
617-367-6717
BostonLawFurman@comcast.net

Donald C. Hill
74 Bay Shore Dr.
Plymouth MA 02360
508-746-5138
ulseinc@aol.com

Michael J. Kelley
167 Milk Street, Suite 428
Boston MA 02109
617-523-1450
nedisability@aol.com

Matthew L. McGrath, III
149 Oak Street
Franklin MA 02038
617-737-3976
kkmg2234@aol.com

Harry L. Miles
77 Pleasant St.
Northampton MA 01061-0210
413-586-8218
harrymiles@aol.com

Charles A. Murphy
50 Burlington Mall Rd., # 100
Burlington MA 01803
781-238-0300
cmurphy@murphyandrandall.com

Michael R. Pizziferri
115 Broad St., First Floor
Boston MA 02110
617-482-4070

Rodney C. Schonland
9 Sever St.
Plymouth MA 02360
508-732-9155
rcs@schonlandlaw.com

Dennis S. Scott
P.O. Box 2164
Danvers MA 01923-5164
978-777-9998
dennis@petervkent.com

William G. Small
110 Winn St., # 202
Woburn MA 01801
781-938-8474

Michigan Attorneys

Robert C. Anderson
148 West Hewitt Ave.
Marquette MI 49855
906-228-6212
rcanders@up.net

Glenn R. Bergmann
11260 Bridlewood Trail
Berrien Springs MI 49103
269-471-1605
bergmannlaw@msn.com

Debra Clancy
3170 Whitfield Ct.
Waterford MI 48329
148-623-0366

James G. Fausone
41820 W. Six Mile Rd., # 103
Northville MI 48167
248-380-0000
jfausone@ftblaw.com

Leonard A. Kaanta
148 W. Hewitt Ave.
Marquette MI 49855
906-228-6212

Paul H. Kullen
1607 East Big Beaver Rd., # 105
Troy MI 48083
248-526-3360
pkullen@macarthur-associates.com

Joseph P. McGill
One Woodward Ave., 10th Fl
Detroit MI 48226-3499
313-965-7978
mcgij1@kitch.com

Joseph E. Mihelich
23801 Gratiot Ave.
Eastpointe MI 48021
810-776-1700
Alphonsus C. Murphy
4572 S. Hagadorn Rd., # 1A
East Lansing MI 48823
517-351-2020

Donald T. Popielarz
409 S. Fayette
Saginaw MI 48602
989-797-4700
dpopielarz@chartermi.net

Richard G. Strenger
100 Bloomfield Hills Pkwy, # 200
Bloomfield Hills MI 48304
248-258-7863
strenger@butzel.com

Michael R. Viterna
41820 W. 6 Mile Rd., # 103
Northville MI 48167
248-380-0000
mviterna@ftblaw.com

Robert P. Walsh
142 West Van Buren St., # 109
Battle Creek MI 49017-3071
269-962-9693
rpwalsh@voyager.net

Wm. Michael White
49 Macomb Place, Suite 53
Mount Clemens MI 48043-2370
586-468-8850

Gregory B. Wilhelm
3433 Tecumseh River Rd.
Lansing MI 48906-3560
517-327-9960
wilhelmesquire@aol.com

Minnesota Attorneys

Theresa A. Capistrant
3009 Holmes Ave., So.
Minneapolis MN 55408
612-827-6300
traci@lawpartner-mn.com

Theodore D. Dooley
301 Fourth Avenue South, # 270
Minneapolis MN 55415
612-339-1453
614grand@winternet.com

Vincent J. Ella
1700 Pillsbury Center S.
220 S. 6th St.
Minneapolis MN 55402-1409
612-339-4295
ellavi@mansfieldtanick.com

Julia L. Finch
333 South Seventh St., # 2000
Minneapolis MN 55402
612-340-7994
jlfinch@riderlaw.com

Fay E. Fishman
3009 Holmes Ave. S
Minneapolis MN 55408
612-827-8123
fay@petersonfishman.com

John W. Geelan
2200 Wells Fargo Center
90 South 7th St.
Minneapolis MN 55402-3901
612-766-7752

Terry Graff
1001 Center Ave., Suite H-1
Moorhead MN 56560-2080
218-291-1429
grafflawoffice@integraonline.com

James T. Hansing
840 Midland Square
331 Second Avenue South
Minneapolis MN 55401
612-333-6113

Peter J. Nickitas
28 Orme Ct
St. Paul MN 55116-2764
651-699-1864
petern5@aol.com

Dennis L. Peterson
3009 Holmes Ave., So.
Minneapolis MN 55408
612-827-8123
dennis@petersonfishman.com

Samuel Rosenstein
2200 Wells Fargo Center
90 South Seventh St.
Minneapolis MN 55402-3901
612-766-7651
srosenstein@faegre.com

Alfred Stanbury
2209 St. Anthony Parkway
Minneapolis MN 55418
612-789-5060
amstanbury@earthlink.net

Thomas B. Wilson
7101 York Ave., South, # 374
Edina MN 55435
952-921-3350
t.b.wilson@worldnet.att.net

Rebecca A. Wong
Capistrant & Associates, P.A.
3009 Holmes Avenue South
Minneapolis MN 55408
612-827-6300
becca@capistrantlaw.com

238\Getting Your Benefits
Ryan J. Wood
3300 Edinborough Way, # 600
Edina MN 55435-5962
952-835-7000
rwood@tn-law.com

Edward A. Zimmerman
201 West Travelers Trail, # 11
Burnsville MN 55337
952-925-2500
mtlenway@hotmail.com

Mississippi Attorneys

Richard Burdine
501 7th St., North, # 1
Columbus MS 39701
662-329-2231

Linda C. Davis
112 Fawnwood Dr.
Brandon MS 39042
601-825-9787
jerdavis@earthlink.net

Marcus D. Evans
535 N. 5th Ave.
Laurel MS 39441
601-425-0400
marcuse@gholson-orr.com

Gregory D. Keenum
219 West College St.
Booneville MS 38829
662-728-1140

Linton C. Kilpatrick
P.O. Box 500
Greenville MS 38702-0500
662-334-9426

Owen Mayfield
P.O. Box 24567
Jackson MS 39225-4567
601-352-1346

Joe M. Ragland
P.O. Box 77
Jackson MS 39205-0077
601-969-5050

Samuel M. Tumey
P.O. Box 113
3025 MS Hwy 569 South
Liberty MS 39645
601-657-8914

Missouri Attorneys

Jeffrey J. Bunten
One Metropolitan Sq, # 2995
211 North Broadway
St. Louis MO 63102
314-241-9666
jeffbunten@earthlink.net

Donald L. Kohl
400 North Fifth St., # 200
St. Charles MO 63301
636-946-9999

Robert A. Martinez
P.O. Box 4929
Springfield MO 65808-4929
417-864-6401
amartinez@aempb.com

Nancy R. Mogab
701 Market St., # 1510
St. Louis MO 63101
314-241-4477
mogabhughe@aol.com

240\Getting Your Benefits
Monte C. Phillips
128 Washington St.
Doniphan MO 63935
573-996-3838
conlaw@clnet.net

Montana Attorneys

Roger E. Carey
116 Wedgewood Lane
Helena MT 59601
406-442-2002
carey@mt.net

Brian P. Fay
125 W. Mendenhall
Bozeman MT 59715
406-586-3084

Robert M. Kampfer
P.O. Box 1946
Great Falls MT 59403-1946
406-727-9540
rkampfer@strainbld.com

Antonia P. Marra
9 Third St North, # 303
Great Falls MT 59401
406-727-5101

Charles J. Tornabene
815 East Front, Suite 4A
Box 7009
Missoula MT 59807-7009
406-327-0800

Kevin E. Vainio
27 West Park St.
Butte MT 59701
406-782-3357
kev722555@aol.com

Nebraska Attorneys

John Stevens Berry
2650 N. 48th St.
Lincoln NE 68504
402-466-8444

John S. Berry, Jr.
2650 N. 48th St.
Lincoln NE 68504
402-466-8444

Stephen G. Charest
2650 N. 48th St.
Lincoln NE 68504
402-466-8444
stephen@jsberrylaw.com

John W. DeCamp
414 S. 11th St.
Lincoln NE 68508
402-477-3974
decamplegal@inebraska.com

Robert A. Laughlin
4521 Leavenworth St., # 22
Omaha NE 68106-1437
402-551-8583
rallaw@radiks.net

Korey L. Reiman
2650 N. 48th St.
Lincoln NE 68504
402-466-8444

Chad Wythers
Berry, Kelley & Reiman
P.O. Box 4554
Lincoln NE 68504
402-466-8444

Nevada Attorneys

John A. Cartner
2533 North Carson St.
Mailstop 3882
Carson City NV 89706
775-841-1659
jaccartner@jaccartner.com

Louis M. DiDonato
245 E. Liberty St., # 250
Reno NV 89501
775-322-7877
lmdatcls@aol.com

S.Denise McCurry
720 S. 4th St., # 301-A
Las Vegas NV 89101
702-671-0013
clintonmccurry@aol.com

Jerry W. Stuchiner
1020 East Charleston Blvd
Las Vegas NV 89104
702-671-0344
paladinlaw@lawyer.com

Robert West
6235 S. Pecos Rd., # 110
Las Vegas NV 89120
702-319-5459
lawyers@usentryvisas.com

New Hampshire Attorneys

Stephanie S. Ferro
84 Bay St.
Manchester NH 03104
603-669-3970

Peter M. Sullivan
P.O. Box 1412
Manchester NH 03101-1412
603-647-5453
peter.sullivan@nhmail.com-BADCKD

New Jersey Attorneys

Ronald E. Aronds
115 North Union Ave., # 201
Cranford NJ 07016
908-272-0111
raronds@excite.com

Michael B. Berman
18 A Robbins St.
Toms River NJ 08753
732-341-2666

Ronald J. Campione
150 JFK Parkway, CN 1000
Short Hills NJ 07078-0999
973-315-4501
rcampione@budd-larner.com

Lewis C. Fichera
773 West Atlantic Ave.
Sewell NJ 08080-1502
856-468-3000
lcfichera@yahoo.com

Vincent A. Giorgio
242 Tremont Ave.
East Orange NJ 07018
913-678-1069
vgior994551@juno.com

Michael A. Katz
382 Springfield Ave., # 217
Summit NJ 07901
908-273-7827
makatz@worldnet.att.net

Frederick W. Klepp
402 Park Blvd.
Cherry Hill NJ 08002
856-663-3344
klepplaw@aol.com

AnnMarie D. Leikauf
3 Frewert Lane
Branchburg NJ 08876-3637
908-218-0598
fedlaw@rcn.com

Gary P. Levin
1442 New Rd., # 3
Northfield NJ 08232
609-646-6100
rxlawyer@prodigy.net

Paul W. Rosenberg
The Executive Mews, # G-37
1930 East Marlton Pike
Cherry Hill NJ 08003
856-424-0500

Dawn R. SanFilippo
411 Pompton Ave.
Cedar Grove NJ 07009
973-239-3100

James B. Smith
266 Lake Ave.
Metuchen NJ 08840
732-494-8404

James B. Smith, Jr
P.O. Box 1040
Asbury Park NJ 07712-1040
732-775-6520
campbelllaw@net.labs.net

Steven J. Wenger
1402 Salem Rd.
Burlington NJ 08016
609-387-3649
swenger51@yahoo.com

New Mexico Attorneys

Patricia Glazek
18 Chapala Rd.
Santa Fe NM 87508
505-466-9777

David N. Greer
P.O. Box 27731
Albuquerque NM 87125
505-842-6117
dngreer@nmia.com

William A. L'Esperance
430 Live Oak Lane, NE
Albuquerque NM 87122
505-266-8482

Michael S. Liebman
P.O. Box 2815
Santa Fe NM 87504-2815
505-982-3164

James C. McKay-NM
1442 South St.Francis Dr., #H
P.O. Box 6250
Santa Fe NM 87502-6250
505-989-3753

Nancy I. Phillips
7917 Woodhaven Dr., NE
Albuquerque NM 87109
505-858-0115
niphilp@aol.com

New York Attorneys

Frank E. Allen
156-36 92nd St.
Jamaica NY 11414-2714
718-835-5969
frank@nete.net

Michael J. Balch
Skadden, Arps, Slate, Meagher & Flom
4 Times Square
New York NY 10036-6522
212-735-2208
mbalch@skadden.com

Nathan M. Barotz
52 Vanbderbilt Ave., 14th Fl
New York NY 10017-3899
212-905-6536
nathanbarotz@onebox.com

Susan F. Bartkowski
421 New Karner Rd.
P.O. Box 15072
Albany NY 12212-5072
518-452-1800
susan.bartkowski@townelaw.com

Edward D. Dowling
132 Foxdale Lane
Port Jefferson NY 11777
631-473-5175

Allan T. Fenley
1373 Union St.
Schenectady NY 12308
518-374-9538
afenley@nycap.rr.com

Rafael L. Franco
P.O. Box 1087
Bronx NY 10453
718-731-5171
rfrancoesq@aol.com

Christopher P. Kissel
2686 East Lake Rd.
Skaneateles NY 13152
315-685-9525

William L. Koslosky
2635 Genesee St.
Utica NY 13501
315-724-5477
polarwlk@dreamscape.com

Mark C. Kujawski
1637 Deer Park Ave.
P.O. Box 661
Deer Park NY 11729-0661
631-242-1600
mark_kujawski@yahoo.com

Bruce D. Lennard
61 Columbia St., # 201
Albany NY 12210
518-447-5218
brucelennard@verizon.net

Edward W. Lundstedt
Main Rd., P.O. Box 366
Laurel NY 11948-0366
516-298-9155

Gil McLean
3760 Express Drive South
Islandia NY 11749
631-582-3700
gilmclean@justice.com

Wesley R. Mead
19-14 22nd Drive, # 1F
Astoria NY 11105
718-606-2878
wmlaw@mail.com

Charles G. Mills, IV
56 School St.
Glen Cove NY 11542-2512
516-759-4300
charles.mills.pc.62@aya.yale.edu

Steven F. Nardizzi
67 Wall St., # 2211
New York NY 10005
212-859-3494
snardizzi@nyc.rr.com

Mark J. O'Connor
5144 Sheridan Drive
Williamsville NY 14221
716-634-8798

Gary Port
100 Cedarhurst Ave.
P.O. Box 435
Cedarhurst NY 11516
516-538-3892
gbport@earthlink.net

Brett A. Preston
313 South Perry St.
Johnstown NY 12095
518-736-5517
brettpres@excite.com

Herbert F. Ryan
1013 - 78th St.
Brooklyn NY 11228-2611
718-836-1797

Peter J. Sebekos
3909 Witmer Rd., # 891
Niagara Falls NY 14305-1239
905-685-1886
sebekos@look.ca

Melvin R. Shaw
82 Wall St., # 1105
New York NY 10005-3601
212-465-3117
shawlaw@lawyer.com

David E. Tobias
3075 Veterans Memorial Hwy, # 200
Ronkonkoma NY 11779
631-580-3700

James P. Trainor
2 Hemphill Pl., # 153
Malta NY 12020
518-899-9200
trainlaw@nycap.rr.com

Mathew B. Tully
P.O. Box 491
Hunter NY 12442
518-263-4249
mtully@tullylegal.com

North Carolina Attorneys

Hugh D. Cox, Jr.
P.O. Box 154
321 Evans Street Mall, #102
Greenville NC 27835-0154
252-757-3977
hughcox@hughcox.com

Vance T. Davis
P.O. Box 754
Lewisville NC 27023
800-393-9496
tate@daviselderlaw.com

Sharon A. Hatton
321 N. Front St.
Wilmington NC 28401
910-772-9455
sharonhatton@bizec.rr.com

250\Getting Your Benefits

Charles J. Hutson
116 W. Main St.
Durham NC 27702
919-667-1000

Craig M. Kabatchnick
103 West Main St., # 200
Everett & Everett
Durham NC 27702
919-682-5691
cmkabatchnick@triad.rr.com

David D. Lennon
176 Mine Lake Ct., # 100
Raleigh NC 27615
919-847-2300
lennonlaw@earthlink.net

Michael A. Leonard
P.O. Box 15085
Wilmington NC 28408
910-452-5544
vetslaw@hotmail.com

Peter J. Sarda
Kirby, Wallace, Creech, Sarda
P.O. Box 12065
Raleigh NC 27605
919-782-9322
psarda@wallacecreech.com

Ohio Attorneys

Randolph W. Alden
470 Olde Worthington Rd., # 250
Westerville OH 43082-8985
614-891-8422 ex
rwa@atd-law.com

Sandra E. Booth
3620 North High St., # 310
Columbus OH 43214
614-784-9451
sbooth@columbus.rr.com

Lawrence E. Chapanar
1312 Beechtree Circle NE
Massillon OH 44646-2530
330-830-2689
chapanar@sssnet.com

Barbara J. Cook
917 Main St., # 300
Cincinnati OH 45202-1314
513-751-4010
bcook@fuse.net

Hugh F. Daly
Legal Aid Society
215 E. 9th St., # 200
Cincinnati OH 45202-2146
513-362-2814

Stephen L. DeVita
1257 Weathervane Lane, # 2 D
Akron OH 44313
937-838-0718
sdevita@aol.com

David K. Frank
250 Civic Center Dr., # 400
Columbus OH 40365
614-781-9476
dfrank@columbus.rr.com

Mark B. Lawson
Legal Aid Society
215 E. 9th St., # 200
Cincinnati OH 45202-2146
513-241-9400
mlawson@lascinti.org

Eddie Lawson, Jr
P.O. Box 104
Springboro OH 45066
937-748-2101
edlawson@woh.rr.com

David C. Love
Fifth Third Center
38 Fountain Square Plaza - - MD 2099D2
Cincinnati OH 45263
513-534-4529
david.love@53.com

Jeffrey T. Lowden
P.O. Box 961
Sylvania OH 43560
419-450-5333
jefflowden@yahoo.com

Michael J. Mooney
917 Main St., # 300
Cincinnati OH 45202-1314
800-977-7919
mjmooney@fuse.net

Michael R. Moran
181Granville St.
P.O. Box 307437
Gahanna OH 43230-7437
614-476-6453
mrmoran@mrmoran.com

Brian M. Ramsey
520 Gardener Bldg
500 Madison Ave.
Toledo OH 43604-1210
419-240-2100
bmrssr@accesstoledo.com

Oklahoma Attorneys

Steven C. Davis
308 NW 13th St., #100
Oklahoma City OK 73103
405-232-0555
steve@davisrasnake.com

Michael L. Harris
P.O. Box 1117
Chickasha OK 73023
580-436-2300

James Harris
6050 South Western Ave.
Oklahoma City OK 73139
405-632-4646
j1d1h1@aol.com

Polly Murphy
1022 Northwest Blvd
Ardmore OK 73401-1533
580-223-2244
v2v2@swbell.net

Gregory R. Rasnack
308 NW 13th St., # 100
Oklahoma City OK 73103
405-232-0555
rasnake@yahoo.com

Lorie R. Rogers
1319 W. Main
Durant OK 74701
580-920-0303
lreesorrogers@hotmail.com

Oregon Attorneys

Jacques P. DePlois
P.O. Box 3159
Coos Bay OR 97420
541-888-6338
jdeplois@charterinternet.com

Thomas J. Flaherty
3032 SE Rood Bridge Dr.
Hillsboro OR 97123
503-245-2500
stahlco@teleport.com

254\Getting Your Benefits
Keith A. Miller
1262 Main St.
Sweet Home OR 97386-1608
541-367-4099

Pennsylvania Attorneys

Margaret C. Abersold
200 Hickory Lane
Valencia PA 16059
724-898-3560

David M. Axinn
P.O. Box 597
Hollidaysburg PA 16648
814-695-5518
daxinn@cohenandaxinn.com

Charles O. Barto, Jr
608 North 3rd St.
Harrisburg PA 17101
717-236-6257
bartovets@comcast.net

William T. Canavan
12 Penns Trail, # 112
Newtown PA 18940
267-756-7136
wtcesq@comcast.net

Maria M. Chesterton
Barto & Assoc
608 North Third St.
Harrisburg PA 17101
717-236-6257
bartovets@comcast.net

Shawn B. Cohen
P.O. Box 597
Hollidaysburg PA 16648
814-695-5518

Felix J. DeGuilio
660 USX Tower
600 Grant St.
Pittsburgh PA 15219
412-261-1972

C.Shawn Dryer
Babst, Calland. Clements & Zomnir
Two Gateway Center
Pittsburgh PA 15222
412-394-5432
sdryer@bccz.com

Andrew R. Eisemann
801 N. Second St.
Harrisburg PA 17102
717-232-5180
aeiseman@psinet.com

Howard Farber
1 Veterans Sq., # 100
Media PA 19063
610-565-3500
hfarber316@aol.com

David W. Francis
114 North Second St.
Harrisburg PA 17101
717-238-9300
dfrancis@powelltrachtman.com

William G. Gardner
623 North Pottstown Pike
Exton PA 19341
610-524-7002
jbgpc@aol.com

Gerald J. Grant
One Penn Center @ Suburban Station
1617 JFK Blvd., # 800
Philadelphia PA 19103
215-557-0099
ggrant@wcblegal.com

Andrew W. Green
P.O. Box 654
103 So. High St.
West Chester PA 19381-0654
610-436-9173

Jerry L. Hogan
810 South Jefferson St., # 9
Allentown PA 18103-8013
610-432-8588

Charles L. Holsworth
HOLSWORTH AND ASSOCIATES, P.C.
5801 Brownsville Road
Pittsburgh PA 15236
412-653-2556
holsworth.law@acba.org

William H. Howard
Cozen O"Connor
1900 Market St.
Philadelphia PA 19103
215-665-2173
whoward@cozen.com

Earl G. Kauffman
The Bourse - Suite 755
111 S. Independence Mall East
Philadelphia PA 19106
215-625-2708
theatty@bellatlantic.net

Lee M. Koch
570 West deKalb Pike, # 113
King of Prussia PA 19406
610-962-9035

Joseph A. Leavengood
61 Seminary Ridge
Gettysburg PA 17325
717-334-4336
joe@leavengood.com

Jess Leventhal
One Oxford Valley, # 317
Langhorne PA 19047
215-757-2010
office2868@aol.com

Peter G. Loftus
1207 N. Abington Rd
Box V
Waverly PA 18471
570-586-8604
llfpc@aol.com

George H. Love, Jr.
P.O. Box 594
Youngstown PA 15696-0594
724-537-0654
ghlove1000@aol.com

Robert D. Marcinkowski
226 West Market St.
West Chester PA 19382
610-431-9480
legal-help@rcn.com

Stephen J. Mascherino
P.O. Box 63
Southampton PA 18966
215-364-0887
rsharer@voicenet.com

Michael R. McCarty
Cozen & O'Connor
1900 Market St., 4th Fl
Philadelphia PA 19103
215-665-2076
mmccarty@cozen.com

Jeffrey A. Mills
212 North Queen St.
Lancaster PA 17601
717-299-3726

258\Getting Your Benefits

Susan Paczak
810 Penn Ave., Fifth Floor
Pittsburgh PA 15222-3614
412-765-2772
sp@abesbaumann.com

John B. Pike
584 Wyoming Ave.
Kingston PA 18704
570-288-7780
jpike@fenderlaw.com

Gerard Plourde
3214 Midvale Ave.
Philadelphia PA 19129
215-843-8203
kgplourde@msn.com

Timothy L. Salvatore
Katherman Briggs & Greenberg, LLP
7 E Market St.
York PA 17401-1205
717-848-3838
tsalvatore@resultsyoudeserve.com

David J. Schramm
Kirkpatrick & Lockhart
535 Smithfield St.
Pittsburgh PA 15222-2312
412-355-6719
dschramm@kl.com

Ronald K. Sharer
P.O. Box 63
Southampton PA 18966
215-364-0887
rsharer@voicenet.com

Gregory J. Spadea
204 East Chester Pike
Ridley Park PA 19078
610-521-0604
gregorys@att.net

Michael P. Toomey
RR # 4, Box 204-S
Sunbury PA 17801
570-988-0872
toom@sunlink.net

James Valentin
One Oxford Valley, # 317
Langhorne PA 19047
215-757-2010

Christopher L. Wildfire
One Oxford Centre, 38th Fl.
Pittsburgh PA 15219
412-263-4368
clw@pbandg.com

Douglas A. Williams
810 Penn Ave., Fifth Floor
Pittsburgh PA 15222-3614
412-765-2772
daw@abesbaumann.com

Jeffrey J. Wood
1720 S. Queen St., # 145
York PA 17403
717-854-3022
jwood@blazenet.net

Peter J. Wymes
1025 Lombard St.
Philadelphia PA 19147
215-627-3899

Preston T. Younkins
200 North Jefferson St.
Kittanning PA 16201
724-548-8166
shortguy@salsgiver.com

Puerto Rico Attorneys

Louis A. DeMier-LeBlanc
P.O. Box 194714
San Juan PR 00919-4714
787-751-3726

Salvador Medina De La Cruz
P.O. Box 21158, R.P. Station
Rio Piedras PR 00928-1185
787-751-6220
leirbag@caribe.net

Daniel Molina-Lopez
416 Ponce de Leon Ave., # 1200
Hato Rey PR 00918
787-753-7910
dml@trdlaw.com

Juan J. Nolla-Acosta
3051 Ave. Juan Hernandez Ortiz, # 12
Isabela PR 00662-3616
787-872-3901
jjnolla@centennialpr.net

William Ramirez-Hernandez
First Federal Bldg, # 1004
1056 Munoz Rivera Ave.
San Juan PR 00927
787-773-0684
wrcivil@cswebmail.com

Republic Of South Korea Attorneys

Damien P. Horigan
EWHA, GSIS
11-1 Daehyun-dong, Seodaemun-gu
Seoul, S. Korea SK 120-750
82-2-3277-3586
damienhorigan@hotmail.com

Rhode Island Attorneys

Vincent J. Chisholm
One Turks Head Place, #1313
Providence RI 02903
401-331-6300

Robert V. Chisholm
One Turks Head Place, #1313
Providence RI 02903
401-331-6300
rchisholm@cck-law.com

Steven J. Coaty
P.O. Box 1293
Newport RI 02840
401-848-7227
coatylaw@netscape.net

William J. Connell
P.O. Box 698
Forestdale RI 02824
401-762-9219
connell72862@aol.com

William J. Ruotolo
2131 Warwick Ave.
Warwick RI 02889
401-739-7404
williamjruotolo@cox.net

South Carolina Attorneys

Harry C. De Pew
2016 Lincoln St.
Columbia SC 29201
803-771-6850

Stephen R. Fitzer
1338 Main St., #702
Columbia SC 29201
803-254-2260

262\Getting Your Benefits

Tammie L. Hoffman
One Carriage Lane, Bldg D
Charleston SC 29407
843-573-4750
tammie.hoffman@scbar.org

Hoyt S. Hooks
2411 Oak St., # 206
Myrtle Beach SC 29577
843-444-1107
shooks@mcnair.net

J. Mitchell Lanier
P.O. Box 1346
Moncks Corner SC 29461
843-761-8164

W F. Partridge, III
SC Attorney Generals Office
P.O. Box 11549
Columbia SC 29211-1549
803-734-7135
partridge@ag.state.sc.us

South Dakota Attorneys

Douglas E. Hoffman
300 N. Dakota Ave., # 510
Sioux Falls SD 57101
605-336-3700
mphblaw@dtgnet.com

Eldon E. Nygaard
1419 East Cherry St.
Vermillion SD 57069
605-624-4500
enygaard@usd.edu

Thomas W. Parliman
141 N. Main Ave., # 400
Sioux Falls SD 57104
605-336-2792
tparliman@qwest.net

Steven R. Pfeiffer
300 N. Dakota Ave., # 510
Sioux Falls SD 57101
605-336-3700
pfeiffer@dtgnet.com

Tennessee Attorneys

Morgan G. Adams
410 McCallie Ave.
Chattanooga TN 37402
423-265-2020
adams@chattanoogainjurylaw.com

William S. Bennett
201 West Main St., # 204
Murfreesboro TN 37130
615-896-3294
wsbennett@hotmail.com

Earl R. Hendry
P.O. Box 220
Roan Mountain TN 37687
423-772-4710
exjudge@mounet.com

J. Myers Morton
900 East Hill Ave., # 175
Knoxville TN 37915
865-523-2000
mortonandmorton@comcast.net

Gregory D. Smith
331 Franklin St., Ste. 1
Clarksville TN 37040
931-647-1299
gregorydsmith@prodigy.net

Robin M. Webb
3604 Wells Ct.
Antioch TN 37013
615-491-4032
kurobinowitz@aol.com

Texas Attorneys

Bryant S. Banes
707 Crossroads Dr.
Houston TX 77079
281-752-6165

Clayte Binion
1810 8th Ave., Suite A
Fort Worth TX 76110
817-927-1800
binion@justice.com

Jeffrey C. Chilton
87 I-H 10 North, # 225
Beaumont TX 77707
409-832-2300
jeff@packardlaw.com

Bruce W. Cobb
7750 Gladys, Suite B
Beaumont TX 77706
409-861-4529
bwcobb@hotmail.com

Robert E. De La Garza
3232 I.H. 10, West, # 202
San Antonio TX 78201
210-736-5166

Linda Evans
One Summit Ave., # 900
Fort Worth TX 76102
817-338-0608

Linda P. Field
2515 Broadway
San Antonio TX 79215
210-227-2700
lpfield@satx.rr.com

Sandra K. Foreman
P.O. Box 201452
Austin TX 78720-1452
512-249-8161
skf@sandrakforeman.com

John P. Galligan
5731 Denmans Loop
Belton TX 76513
254-933-9817
galligan@vvm.com

Warren H. Gould
One Summit Ave., # 900
Fort Worth TX 76102
817-338-0608

Joseph R. Gutheinz, Jr.
205 Woodcombe
Houston TX 77062
281-488-1280

Robert C. Hardy
1900 North Loop West, # 690
Houston TX 77018
713-529-8888

Don A. Harper
1003 Wirt Rd., # 306
Houston TX 77055-6832
713-467-8555
dharperlaw@aol.com

Michael W. Hatfield
112 E. Pecan, # 3000
San Antonio TX 78205
210-224-4491
mhatfield@scs-law.com

Maurice D. Healy
P.O. Box 860218
Plano TX 75086-0218
972-881-7100
mdhealy@sysmatrix.net

John R. Heard
3737 Broadway, # 310
San Antonio TX 78209
210-820-3737
jrhatty@heardandsmith.com

C. Ray Holbrook, Jr.
1420 Avenue L
Santa Fe TX 77510
409-925-7919
craymary@aol.com

Webb M. Jones
P.O. Box 752501
Houston TX 77275-5201
713-664-5132
webbmilas@hotmail.com

Joel Lambert
2300 First City Tower
1001 Fannin Street
Houston TX 77002-6760
713-758-2993
jlambert@velaw.com

Stuart L. Leeds
303 Texas Ave., # 1003
El Paso TX 79901
915-577-0880

Darla J. Lilley
P.O. Box 1135
Hughes Springs TX 75656
785-979-7044

Jill Mitchell
21211 La Pena Dr.
San Antonio TX 78258
210-481-5986
mmitchell9@satx.rr.com

Julia C. Perales-Leisk
3508 Sumter Glade
Schertz TX 78154
210-659-3197
jcperales@aol.com

Stephen M. Rapkin
206 E. Locust St., # 111A
San Antonio TX 78212
210-520-9646

Elizabeth Rapkin
206 East Locust St., # 111A
San Antonio TX 78212
210-212-6700

Gordon W. Sargent
2504 Glen Springs Way
Austin TX 78741
512-473-9340
gwsargent@hotmail.com

Jason P. Sharp
3 Greenway Plaza, # 2000
Houston TX 77046
713-653-5748
jsharp@coatsrose.com

Beverly E. Smith
8930 Fourwinds Dr., # 251
San Antonio TX 78239
210-599-4722
bslaw2002@yahoo.com

Victor M. Valdes Santiago
111 Soledad St., # 300
San Antonio TX 78205
210-229-9652

Suzanne Villalon-Francisco
3737 Broadway, # 310
San Antonio TX 78209-6547
210-820-3737
svfatty@heardandsmith.com

Bruce D. Williams
1305 Prairie, # 300
Houston TX 77002
713-221-1916
b.d.williams-atty@juno.com

Joseph R. Willie, II
1301 Leeland, # 210
Houston TX 77022-7732
713-659-7330
jwillieii@aol.com

Utah Attorneys

Martin S. Blaustein
2944 Imperial St.
Salt Lake City UT 84106
801-328-8891

Alicia P. Henning
P.O. Box 1347
Bountiful UT 84011
801-699-0402
alihenning@msn.com

Vermont Attorneys

Brett E. Bacon
316 Main St., # 1
P.O. Box 1000
Norwich VT 05055-1000
802-649-5557
brettbacon@msn.com

Virgin Islands Attorneys

Fred Vialet, Jr.
P.O. Box 354
St. Thomas
U.S. Virgin Islands VI 00804
340-776-5660

Virginia Attorneys

Frank G. Aschmann
209 South Alfred St.
Alexandria VA 22314
703-683-1142
aschmannlaw@aol.com

Frederick S. Avery, III
1527 Maurice Dr.
Woodbridge VA 22191-1922
703-690-1669

Mark L. Bellamy
133 Dogwood Dr.
Marion VA 24354
540-783-9669
mohawk23@aol.co

David E. Boelzner
411 East Franklin St., 4th Fl
Richmond VA 23219
804-782-1803
dboelzner@wrightrobinson.com

Mary R. Brett
11797 Bayfield Ct.
Reston VA 20194-1510
703-689-3527
dcmaryesq@aol.com

Julie Clifford
124 South Royal St.
Alexandria VA 22314
703-548-7811
cliffordjc@aol.com

Michael E. Hendrickson
211 N. Union St., # 100
Alexandria VA 22314
703-838-5577
mehendrickson@justice.com

David A. Horne
1641 Mount Eagle Place
Alexandria VA 22302-2122
703-998-8657
dhatalaw@aol.com

Thomas D. Hughes
616 North Washington St.
Alexandria VA 22314-1991
703-836-9590

D.Michael Hurst, Jr
151 Hilton St.
Alexandria VA 22314
703-548-3980

Richard R. James
P.O. Box 6448
Glen Allen(Richmond) VA 23058-6448
804-360-3120
rjamesesq@verizon.net

Robert E. Kelly
P.O. Box 119
Annandale VA 22003-0119
703-447-3117

Thomas K. Kirui
60 S. Van Dorn St., # F-405
Alexandria VA 22304
240-535-1282
wakili@wakili.us

Grant E. Lattin
11970 Shorewood Ct.
Woodbridge VA 22192
703-490-0000
grantlattin@aol.com

James T. Martin, Jr.
200 High St., # 407
Portsmouth VA 23704
757-391-3110
jmartin@portslaw.com

Marissa D. Mitchell
411 E. Franklin St., 4th Fl
Richmond VA 23219-2205
804-783-1118
mmitchell@wrightrobinson.com

Michael K. Murphy
10560 Main St., PH 15
Fairfax VA 22030-7182
703-385-9330
mkmurph@aol.com

Denis R. O'Brien
P.O. Box 1590
Amherst VA 24521
434-946-0280
huminboid@aol.com

Lella Amiss E. Pape
8133 Leesburg Pike, 9th Fl
Vienna VA 22182
703-790-1911
lpape@rbdlaw.com

Lisa K. Piper
2009 North 14th St., # 410
Arlington VA 22201
703-469-3750
lisakaypiper@yahoo.com

Marshall O. Potter, Jr.
912 Cottage St.
Vienna VA 22180
703-938-3220

Jose A. Raffucci, Jr.
6934-B Little River Turnpike
Annandale VA 22003
703-750-3100

Helen Randolph
P.O. Box 17416
Arlington VA 22216
703-525-0808

272\Getting Your Benefits

Noelle L. Shaw-Bell
411 East Franklin St., 4th Fl
Richmond VA 23219-2205
804-783-1112
nshawbell@wrightrobinson.com

Kevin P. Shea
34 West Queens Way
Hampton VA 23669
757-727-7767
kevinpshea@justice.com

Thomas J. Short
5426 Hudship Court
Burke VA 22015
703-426-2554
tshort5555@aol.com

Daniel J. Smith
P.O. Box 332
Charlottesville VA 22902
434-249-8270

Christopher A. Somers
7015 Old Keene Mill Rd., # 202
Springfield VA 22150-2805
703-569-0400
chrissome@aol.com

Patrick H. Stiehm
4308 Lawrence St.
Alexandria VA 22309
703-360-1089
stiehm.law@juno.com

William D. Teveri
1300 Army Navy Drive, # 214
Arlington VA 22202-2000
703-979-8309
teverilaw@aol.com

Jenny Y. Twyford
P.O. Box 385
Waterford VA 20197
540-882-4199
jennytwyford@yahoo.com

Glenn S. Wainer
5827 Columbia Pike, # 505
Falls Church VA 22041
703-931-6067

Robert J. Warner
2400 Clarendon Blvd.
Arlington VA 22201
703-528-4554

Sandra W. Wischow
411 East Franklin St., 4th Fl
Richmond VA 23219-2205
804-783-1162
swischow@wrightrobinson.com

Norman R. Zamboni
7508 Parkwood Ct., # 101
Falls Church VA 22042
877-274-5612
normzamboni@erols.com

Washington Attorneys

Richard A. Baum
114 W. Magnolia St., # 420
Bellingham WA 98225-4349
360-671-2296
mcsrab@crownoffices.com

John R. Crickman
P.O. Box 637
Friday Harbor WA 98250-0637
360-378-2119

Joseph W. Evans
P.O. Box 2570
Silverdale WA 98383-2570
360-692-4386
josephwevans@hotmail.com

George A. Fields
101 Broadway Ave., East
Seattle WA 98102
206-622-5679
gafields2000@aol.com

Robert A. Friedman
3410 Broadway
Everett WA 98201
425-252-5551
rafnmi@aol.com

George R. Guinn
605 East Holland Ave., # 113
Spokane WA 99218-1246
509-464-2410
georgeguinn@qwest.net

Elie Halpern
1800 Cooper Pt Rd, SW, Bldg #19
Olympia WA 98502
360-753-8055
elieh@hycl.com

Troy X. Kelley
2521 N. Fremont St.
Tacoma WA 98406
425-687-8844

Kim Krummeck
6211 26th Ave., N.E.
Seattle WA 98115
206-985-2120
kkrummecklaw@earthlink.net

Christopher T. Lyons
640 E. Whidbey Ave.
Oak Harbor WA 98277
360-675-9310
trulylaw@whidbey.net

MaryAnne Royle
6806 N.W. Dogwood Dr.
Vancouver WA 98663
360-993-0364
roylelaw@aol.com

George F. Wolcott
P.O. Box 770
1177 Jadwin Avenue
Richland WA 99352
509-946-3588
wolcottsd@aol.com

West Virginia Attorneys

Richard P. Cohen
P.O. Box 846
Morgantown WV 26507-0846
304-292-1911
rpc116c@netscape.net

John T. Miesner
22 Capitol St.
Charleston WV 25301
304-244-9821
john@hhsmlaw.com

Edward P. Tiffey
P.O. Box 6397
Charleston WV 25362-0397
304-344-3200
ed@tiffeylaw.com

Wisconsin Attorneys

Gregory C. Burce
324 E. Wisconsin Ave., # 1200
Milwaukee WI 53202-4309
414-273-2001
gcb@hall-legal.com

William Drengler
P.O. Box 5152
Wausau WI 54402-5152
715-849-9800
drengler@dwave.net

Terry J. Klippel
2433 N. Mayfair Road, # 207
Wauwatosa WI 53226-1406
414-453-8500

Ryan D. Lister
408 3rd St., # 205
Wausau WI 54403
715-843-6516
listerlaw@dwave.net

Stephen M. Needham
135 W. Wells St., # 340
Milwaukee WI 53203
414-287-1190

Diane E. Sapp
1448 220th Ave
Milltown WI 54858-2806
715-825-3883

William P. Wetz
147 West Wilson St., # 2
Madison WI 53703
608-255-3907

Just like the Board of Veterans Appeals and a few special appeals court, there are some non-attorneys who are authorized to practice before this court. Below is the most recent list of non-attorney practitioners:

California Non-Attorneys

Paula Hart
6355 Topanga Canyon Blvd
Suite 529
Woodland Hills CA 91367
818-992-4225

Richard D. Little
1309 East Seventh St.
Los Angeles CA 90021
213-489-9010
veteraninfo@aol.com

Spencer Lord
Bet Tzedek Legal Services
145 South Fairfax Ave., 3 200
Los Angeles CA 90036-2172
323-549-5834
spencerlord@bettzedek.org

Charles W. Spellman
924 Waterbury Lane
Ventura CA 93001
805-648-7043

Colorado Non-Attorneys

Peter Link
Blinded Veterans Association
P.O.Box 25126
Denver CO 80225
303-914-5831
vsoplink@vba.va.gov

District of Columbia Non-Attorneys

Jacqueline M. Jefferson
5335 Wisconsin Ave., NW, # 920
Washington DC 20015
202-895-7205
jjefferson@wrightrobinson.com

278\Getting Your Benefits

Kevin P. McCarthy
5335 Wisconsin AVe., NW, # 920
Washington DC 20015-2030
202-895-7211
kmccarthy@wrightrobinson.com

Josh Niewoehner
5335 Wisconsin Ave., NW, # 920
Washington DC 20015
202-895-7205

Indiana Non-Attorneys

Brandy L. Bilbee
P.O. Box 1223
Marion IN 46952
765-668-7531

Louisiana Non-Attorneys

Richwell Ison
1515 Poydras St., # 2222
New Orleans LA 70112
504-581-2233
richwelli@aol.com

Maryland Non-Attorneys

James Doran
AMVETS
4647 Forbes Blvd
Lanham MD 20607
301-459-9600
amvets@amvets.org

Mississippi Non-Attorneys

James C. Davis
112 Fawnwood Dr.
Brandon MS 39042
601-825-9787
jcrdavis@earthlink.net

North Dakota Non-Attorneys

James W. Deremo
P.O. Box 11044
Fargo ND 58106
701-271-8529

Nebraska Non-Attorneys

Margie S. Phillipson
2650 N. 48th St.
Lincoln NE 68504
402-466-8444
margie@jsberrylaw.com

New York Non-Attorneys

Brian A. Campbell
4055 State Route 3
Fulton NY 13069
315-593-8309
vt1192@aol.com

Arthur E. Dessureau
Law Office of Melvin R. Shaw
82 Wall St., # 1105
New York NY 10005-3600
212-465-3117
adessureau@lawyer.com

Ohio Non-Attorneys

Riccardo V. Haynes
15288 Howe Rd.
Strongsville OH 44136
440-846-8751
rvh051864@aol.com

Pennsylvania Non-Attorneys

Lois Bartolomei
309 Marlyn Lane
Wallingford PA 19086
610-565-7206
bbpasta@erols.com

Pamela E. Benner
Suite 200, The Pavilion
Jenkintown PA 19046
800-681-7000
pam@shorlevin.com

George J. Wilson
1902 Glendale Ave.
Bethlehem PA 18018
610-691-7007
gwilson@enter.net

Rhode Island Non-Attorneys

Richard J. Levesque
Vietnam Veterans of America
380 Westminstor St.
Providence RI 02903
401-223-3693
nsorleve@vba.va.gov

Washington Non-Attorneys

Mark T. Bean
1800 Cooper Pt. Rd SW, Bldg # 19
Olympia WA 98502
360-753-8055

Allen G. Norman
P.O. Box 2347
Seattle WA 98111
206-682-2599
plclawrs@ix.netcom.com

Wisconsin Non-Attorneys

Sheryl S. Lister
408 3rd St., # 205
Wausau WI 54403
715-843-6516
listerlaw@dwave.net

PART VII

A CLOSER LOOK AT BENEFITS

CHAPTER TWENTY-FIVE

PAYMENTS

For the purposes of this chapter, we are going to assume that your request for service connection disability benefits was approved. After all, the payments that I will be discussing are only made to those veterans who have had their benefit claims approved.

In the previous chapter I talked about the fact that in certain situations the VA made payments to veterans. I talked about two broad programs that compensated the veteran for disabilities. One program was disability compensation and the other was disability pension. There is a major difference between these two programs that should be understood by the veteran and there are certain other compensation programs that will be discussed in this chapter.

There is no question that military service is a dangerous occupation and many leave the service with disabilities that cannot be corrected. In order to compensate these people for their disabilities, a number of programs were instituted to give the veteran additional compensation.

These programs were originally created to compensate those who had lost limbs or were permanently crippled during war, but today the majority of those who draw disability compensation payments do not fall into this category. They are veterans who have permanent ailments that were incurred during either while on active duty or performing periods of reserve service.

Disability compensation payments are paid to eligible recipients by both the military services and the Department of Veterans Affairs for all of those who have established their entitlement to such payments. It is possible to get disability payments from both the military as well as the VA, but as will be discussed later, at the time of this writing, veterans who do receive payments from both the military and the VA lose one dollar in entitlement from the active military for each dollar received from the VA. This is neither fair nor equitable, but it is the law.

Disability Compensation

One of the best known compensation programs within the VA deals with payments made to veterans for disabilities that are determined to be service connected. Those receiving such payments do so as a result of lingering effects of illnesses or injuries that occurred while on active duty or during reserve service. These payments are made to the qualified veteran on a monthly basis. Historically, each year Congress increases the amounts of these payments with cost of living increases. These payments are also fully exempt from federal, state, and local income taxes.

Eligibility

To be eligible to receive such payments the veteran must simply have served in the military, including periods of Reserve and National Guard service. This requirement means that anyone who even served in the military for a single day is eligible to receive disability compensation. There is no minimum time that the applicant must have spent in uniform to qualify.

To illustrate this point, I know of one case where the individual in question served less than one week on active duty before being injured to the point he was no longer able to perform his duties. A medical board determined he was totally disabled and he was medically retired from the United States Army. He has been drawing disability compensation at the 100% level since he was 21 years old.

However, keep in mind that these programs were designed as "rewards" for those who served their country faithfully. With this thought in mine, as with every VA program there are, however, certain groups of veterans who are not qualified to receive such payments. These groups are:

1. Those who received discharges rated as "under dishonorable conditions",

   and

2. Those whose disabilities were caused by "willful misconduct." Willful misconduct would cover such situations as the disability being incurred during the commission of a crime or while on unauthorized absences (AWOL) or as a result of alcohol or drug abuse.

The Concept

The concept behind the creation of the disability compensation programs was to make payments to disabled veterans to offset their loss in earning power that came about as a result of the disability incurred while on active duty.

The perceived disability is expressed as a percentage of loss of earning power with compensation beginning at the 10% level. From 10%, the rated disability will increase by 10% until reaching the 100% level. For each level, there is an assigned disability payment. These amounts increase each year as Congress authorized cost of living increases.

In an unusual move that showed surprising foresight, Congress also realized that the loss of earning power suffered by a disabled veteran also applied to the spouse and any children of that veteran. As a result, there are supplemental payments added to the amount authorized for those whose disabilities are rated as 30% and above that are for the spouse and children.

There are also situations were the veteran may be the sole support for the veteran's parents. In these instances there are also supplemental payments available to assist due to the perceived loss in earning power of the disabled veteran.

As an example, in 2004 someone who is unmarried and is rated as 30% disabled would receive a monthly payment of $324.00 per month. If this same individual were married, for this 30% disability, he or she would receive $363.00 per month. If the disabled veteran were married and supporting his or her parents, for this same 30% disability, the monthly payment would be $425.00 per month.

If a disabled veteran who is married and has one child is rated as 30% disabled, he or she would receive $391.00 per month. For each additional child under the age of 18, the veteran would receive an additional $19.00 per month.

At the 100% level, a veteran who is married would receive $2,429.0 per month, tax free.

Special Monthly Compensation

In addition to the disability payments discussed above that are the basis of the program there are a number of other payments that may be authorized in addition to the disability compensation to compensate the veteran for loss of specific body parts.

For example, a veteran rated as a 100% disabled who is married and also is rated for special compensation for loss of use of legs or feet would receive $2,990.00 per month. This sum includes an amount that is designated for attendant care for the veteran.

DISABILITY PENSION

Disability Pension is a benefit paid to wartime veterans with limited income who are no longer able to work. You may be eligible if:

•you were discharged from service under other than dishonorable conditions, AND

•you served 90 days or more of active duty with at least 1 day during a period of war time. However, 38 CFR 3.12a requires that anyone who enlists after 9/7/80 generally has to serve at least 24 months or the full period for which a person was called or ordered to active duty in order to receive any benefits based on that period of service. With the advent of the Gulf War on 8/2/90 (and still not ended by Congress to this day), veterans can now serve after 9/7/80 during a period of war time. When they do, they generally now must serve 24 months to be eligible for pension or any other benefit. But note the exclusions in 38 CFR 3.12(d), AND

•you are permanently and totally disabled, or are age 65 or older, AND

•your countable family income is below a yearly limit set by law

FAMILY INCOME LIMITS (EFFECTIVE DECEMBER 1, 2004)[48]

If you are a...   Your yearly income must be less than...

- Veteran with no dependents $10,162
- Veteran with a spouse or a child $13,309

(Veterans with additional children: add $1,734 to the limit for EACH child)

- Housebound veteran with no dependents $12,419
- Housebound veteran with one dependent $15,566
- Veteran who needs aid and attendance and has no dependents $16,955
- Veteran who needs aid and attendance and has one dependent $20,099

How Much Does VA Pay?

VA pays you the difference between your countable family income and the yearly income limit which describes your situation (see chart above). This difference is generally paid in 12 equal monthly payments rounded down to the nearest dollar. Call the toll-free number below for details.

---

[48] Some income is not counted toward the yearly limit (for example, welfare benefits, some wages earned by dependent children, and Supplemental Security Income)

How Can You Apply?

You can apply by filling out VA Form 21-526, Veteran's Application for Compensation Or Pension. If available, attach copies of dependency records (marriage & children's birth certificates) and current medical evidence (doctor & hospital reports). You can also apply on line through our website at http://vabenefits.vba.va.gov/vonapp.

Related Benefits

- Vocational Rehabilitation Program

- Medical Care

<u>Dependent Indemnity Compensation (DIC)</u>

DIC is a monthly benefit paid to eligible survivors of a

•Military service member who died while on active duty, OR

•Veteran whose death resulted from a service-related injury or disease, OR

•Veteran whose death resulted from a non service-related injury or disease, and who was receiving, or was entitled to receive, VA Compensation for service-connected disability that was rated as totally disabling

1. for at least 10 years immediately before death, OR

2. since the veteran's release from active duty and for at least five years immediately preceding death, OR

3. for at least one year before death if the veteran was a former prisoner of war who died after September 30, 1999.

<u>Who is Eligible</u>

The surviving spouse is eligible for this benefit if he or she:

•validly married the veteran before January 1, 1957, , OR

•was married to a service member who died on active duty, OR

•married the veteran within 15 years of discharge from the period of military service in which the disease or injury that caused the veteran's death began or was aggravated, OR

•was married to the veteran for at least one year, OR

•had a child with the veteran, AND

•cohabited with the veteran continuously until the veteran's death or, if separated, was not at fault for the separation, AND

•is not currently remarried[49].

The surviving child(ren), is/are eligible if he/she is:

•not included on the surviving spouse's DIC

•unmarried, AND

•under age 18, or between the ages of 18 and 23 and attending school.[50]

The surviving parent(s) may be eligible for an income-based benefit. See our fact sheet, Parents' DIC, or call the toll-free number below for more information.

Payment Amount

The basic monthly rate of DIC is $993 for an eligible surviving spouse. The rate is increased for each dependent child, and also if the surviving spouse is housebound or in need of aid and attendance. VA also adds a transitional benefit of $250 to the surviving spouse's monthly DIC if there are children under age 18. The amount is based on a family unit, not individual children. It is paid for two years from the date that entitlement to DIC commences, but is discontinued earlier when there is no child under age 18 or no child on the surviving spouse's DIC for any reason.

Benefit rate tables, including those for children alone and parents, can be found on the Internet at http://www.vba.va.gov/bln/21/Rates, or call the toll-free number below.

---

[49] A surviving spouse who remarries on or after December 16, 2003, and on or after attaining age 57, is entitled to continue to receive DIC.
[50] Certain helpless adult children are entitled to DIC. Call the toll-free number below for the eligibility requirements for those survivors

How to Apply

Claimants should complete VA Form 21-534 (Application for Dependency and Indemnity Compensation, Death Pension and Accrued Benefits by a Surviving Spouse or Child), and submit it to the VA regional office serving the claimant's area. Call the toll-free number below for information about supporting materials that VA may need to process a DIC claim.

Related Benefits

- Health Care (CHAMPVA)
- Federal Employment Preference
- Home Loan Guaranty
- Survivors' & Dependents' Educational Assistance

PARENTS' DIC

Parents' DIC is an income-based monthly benefit for the parents, or parent, of a military service member or veteran (hereafter referred to as "veteran") who died from

- a disease or injury incurred or aggravated while on active duty or active duty for training, OR
- an injury incurred or aggravated in line of duty while on inactive duty for training, OR
- a service-connected disability.

Who are eligible parents?

The term "parent" includes a biological, adoptive, and foster parents. A foster parent is a person who stood in the relationship of a parent to the veteran for at least one year before the veteran's last entry into active duty.

Payment Amount

The following are the maximum annual rates paid[51]. Rates are reduced based on the countable income of the parent or parents.

---

[51] Benefit rates are effective December 1, 2003. Rates change annually.

- Sole Surviving Parent Living or Not Living With a Spouse $5,844
  with Aid & Attendance Allowance (A&A)   9,000
- One of Two Parents Not Living with a Spouse   4,224
  with A&A   7,296
- One of Two Parents Living with a Spouse   3,960
  with A&A   7,116

Why is Parents' DIC an "income based" benefit?

Eligibility to Parents' DIC is based on need[52]. When countable income exceeds the limit set by law, no benefit is payable. Eligible parents must report all sources of income to VA; for example, gross wages, retirement annuity, insurance proceeds or annuity, interest, and dividends. The spouse's income must also be included if living with a spouse. A spouse may be the other parent of the deceased veteran, or from remarriage. The following are the current income limits:

Sole Surviving Parent, or One of Two Parents Not Living With a Spouse $11,560

Sole Surviving Parent Living with a Spouse, or One of Two Parents Living With a Spouse 15,538

Reducing the parents' countable income.

There are a few ways that the eligible parents can reduce the income that counts toward Parents' DIC. This would include such things as unusual medical expenses may be used to reduce countable income. This includes amounts actually paid by parents during the calendar year for medical expenses for themselves and for relatives they are under an obligation to support, for which they are not reimbursed by insurance.

In computing the parents' income, VA will deduct the amount the parents paid for medical expenses, if found qualified, by use of a formula provided by law.

How to Apply?

You can apply by filling out VA Form 21-535 [*Application for Dependency and Indemnity Compensation by Parent(s)*], and submitting it to the

---

[52] Income limits are effective December 1, 2003. Limits change annually.

VA regional office that serves your area. Call the toll-free number below for information about supporting materials that VA may need to process your claim.

DEATH PENSION

Death Pension is a benefit paid to eligible dependents of deceased wartime veterans.

Who Is Eligible?

You may be eligible for death benefits if:

•the deceased veteran was discharged from service under other than dishonorable conditions, AND

•he or she served 90 days or more of active duty with at least 1 day during a period of war time. However, 38 CFR 3.12a requires that anyone who enlists after 9/7/80 generally has to serve at least 24 months or the full period for which a person was called or ordered to active duty in order to receive any benefits based on that period of service. With the advent of the Gulf War on 8/2/90 (and still not ended by Congress to this day), veterans can now serve after 9/7/80 during a period of wartime. When they do, they generally now must serve 24 months to be eligible for pension or any other benefits. But note the exclusions in 38 CFR 3.12(d), AND

•you are the surviving spouse or unmarried child of the deceased veteran, AND

•your countable income is below a yearly limit set by law

INCOME LIMITS (EFFECTIVE DECEMBER 1, 2004)

If you are a...   Your yearly income must be less than[53]...

- Surviving spouse with no dependent children $ 6,814

---

[53] Some income is not counted toward the yearly limit (for example, welfare benefits, some wages earned by dependent children, and Supplemental Security Income)

- Surviving spouse with one dependent child $ 8,921

    (Add $1,734 to the limit for EACH additional child)

- Housebound surviving spouse with no dependents $ 8,328

- Housebound surviving spouse with one dependent $10,432

- Surviving spouse who needs aid and attendance
    with no dependents $10,893

- Surviving spouse who needs aid and attendance
    with one dependent $12,996

- Surviving child (no eligible parent) $1,734

Payment Amount

VA pays you the difference between your countable income and the yearly income limit which describes your situation (see chart above). This difference is generally paid in 12 equal monthly payments rounded down to the nearest dollar. Call the toll-free number below for details.

How to Apply

You can apply by filling out VA Form 21-534, *Application for Dependency and Indemnity Compensation Or Death Pension by Surviving Spouse or Child.* If available, attach copies of dependency records (marriage & children's birth certificates).

BURIAL AND PLOT ALLOWANCES

VA Burial Allowance

A VA burial allowance is a partial reimbursement of an eligible veteran's burial and funeral costs. When the cause of death is not service-related, the reimbursement is generally described as two payments:
(1) a burial and funeral expense allowance, and

(2) a plot interment allowance.

Who Is Eligible

You may be eligible for a VA burial allowance if:

- you paid for a veteran's burial or funeral, AND

- you have not been reimbursed by another government agency or some other source, such as the deceased veteran's employer, AND

- the veteran was discharged under conditions other than dishonorable.

In addition, at least one of the following conditions must be met:
- the veteran died because of a service-related disability. OR

- the veteran was receiving VA pension or compensation at the time of death, OR

- the veteran was entitled to receive VA pension or compensation but decided not to reduce his/her military retirement or disability pay, OR

- the veteran died in a VA hospital or while in a nursing home under VA contract, or while in an approved state nursing home.

Payment Amount

Service-Related Death. VA will pay up to $1,500 toward burial expenses for deaths prior to September 10, 2001. For deaths on or after September 11, 2001, VA will pay $2,000. If the veteran is buried in a VA national cemetery, some or all of the cost of moving the deceased may be reimbursed.

Non-service-Related Death. VA will pay up to $300 toward burial and funeral expenses, and a $150 plot interment allowance for deaths prior to December 1, 2001. The plot-interment allowance is $300 for deaths on or after December 1, 2001. If the death happened while the veteran was in a VA hospital or under contracted nursing home care, some of all of the costs for transporting the deceased's remains may be reimbursed.

How To Apply

You can apply by filling out VA Form 21-530, *Application for Burial Allowance*. You should attach proof of the veteran's military service (DD 214), a death certificate, and copies of funeral and burial bills you have paid.

Related Benefits

- Burial in VA National Cemeteries
- Headstones and Markers

- Presidential Memorial Certificates

- Burial Flags

BURIAL FLAGS

A United States flag is provided, at no cost, to drape the casket or accompany the urn of a deceased veteran who served honorably in the U. S. Armed Forces. It is furnished to honor the memory of a veteran's military service to his or her country. Eligibility for Former Members of Selected Reserve were added by Section 517 of Public Law 105-261.

Who Is Eligible To Receive The Burial Flag

Generally, the flag is given to the next-of-kin, as a keepsake, after its use during the funeral service. When there is no next-of-kin, VA will furnish the flag to a friend making the request for it. For those VA National Cemeteries with an Avenue of Flags, families of veterans buried in these national cemeteries may donate the burial flags of their loved ones to be flown on patriotic holidays.

How To Apply

You may apply for the flag by completing VA Form 2008, *Application for United States Flag for Burial Purposes.* You may get a flag at any VA regional office or U.S. Post Office. Generally, the funeral director will help you.

Replacement of the Burial Flag

The law allows the VA to issue one flag for a veteran's funeral. The VA cannot replace the flag if it is lost, destroyed, or stolen. However, some veterans' organizations or other community groups may be able to help you get another flag.

Displaying the Burial Flag

The proper way to display the flag depends upon whether the casket is open or closed. VA Form 2008 provides the correct method for displaying and folding the flag. The burial flag is not suitable for outside display because of its size and fabric. It is made of cotton and can easily be damaged by weather.

DISABILITY COMPENSATION FOR SEXUAL OR PERSONAL TRAUMA

Some veterans (both women and men) have suffered sexual or other personal trauma while serving on active military duty. The veterans might still struggle with fear, anxiety, embarrassment, or profound anger as a result of these experiences. Nothing can undo the past, but if a veteran suffers from the effects of trauma in the service, VA may be able to help them.

VA Definition of Sexual or Personal Trauma

Sexual or personal trauma are events of human design that threaten or inflict harm. Trauma is defined as any lingering physical, emotional, or psychological symptoms. Examples of sexual or personal trauma might be:

- •Rape,

- •Physical assault,

- •Domestic battering, and

- •Stalking

Disability Compensation

Disability Compensation is a monthly payment to a veteran disabled by an injury or a disease incurred or aggravated on active service. The veteran must have been discharged under other than dishonorable conditions to be eligible, and must current suffer from disabling symptoms to receive compensation. Post Traumatic Stress Disorder (PTSD) Secondary to Sexual or Personal Trauma can certainly cause disabling symptoms.

PTSD is a recurrent emotional reaction to a terrifying, uncontrollable or life-threatening event. The symptoms may develop immediately after the event or may be delayed for years. The symptoms include:

- •Sleep disturbances and nightmares,

- •Emotional instability,

- •Feelings of fear and anxiety,

- •Impaired concentration,

- •Flash-backs, and

•Problems in intimate and other interpersonal relations.

How the Application Process Works

You can apply by filling out VA Form 21-526, *Veterans Application for Compensation or Pension.* VA counselors and Women Veterans Coordinators are available for assistance.

CHAPTER TWENTY-SIX

BENEFITS FOR SELECTED RESERVE AND NATIONAL GUARD MEMBERS

Selected Reserve and National Guard members who served on regular active duty are eligible for the same VA benefits as other veterans. The member must meet the same length of service required for any benefit.

The following are VA benefits, based on non-active duty service, for which Selected Reserve and National Guard Members may be eligible:

•**COMPENSATION** – This is a monthly benefit that is paid for disabilities that resulted from a disease or injury incurred while on active duty for training, or an injury, heart attack or stroke incurred during inactive duty for training. Such disabilities are considered "service-connected."

•**MEDICAL CARE** - VA will provide medical care for service-connected disabilities. Medical care for non service-connected conditions is determined by current Veterans Health Administration criteria.

•**EDUCATION AND TRAINING** – Selected Reservists and National Guard members may be entitled to receive up to 36 months of benefits under the Montgomery GI Bill – Selected Reserve (Chapter 1606).

Benefit entitlement ends either (a) 10 years from the date of eligibility for the program, or until released from service; or (b) 14 years if eligibility began on or after October 1, 1992.

To qualify for these benefits, the participant must:

- have a six-year obligation to serve in the in the Selected Reserve or National Guard (officers must agree to serve six years in addition to the original obligation),

- have completed initial active duty for training (IADT),

- meet the requirements to receive a high school diploma or equivalency certificate before applying for benefits, and

- remain in good standing while serving in a Selected Reserve or National Guard unit.

•**VOCATIONAL REHABILITATION & EMPLOYMENT** – This program helps individuals who have service-connected disabilities by offering them services and assistance to help them prepare for, find and keep suitable employment. For individuals with serious service-connected disabilities, VA also offers services to improve their ability to live as independently as possible.

•**HOME LOAN** - VA guarantees loans to purchase a home, manufactured home, manufactured home and lot, certain types of condominiums, or to build, repair, and improve a home. This benefit may be used to refinance an existing home loan. Certain disabled veterans can receive grants to have their home specially adapted to their needs. Native Americans living on Trust Land may qualify for a direct loan.

To qualify, the individual must have completed six years of service in the Selected Reserves or National Guard with an honorable discharge. If he/she was discharged due to service-connected disability, the required service time could be less. (Note: this eligibility expires on September 30, 2009.)

•**LIFE INSURANCE** – There are three programs that affect Selected Reserve and National Guard members:

- SGLI (Servicemembers' Group Life Insurance) is low-cost life insurance for servicemembers and reservists. It is available in $10,000 increments up to a maximum of $250,000. SGLI coverage begins when the servicemember enters service. Coverage continues for 120 days from date of separation, or up to one year if totally disabled at the time of separation from service.

- VGLI (Veterans' Group Life Insurance) is renewable term life insurance for veterans. It is available in amounts up to $250,000 but not to exceed the amount of SGLI coverage in force at the time of the servicemember's separation from service. Premiums are age-based. Participants must apply within 120 days of separation, or 1 year and 120 days if proof of good health is provided

- FGLI (Family Group Life Insurance) is low cost life insurance extended to the spouse and children of servicemembers insured under SGLI. Spousal coverage is available up to a maximum of $100,000, but may not exceed the servicemember's coverage amount. Dependent children are automatically covered for $10,000 for which there is no cost. Coverage terminates 120 days after the servicemember is released from service. The spouse may convert policy to a commercial policy

•BURIAL IN A NATIONAL CEMETERY, AND HEADSTONE/MARKER

These benefits are available to individuals who:

- died as a result of a disease or injury incurred or aggravated in line of duty during a period of active duty for training or inactive duty training, or

- was disabled as a result of a disease or injury incurred or aggravated in line of duty during a period of active duty for training or inactive duty training, or

- died while hospitalized or undergoing treatment at the expense of the United States for injury or disease contracted or incurred under honorable conditions while performing active duty for training or inactive duty training, or undergoing such hospitalization or treatment, or
- at the time of death, was entitled to retired pay based on Selected Reserve or National Guard service or would have been entitled but for being under the age of 60, or

- died under honorable conditions as a member of the Reserve Officers' Training Corps of the Army, Navy, or Air Force while attending an authorized training camp or on an authorized cruise, while performing authorized travel or from that camp or cruise, or while hospitalized or undergoing treatment at the expense of the United States for injury or disease contracted or incurred under honorable conditions while engaged in one of those activities.

•BURIAL FLAG

A U.S. flag for burial purposes is issued for individuals:

- who completed at least one enlistment in the Selected Reserves or National Guard, or was discharged due to service-connected disability, or
- whose death is related to his/her service, or
- who, at the time of death, was eligible for retirement pay based on Selected Reserve or National Guard service, or would have been entitled had the member attained age 60.

Department of Veterans Affairs
Veterans Benefits Timetable

Information for Veterans Recently Separated from Active Military Service

Disability Compensation: VA pays monthly compensation to veterans for disabilities incurred or aggravated during military service. This benefit is not subject to federal or state income tax. Entitlement is established from the date of separation if the claim is filed within one year from separation. Generally, military retirement pay is reduced by any VA compensation received. Income from Special Separation Benefits (SSB) and Voluntary Separation Incentives (VSI) affects the amount of VA compensation paid

Time Limit: None   Where to Apply - Any VA office or call 1-800-827-1000 or file at www.va.gov

Disability Pension: This income-based benefit is paid to veterans with honorable war-time service who are permanently and totally disabled due to non service-connection disability (or age 65 or older).

Time Limit: None   Where to Apply: Same as above

Medical: VA provides a wide range of health care services to veterans including treatment for military sexual trauma, and for conditions possibly related to exposure to Agent Orange, ionizing radiation, and other environmental hazards in the Persian Gulf. Generally, veterans must be enrolled in VA's Health Care System to receive care.

Combat Veterans - VA will provide combat veterans free health care for any illness possibly associated with service against a hostile force in a war after the Gulf War or during a period of hostility after November 11, 1998.

Time Limit: Two years from release from active duty. Where to Apply: Any VA medical facility or call 1-877-222-8387 or file at www.va.gov

Dental: Veterans may receive one-time dental treatment if they were not provided treatment within 90 days before separation from active duty. The time limit does not apply to veterans with dental conditions resulting from service-connected wounds or injuries.

Time Limit: 90 days from separation   Where to Apply: Same as above

Education and Training: Up to 36 months of benefits for

•Montgomery GI Bill – Active Duty (Chapter 30), or

•Veterans Educational Assistance Program (VEAP) (Chapter 32), or

•Montgomery GI Bill – Selected Reserve (Chapter 1606)

Time Limit: 10 years from release from last period of active duty. Limited extensions available

10 years from the date of eligibility for the program, or until released from the Selected Reserve or National Guard. 14 years if eligibility began on or after October 1, 1992. If activated under title 10, eligibility period is extended by time on active duty plus 4 months. Separate extension for each activation. Extension not available if activated under title 32

Where to Apply: Any VA office or call 1-800-442-4551 or file at www.va.gov

Vocational Rehabilitation and Employment: VA helps veterans with service-connected disabilities prepare for, find and keep suitable employment. For veterans with serious service-connected disabilities, VA also offers services to improve their ability to live as independently as possible. Some of the services offered are: job search, vocational evaluation, career exploration, vocational training, education training, and rehabilitation service.

Time Limit: Generally 12 years from VA notice to veteran of at least a 10 percent disability rating   Where to Apply: Any VA office or call 1-800-827-1000 or file at www.va.gov

Home Loan: Veterans with qualifying service are eligible for VA home loan services including guaranteed loans for the purchase of a home, manufactured home, manufactured home and lot, certain types of condominiums, or to build, repair, and improve homes. This benefit may be used to refinance an existing home loan. Certain disabled veterans can receive grants to have their homes specially adapted to their needs. Native Americans living on Trust Land may qualify for a direct home loan.

Time Limit: None   Where to Apply: Any VA office or call 1-800-827-1000

Life Insurance:

•SGLI (Servicemembers' Group Life Insurance) is low-cost life insurance for servicemembers and reservists. It is available in $10,000 increments up to a maximum of $250,000. SGLI coverage begins when the servicemember enters service.

•VGLI (Veterans' Group Life Insurance) is renewable term life insurance for veterans. It is available in amounts up to $250,000 but not to exceed the amount of SGLI coverage in force at the time of the servicemember's separation from service. Premiums are age-based.

•FGLI (Family Group Life Insurance) is low cost life insurance extended to the spouse and children of servicemembers insured under SGLI. Spousal coverage is available up to a maximum of $100,000, but may not exceed the servicemember's coverage amount. Dependent children are automatically covered for $10,000 for which there is no cost.

•SDVI (Service-Disabled Veterans' Insurance), also called "RH" insurance, is life insurance for service-disabled veterans. The basic coverage is $10,000. A $20,000 supplemental policy is available if premium payments for the basic policy are waived due to total disability.

•VMLI (Veterans' Mortgage Life Insurance) is mortgage protection insurance issued to those severely disabled veterans who have received grants for Specially Adapted Housing from VA. Maximum coverage of $90,000.

Coverage continues for 120 days from date of separation, or up to one year if totally disabled at the time of separation from service

Time Limit: Must apply within 120 days of separation, or 1 year and 120 days if proof of good health is provided

Coverage terminates 120 days after servicemember is released from service. Spouse may convert policy to a commercial policy

For basic must apply within two years from date of notification of service-connected disability. For supplemental must apply within one year of approval of waiver of premiums.

Must apply before the age of 70 Where to Apply: Any VA office or call 1-800-669-8477

Reemployment: The Department of Labor's web site www.dol.gov contains information on employment and reemployment rights of members of the uniformed services.

For military service over 180 days, must apply for reemployment with employer within 90 days after separation. Shorter periods to apply if service is less than 180 days. Where to apply - Former employer

Unemployment Compensation: The Unemployment Compensation for Ex-servicemembers program is administered by the States as agents of the Federal government. The Department of Labor's web site www.dol.gov contains links for each state's benefits, including the District of Columbia and Puerto Rico.

Limited time   State Employment Office (bring your DD-214)

PROTECT YOUR IDENTITY

Your DD-214 contains personal information. Keep it in a safe place. Protect yourself from identify theft. If you decide to file your DD-214 at a public records facility such as a court house or vital statistics agency, you may want to inquire about the level of security in place to
limit public access to your document.

Compensation & Pension Service – April 2003

Special Benefit Allowances Rate Table

Benefit Rate Da   ged Public Law

Automobile Allowance $ 2-16-2003 PL 108-183

Clothing Allowance $616   -01-2004* PL 108-363[54]

---

[54] The clothing allowance increase, while effective the date of the law, is not payable until the following August 1st. (Example: PL 97-306 effective October 1, 1982, increased the clothing allowance to $327.00. This rate was payable August 1, 1983.)

Medal of Honor Pension $1027 per month 12-01-2004 2.7% COLA

CHAPTER TWENTY-SEVEN

EDUCATIONAL PROGRAMS

There are several educational programs that are conducted by the Department of Veterans Affairs. They are outlined below:

Montgomery GI Bill

The Montgomery GI Bill (MGIB) is the current educational program for those on active duty and is authorized under Chapter 30. This program provides up to 36 months of education benefits for those eligible. The programs must be approved for VA training, but generally, this education may be provided to the veteran by:

- College, Business, Technical or Vocational school
- Tuition assistance "Top-up"
- Apprenticeship/Job Training
- Correspondence Courses
- Remedial, Deficiency, and Refresher Training (in some cases)
- Flight Training (in some cases)
- The cost of tests for licenses or certifications needed to get, keep, or advance in a job

Eligibility

If you are in service, you may be eligible for training under this program after 2 years of active duty. Please consult with the Education Services Officer at your installation, or call the toll-free number below, for information about your eligibility.

If you are separated from service, you may be an eligible veteran if you[55]:

- Entered active duty for the first time after June 30, 1985;

- Got a high school diploma or equivalent (or, in some cases, 12 hours of college credit) before the end of your first obligated period of service;

- Got an honorable discharge;

- Continuously served for 3 years, OR
    1. 2 years if that is what you first enlisted for, OR
    2. 2 years if you have an obligation to serve four years in the Selected Reserve AND entered Selective Reserve within a year of leaving active duty.

You should be aware that the following pitfalls could cause you to lose all MGIB benefits:

Honorable Discharge.   You must have an honorable discharge. A "general" or "under honorable condition" is not qualifying.

Early Discharge.   To be eligible with an early discharge, your separation reason must meet certain requirements. Call the VA toll-free number below (or check with your Education Services Officer if you're on active duty) for more information.

How Much Does VA Pay?

The monthly benefit paid to you is based on the type of training you take, length of your service, your category, and if DOD put extra money in your MGIB

---

[55] Different rules apply if you entered active duty before July 1, 1985, and in certain other cases. Call the VA toll-free number below for more information.

Fund (called "kickers"). You usually have 10 years to use your MGIB benefits, but the time limit can be less, in some cases, and longer under certain circumstances. For those with 3 years of service, full-time rates are $800 per month.

How To Apply

You can apply by filling out VA Form 22-1990, *Application for Education Benefits.* You can also apply on line through our website at http://vabenefits.vba.va.gov/vonapp.

VOCATIONAL REHABILITATION – CHAPTER THIRTY-ONE

Another educational program available under the Department of Veterans Affairs is Vocational Rehabilitation. Vocational Rehabilitation is a program which helps eligible disabled veterans get and keep lasting, suitable jobs. It also helps seriously disabled veterans achieve independence in daily living.

The program offers a number of services to help each eligible disabled veteran reach his or her rehabilitation goal. These services include vocational and personal counseling, education and training, financial aid, job assistance, and, if needed, medical and dental treatment. Services generally last up to 48 months, but they can be extended in certain instances.

Eligibility

Usually, you must first be awarded a monthly VA Disability Compensation payment. In some cases, you may be eligible if you aren't getting VA compensation (for example, you are awaiting discharge from the service because of a disability, OR you are entitled to VA compensation but have decided not to reduce your military retirement or disability pay).

Eligibility is also based on you meeting the following conditions[56]:

- You served on or after September 16, 1940 AND

- Your service-connected disabilities are rated at least 20% disabling by VA, AND

- You need Vocational Rehabilitation to overcome an employment handicap, AND

- It has been less than 12 years since VA notified you of your eligibility

How Much Does VA Pay?

If you need training, VA will pay your training costs, such as tuition and fees, books, supplies, equipment, and, if needed, special services. While you are in training, VA will also pay you a monthly benefit to help with living expenses, called a subsistence allowance. For details, call the toll-free number below.

---

[56] You may be eligible for Vocational Rehabilitation if you are rated 10% disabled, and you have a serious employment handicap. You may have longer than 12 years to use this benefit if certain conditions prevented you from training.

How To Apply?

You can apply by filling out VA Form 28-1900, *Disabled Veterans Application for Vocational Rehabilitation,* and mail it to the VA regional office that serves your area. You can also apply on line through our website at http://vabenefits.vba.va.gov/vonapp.

Related Benefits

- Work Study Allowance
- Tutorial Assistance
- Revolving Fund Loan

POST-VIETNAM VETERANS' EDUCATIONAL ASSISTANCE PROGRAM (VEAP) CHAPTER THIRTY-TWO

The Post-Vietnam Veterans' Educational Assistance Program, or "VEAP" for short, is an education benefit for veterans who paid into VEAP while they were in the service. Eligible veterans may be entitled to as much as 36 months of training. Eligibility usually ends 10 years after getting out of the service, but the time limit can be longer in certain cases. Eligible veterans may pursue any of the following types of training[57]:

- College or University Programs

- Correspondence Courses

- Business, Technical or Vocational Training

- Flight Training, in some cases

- Apprentice/On-the-Job Training

- High School Diploma or equivalent

- Remedial, Deficiency, and Refresher Training (in some cases)

- The cost of tests for licenses or certifications needed to get, keep, or advance a job

Eligibility

You may be eligible if you're still on active duty, call the toll-free number below for details about your eligibility for VEAP or to find out if you may switch to the Montgomery Bill.

- You were discharged under conditions other than dishonorable, AND

- You first entered active duty after December 31, 1976, and before July 1, 1985, AND

- You contributed to VEAP before April 1, 1987, AND

- You served long enough to qualify (See below)

Length of Service Requirement:

You generally had to complete 24 continuous months of active duty. Please contact the toll-free number if you have less service, as there are some

---

[57] The program must be approved for VA training.

exceptions. Contributions to the program may also be refunded. Please call toll-free number below for more information.

What Does VA Pay?

The total dollar amount of your benefits is the sum of:
- Your total contributions, PLUS

- Matching funds from VA equal to 2 times your contributions, PLUS

- Any DOD contributions or "kickers"

The monthly amount you'll receive is based on the total (above), the number of months you contributed, the type of training you're in, and your training time.

How To Apply?

When you find a program approved for VA training, you can apply for VEAP by filling out VA Form 22-1990, *Application for Education Benefits.* You can also apply on line through the website at http://vabenefits.vba.va.gov/vonapp.

Related Benefits
- Work-Study Program

- Tutorial Assistance

- Noncontributory VEAP (Sec. 903)

- Refund of Contributions

SURVIVORS & DEPENDENTS' EDUCATIONAL ASSISTANCE – CHAPTER THIRTY-FIVE

Survivors' & Dependents' Educational Assistance is an education benefit for eligible spouses and children of certain veterans. Eligible persons can receive up to 45 months of full-time or equivalent benefits for[58]:

- College, Business, Technical or Vocational Courses,

- High School Diploma or GED, Independent Study or Distance Learning courses

- Correspondence Courses (Spouses Only), Apprenticeship/Job Training

- Remedial, Deficiency, and Refresher Training (in some cases)

- The cost of tests for licenses or certifications needed to get, keep, or advance in a job

Eligibility

A claimant must be the son, daughter, or spouse of:

- a veteran who died or is permanently and totally disabled as the result of a service-connected disability. The disability must arise out of active service in the Armed Forces.

- a veteran who died from any cause while such service-connected disability was in existence.

- a service member missing in action or captured in line of duty by a hostile force.

- a service member forcibly detained or interned in line of duty by a foreign government or power.

---

[58] Schools and programs must be approved by a State Approving Authority (SAA) for VA training.

How Long Is the Period During Which This Benefit May Be Used?

As with so many VA programs, there is a limit to the time during which this benefit is available to someone who is eligible[59].

- Spouse/Surviving Spouse: 10 years from the date VA establishes eligibility. For surviving spouses of veterans who died while on active duty, 20 years from the date of the veteran's death (benefits can't be paid before December 10, 2004 for anyone whose 10 year period ended prior to that date).

- Children: between ages 18 and 26.

How Much Does VA Pay?

The amount VA pays is based on the type of training program, and training time. Benefits are paid in arrears and monthly. For example for Fiscal Year 2005, VA pays $803 monthly for full-time training for a full month at a college or university. If attendance is less than a month or less than full-time, payments are reduced proportionately. Rate tables can be found on the Internet Website or by calling the toll-free number shown below.

How To Apply?

After finding a program approved for VA training, complete VA Form 22-5490, *Application for Survivors' and Dependents' Educational Assistance.* Send it to the VA regional office with jurisdiction over the State where you will train, or apply on-line at the Internet Website shown below.

Related Benefits

- Special Benefits for Children with Disabilities

- Educational Counseling Services

- Work-Study Employment

- Tutorial Assistance

---

[59] These time limits can be extended under certain circumstances. Call the toll-free number or visit the Internet Website shown below for details.

MONTGOMERY GI BILL – SELECTED RESERVE – CHAPTER ONE HUNDRED AND SIX

The Montgomery GI Bill - Selected Reserve is an education program that provides up to 36 months of benefits to members of the Selected Reserve. This includes the Army, Navy, Air Force, Marine Corps, and Coast Guard Reserves, as well as the Army National Guard and the Air Guard. It is the first program that doesn't require a person to serve on active duty in the regular Armed Forces to qualify.

An eligible reservist may get education benefits while in a program approved for VA training. For information about the types of training available, call the toll-free number below.

Eligibility

You may be an eligible Reservist or National Guard member if[60]:

- after 6/30/85, you signed a six-year obligation to serve in the Selected Reserve, AND

- you completed your Initial Active Duty for Training (IADT), AND

- you got your High School Diploma or GED before you completed your IADT, AND

- you are in good standing in a drilling Selected Reserve unit

If you stay in the Selected Reserves, benefits generally end 10 years from the date you become eligible for the program. You may have longer if you couldn't train because of a service-related disability. Your eligibility generally ends when you leave the Selected Reserves.

How Much Does VA Pay?

The monthly benefit paid to you is based on the type of training you're in. If you're attending school, your payment is based on your training time. The full-time rate for College training is $272 per month.

---

[60] If you are an officer in the Selected Reserve, OR if you entered active duty from the Selected Reserve after 11/29/89, call the toll-free number below for details.

How To Apply?

Your unit will give you a *Notice of Basic Eligibility* (DD Form 2384 or 2384-1) when you become eligible. When you find a program approved for VA training, fill out VA Form 22-1990, *Application for Education Benefits*. Send it to the VA regional office that serves the state where you will train. You can also apply on line through our website at http://vabenefits.vba.va.gov/vonapp.

Related Benefits

- Work-Study Program
- Tutorial Assistance
- Educational and Vocational Counseling

CHAPTER TWENTY-EIGHT

SPECIAL AND LIMITED BENEFITS

There are a number of programs that are available for special purposes as a limited benefit. These health care benefits are offered only to certain veterans or to veterans under special situations. These programs are:

- Agent Orange Exposure Treatment and Registry Examination

- Automobile Assistance

- Beneficiary Travel (Including Ambulance)

- Bereavement Counseling

- Blind Veterans Services

- Combat Veteran Eligibility

- Dental Care

- Domiciliary Care

- Emergency Care in Non-VA Facilities

- Extended Care

- Eyeglasses

- Foreign Medical Care

- Gulf War Illness

- Hearing Aids

- Home Health Care

- Home Improvement and Structural Alterations

- Homeless Programs

- Ionizing Radiation Exposure, Treatment and Registry Examination

- Long Term Care

- Maternity Care

- Medical Equipment and Aids

- Military Sexual Trauma Counseling

- Non-VA Health Care Services

- Nose or Throat Radium Treatment

- Nursing Home Care

- Project 112/SHAD Participants

- Readjustment Counseling

- Women Veterans Services

Agent Orange Exposure Treatment and Registry Examination

Vietnam veterans exposed to Agent Orange while in Vietnam are eligible for cost-free hospital care, medical services, and nursing home care for any disability that may be associated with the exposure. In addition, these veterans are eligible for enrollment in Priority Group 6, unless they are eligible for placement in a higher priority. This special treatment authority is limited to those veterans who:

Served on active duty in the Republic of Vietnam during the period beginning on January 9, 1962, and ending on May 7, 1975; and

Have conditions for which the National Academy of Sciences found evidence of a possible association with herbicide exposure.

Those conditions are:

- Adult-onset (Type 2) diabetes,

- Chronic lymphocytic leukemia (CLL)

- Hodgkin's disease

- Multiple myeloma

- Non-Hodgkin's lymphoma

- Acute and subacute peripheral neuropathy

- Porphyria cutanea tarda, chloracne, prostate cancer

- Respiratory cancers (cancer of the lung, bronchus, larynx, or trachea)

- Soft-tissue sarcoma (other than osteosarcoma, chondrosarcoma, Kaposi's sarcoma, or mesothelioma).

Extensive medical examinations are offered at all VA medical centers for eligible concerned veterans who may have been exposed to Agent Orange or other herbicides during their military service, Veterans who are interested in participating in this program should contact the nearest VA medical center for an examination.

There have been a number of informational brochures published about Agent Orange and medical problems. What follows is one of them.

Agent Orange Information for Veterans Who Served in Vietnam
GENERAL INFORMATION
Environmental Agents Service
Department of Veterans Affairs
810 Vermont Avenue, N.W.
Washington, DC 20420

Agent Orange was used in Vietnam to protect U.S. troops. Agent Orange was a herbicide used in Vietnam to kill unwanted plants and to remove leaves from trees that otherwise provided cover for the enemy. The name, "Agent Orange," came from the orange stripe on the 55-gallon drums in which it was stored. Other herbicides, including Agent White and Agent Blue, were also used in Vietnam to a much lesser extent.

When and where Agent Orange was used in Vietnam.

Between 1961 and 1971, the U.S. military in South Vietnam used more than 19 million gallons of herbicides for defoliation and crop destruction. Several types and combinations of chemicals were used. These mixtures were identified by the color of the stripe on the storage drums.

The three most common mixtures were Agent Orange, Agent White, and Agent Blue. Fifteen different herbicides were shipped to and used in Vietnam. Most of the herbicides sprayed in Vietnam were Agent Orange, which was used between January 1965 and April 1970. Herbicides other than Agent Orange were used in Vietnam prior to 1965, but to a very limited extent. The total area sprayed with herbicides between 1962 and 1965 was quite small. However, some of the herbicides used in the early years contained greater concentrations of dioxin. Spraying occurred in all 4 military zones of Vietnam.

Heavily sprayed areas included inland forests near the demarcation zone; inland forests at the junction of the borders of Cambodia, Laos, and South Vietnam; inland forests north and northwest of Saigon; mangrove forests on the southernmost peninsula of Vietnam; and mangrove forests along major shipping channels southeast of Saigon.

Long-term Effects of Exposure to Agent Orange.

In the 1970's some veterans became concerned that exposure to Agent Orange caused health problems. One of the chemicals in Agent Orange contained minute traces of TCDD (dioxin), which caused a variety of illnesses in laboratory animals. More recent studies have suggested that the chemical may be related to a number of cancers and other health problems.

What concerned Vietnam veterans can do.

In 1978, the Veterans Administration, now known as the Department of Veterans Affairs (VA), set up the Agent Orange Registry Health Examination Program for Vietnam veterans concerned with the possible long-term medical effects of exposure to Agent Orange. Vietnam veterans who are interested in participating in this program should contact the nearest VA medical center for an examination. More than 315,000 Vietnam Veterans have completed this examination.

What a veteran can expect from this examination.

Veterans who participate in this examination are asked about their possible exposure to herbicides in Vietnam. A medical history is taken, a physical examination is performed, and a series of basic laboratory tests, such as a chest x-ray (if appropriate), urinalysis, and blood tests, are done. If medically required, consultations with other health specialists are scheduled.

However, no special Agent Orange tests are offered because there is no way to show that Agent Orange or other herbicides used during Vietnam caused individual medical problems. There are tests that show body dioxin levels, but VA does not perform them because there is serious question about their value to veterans. VA also makes a presumption of Agent Orange exposure for Vietnam veterans.

In its 1994 report on Agent Orange, the National Academy of Sciences (NAS) concluded that individual TCDD levels in Vietnam veterans usually are not meaningful because of background exposures to TCDD in all Americans, poorly understood variations among individuals in TCDD metabolism, relatively large measurement errors, and exposure to herbicides that did not contain TCDD.

How a veteran benefits from taking VA's Agent Orange Registry examination.

The veteran is informed of the results of the examination during a personal interview and gets a follow-up letter further describing the findings. Each veteran is given the opportunity to ask for an explanation and advice. Sometimes a follow-up examination or additional laboratory tests are scheduled because of the possibility of previously undetected medical problems being present. These discoveries can help veterans get prompt treatment for their illnesses. Some veterans think they are in good health, but are worried that exposure to Agent Orange and other substances may have caused some hidden illnesses. The knowledge that a complete medical examination does not show any problems can be reassuring or helpful to Registry participants. All examination and test results are kept in the veteran's permanent medical record. These data are entered into the VA Agent Orange Registry.

Vietnam veterans can get medical treatment for Agent Orange-related illnesses.

Under Section 102, Public Law 104-262, the Veterans' Health Care Eligibility Reform Act of 1996, VA shall furnish hospital care, medical services and may furnish nursing home care to veterans exposed to herbicides in Vietnam. These veterans will be furnished health care and without the requirement of a co-payment. There are some restrictions. VA cannot provide such care for a:

(1) disability which VA determines did not result from exposure to Agent Orange, or

(2) disease which the NAS has determined that there is "limited/suggestive" evidence of no association between occurrence of the disease and exposure to a herbicide agent.

Some Vietnam veterans get disability compensation for Agent Orange-related illnesses.

VA pays disability compensation to Vietnam veterans with injuries or illnesses incurred in or aggravated by their military service. Veterans do not have to prove that Agent Orange caused their medical problems to be eligible for compensation. Rather, VA must determine that the disability is "service-connected." A Veterans Services Representative, at a VA medical center or regional office, can explain the compensation program in greater detail and assist veterans who need help in applying. For more information about the VA's Agent Orange program call the toll-free helpline: 1-800-749-8387; for disability compensation program information, call toll-free: 1-800-827-1000.

"Service-Connection" Based on Evidence of an Association with Agent Orange (or other herbicides used in Vietnam).

The number of diseases that VA has recognized as associated with (but not necessarily caused by) Agent Orange exposure has expanded considerably during the 1990's. The following conditions are recognized for service-connection for these veterans:

- Phloracne (a skin disorder),

- Porphyria cutanea tarda,

- Acute or subacute peripheral neuropathy (a nerve disorder),

- type 2 diabetes, and

- numerous cancers [non-Hodgkin's lymphoma, soft tissue sarcoma, Hodgkin's disease, multiple myeloma, prostate cancer, and respiratory cancers (including cancers of the lung, larynx, trachea, and bronchus)].

VA is in the process of adding chronic lymphocytic leukemia to this list. In addition, Vietnam veterans' children with the birth defect spina bifida are eligible for certain benefits and services. Furthermore, VA was now provides certain benefits, including health care, for children with birth defects who were born to female Vietnam veterans.

Other VA efforts are underway to help Vietnam veterans who were exposed to Agent Orange.

In addition to the efforts described above (that is, Agent Orange Registry examination program, medical treatment, and disability compensation), VA is doing research to learn more about the possible adverse health effects of military service in Vietnam. The Environmental Epidemiology Service (EES) is the premiere office for Vietnam/Agent Orange-related research within VA. EES investigators have completed numerous studies on this subject; summaries are available at http://www.va.gov/agentorange/.

What other government departments and agencies are doing.

Many other Federal departments and agencies have pursued and/or are conducting scientific studies on this subject. The Centers for Disease Control and Prevention (CDC), Air Force (USAF), National Institute for Occupational Safety and Health (NIOSH), National Cancer Institute (NCI), and Environmental Protection Agency (EPA) have all been involved in research.

In 1984, the CDC published an important study, partially funded by VA, regarding Vietnam veterans' risks of fathering babies with birth defects. VA also funded the CDC Vietnam Experience Study published in 1987 and 1988, and the CDC Selected Cancers Study published in 1990.

For additional information about the CDC effort, see www.cdc.gov/mmwr/mmwrpvol.htmwww.html for August 17, 1984, February 13, and July 24, 1987, and May 27, 1988. The USAF is conducting a long-term study of illnesses and death among the men involved in the herbicide spraying missions. Air Force researchers have issued numerous reports regarding their findings in this ongoing project.

Several states have undertaken research efforts to learn more about the possible health effects of Agent Orange and the Vietnam experience upon our Nation's veterans.

The National Academy of Sciences' Institute of Medicine has a major role in this issue. Under Public Law 102-4, the Agent Orange Act of 1991, the Institute of Medicine (IOM) of National Academy of Sciences, a non-governmental organization, has reviewed and continues to evaluate all relevant scientific literature and to provide advice to the Secretary of Veterans Affairs on health effects of herbicides exposure. The IOM project is being undertaken in accordance with Public Law 102-4. The IOM reported its initial findings in July 1993. Updates were released in March 1996, February 1999, April 2001, and January 2003. A special report on type 2 diabetes was released in October 2000. A special report on acute myelogenous leukemia in the children of Vietnam veterans was issued in February 2002. Future reports are anticipated approximately every two years. The IOM and its subcontractor also developed a historical herbicide exposure reconstruction model that could be used in Agent Orange-related research efforts. For additional information and a complete version of the IOM reports, see www.nap.edu.

The IOM recently concluded that with the current technology, a health study of Vietnam veterans is feasible. However, VA now makes the presumption of exposure to Agent Orange for Vietnam veterans. This means that a Vietnam veteran is not required to prove exposure to herbicides in Vietnam. Some researchers are interested in producing better information to accurately estimate the exposure of individual veterans.

Certain Vietnam-era veterans who served in Korea also can get the Agent Orange Registry examination. So can certain other veterans who were exposed to herbicides elsewhere.

In September 2000, VA recognized that Agent Orange was used in Korea in the late 1960's and approved Agent Orange examinations for U.S. veterans who served in Korea in 1968 or 1969. VA took this action despite reports that Republic of Korea troops, not U.S. military personnel, did the actual spraying.

In March 2001, Secretary Principi ordered that those examinations be made available to all other veterans who may have been exposed to dioxin or other toxic substances in a herbicide or defoliant during the conduct of or as the result of testing, transporting, or spraying of herbicides for military purposes.

Additional information is available.

There is at each VA medical center an "Environmental Health Clinician" responsible for the conduct of Agent Orange Registry exams. These health care providers participate in national conference calls conducted by the Environmental Agents Service (EAS), and receive frequent mailings from VA headquarters updating them on the latest developments on Agent Orange issues. Each facility also has an "Environmental Health Coordinator" to facilitate the Agent Orange program.

The Agent Orange Review newsletter, prepared by the VA Environmental Agents Service, provide Agent newsletter, prepared by the VA Environmental Agents Service, provides updated information on Federal government studies and activities related to Agent Orange and the Vietnam experience. Registry participants are automatically added to the mailing list; others can contact the EAS at the address below.

The Agent Orange Brief fact sheets, prepared and updated by the VA Environmental Agents Service (EAS), are available from EAS and at VA medical centers.

The following Agent Orange Briefs are now available:

- General:

A1. General Information
A2. Class Action Lawsuit

- VA Programs (Except Research):

B1. Agent Orange Registry
B2. Health Care Eligibility
B3. Disability Compensation
B4. Information Resources

- Research:

C1. The Problem Encountered in Research
C2. Agent Orange/Vietnam Related Research-VA Efforts
C3. Agent Orange/Vietnam Related Research-Non-VA Efforts

- Medical Conditions:

D1. Birth Defects
D2. Chloracne
D3. Non-Hodgkin's Lymphoma
D4. Soft Tissue Sarcomas
D5. Peripheral Neuropathy
D6. Hodgkin's Disease
D7. Porphyria Cutanea Tarda
D8. Multiple Myeloma
D9. Respiratory Cancers
D10. Prostate Cancer
D11. Spina Bifida
D12. Diabetes
D13. Chronic Lymphocytic Leukemia

Copies of the newsletters, fact sheets, and additional information is available online at www.va.govwww.gov/agentorange. Vietnam veterans and their families are also encouraged to call the Gulf War/Agent Orange Helpline. The toll-free telephone number for the Helpline is 1-800-749-8387.

Contact the EAS (131), Department of Veterans Affairs, 810 Vermont Ave., N.W., Washington, DC 20420, for additional information on Agent Orange. Veterans service organizations and State government entities (including Agent Orange Commissions, Departments or Divisions of Veterans Affairs, Departments of Health) also help individuals seeking information on this subject. The initial and follow-up IOM reports are available on-line at www.nap.edu or for purchase from the National Academy Press, 2101 Constitution Avenue, N.W., Lockbox 285, Washington, DC 20055. The telephone numbers are 1-800-624-6242 and 202-334-3313. Copies of these books were sent to all VA medical center libraries[61].

Toll-Free Telephone Gulf War/ Agent Orange Helpline
*** 1-800-749-8387 ***
Environmental Agents Service
Department of Veterans Affairs
810 Vermont Avenue, NW
Washington, DC 20420

---

[61] For more information about VA benefits for veterans exposed to Agent Orange, go to: http://www.vba.va.gov/bln/21/benefits/Herbicide/index.htm

Agent Orange Benefits for Family Members

Vietnam veterans' children with the birth defect spina bifida are eligible for certain benefits and services. In addition, VA was now provides certain benefits, including health care, for children with birth defects who were born to female Vietnam veterans. These programs are administered by the Health Administration Center.

Automobile Assistance

You may qualify for automobile assistance for this VA benefit if you have:

- A service connected loss or permanent loss of use of one or both hands or feet; or

- A permanent impairment of vision of both eyes to a certain degree; or

- Entitlement to compensation for ankylosis (immobility) of one or both knees or one of both hips.

VA provides a one time payment of not more than $11,000 toward the purchase of an automobile or other vehicle. VA pays for adaptive equipment and for repair, replacement or reinstallation required because of disability.

To apply for this benefit or request further information, contact your nearest VA Regional Office or you call 1-800-827-1000.

Beneficiary Travel (Including Ambulance)

VA currently reimburses eligible veterans $ .11 per mile for travel to the nearest VA health care facility that can provide their needed care. Veterans traveling for their Compensation and Pension (C&P) exams are also reimbursed $.11 per mile. However, veterans are reimbursed $.17 per mile if, through no fault of their own, they have to return to VA to repeat a lab test, x-ray or other exam in order to complete their C&P exam.

In most cases, travel benefits are subject to a deductible of $3 each way. A maximum of $18 per month may be deducted.

Here's an example of how VA computes travel benefits:

A veteran who is eligible for travel reimbursement lives 35 miles from the nearest VA health care facility that could treat his condition (70 miles round trip). His travel reimbursement is computed as follows:

Sample Type Sample Numbers

Round trip mileage 70 miles

Multiply by the mileage reimbursement rate $.11 per mile

Gross Total reimbursement $7.70

Subtract $3.00 deductible for each one-way trip $6.00

The veteran will be reimbursed $1.70

Bereavement Counseling

VA health care facilities offer bereavement counseling to veterans and their family members who are receiving VA health care benefits. Bereavement counseling is also provided parents, spouses and children of Armed Forces personnel who died in the service of their country. Also eligible are family members of reservists and National Guardsmen who die while on duty. Counseling is provided at Vet Centers.

The nearest Vet Center locations can be found by calling 1-800-827-1000 or by going to http://www.va.gov/rcs/index.htm

Blind Veterans Services

Blind veterans may be eligible for services at a VA Medical Center or for admission to a VA blind rehabilitation center or clinic. Services are available at all VA medical facilities through the Visual Impairment Services (VIST) Coordinator. Aids and services for blind veterans include:

- A total health and benefits review by a VA Visual Impairment services team

- Adjustment to blindness training

- Home improvements and structural alterations to homes

- Specially adapted housing and adaptations

- Low vision aids and training in their use

- Electronic and mechanical aids for the blind, including adaptive computers and computer-assisted devices such as reading machines and electronic travel aids

- Guide dogs, including the expense of training the veteran to use the dog and the cost of the dog's medical care

- Talking books, tapes and Braille literature

Combat Veteran Eligibility

If you served in a theater of combat operations in combat against a hostile force during a period of hostilities after November 11, 1998, you are eligible for cost-free care of conditions potentially related to combat for two years following discharge from active duty. During this timeframe, you are also eligible for enrollment in Priority Group 6, unless you are eligible for a higher priority due to other eligibility factors.

VA asks your help in establishing your status as a combat veteran by showing the Enrollment Coordinator at your local facility one of the following pieces of evidence when you apply for care, or any time.

- Your DD 214 indicating service in a designated combat theater of operations; or

- Proof of receipt of the Afghanistan Campaign Medal; Iraq Campaign Medal; Armed Forces Expeditionary Medal; Kosovo Campaign Medal; Global War on Terrorism Expeditionary Medal (does not include Global War on Terrorism Service Medal); or Southwest Asia Campaign Medal; or

- Proof of receipt of Hostile Fire or Imminent Danger Pay (commonly referred to as "combat pay") after November 11, 1998; or

- Proof of exemption of Federal tax status for Hostile Fire or Imminent Danger Pay after November 11, 1998.

Dental Care

Eligibility for VA dental benefits is based on very specific guidelines and differs significantly from eligibility requirements for medical care.

You are eligible for outpatient dental treatment if you meet one of the following criteria:

If you:

- Have a service-connected compensable dental disability or condition - **Any needed dental care**

- Are a former prisoner of war - **Any needed dental care**

- Have service-connected disabilities rated 100% disabling (even if you have a temporary 100% service-connected rating) or are unemployable due to service-connected conditions - **Any needed dental care**

- Are participating in a VA vocational rehabilitation program - **Dental care needed to complete the program.**

- Have a service connected and/or non-compensable dental condition or disability that existed at the time of discharge or release from active duty of at least 180 days or 90 days during the Gulf War Era - **One-time dental care if you apply for dental care within 90 days of separation from active duty and the certificate of discharge does not include certification that all appropriate dental treatment had been rendered prior to discharge.**

- Have a service-connected non-compensable dental condition or disability resulting from combat wounds or service trauma - **You are eligible for needed care for the service-connected condition(s).**

- You have a dental condition clinically determined by VA to be currently aggravating a service-connected medical condition. - **You are eligible for dental care to resolve the problem.**

- You are receiving outpatient care or scheduled for inpatient care and require dental care for a condition complicating a medical condition currently under treatment.- **You are eligible for dental care to resolve the problem.**

- Certain veterans enrolled in a VA Homeless Program for 60 consecutive days or more may receive certain medically necessary outpatient dental services.

Domiciliary Care

VA may provide domiciliary care to veterans whose annual income does not exceed the maximum annual Improved Disability VA Pension Rate or to veterans who have been determined to have no adequate means of support.

Emergency Care in Non-VA Facilities

Emergency Care in Non-VA facilities is provided as a safety net for veterans under specific conditions. You are eligible if the non-VA emergency care is for a service-connected condition or, if enrolled, you have been provided care by a VA clinician or provider within the past 24 months and have no other health care coverage. Also, it must be determined that VA health care facilities were not feasibly available; that a delay in medical attention would have endangered your life or health, and that you are personally liable for the cost of the services.

Extended Care

VA provides institutional long term care to eligible veterans through VA Nursing Homes, Community Nursing Homes, State Veterans Homes, and Domiciliaries. Other services include:

1. Hospice

2. Respite Care

3. Geriatric Evaluation and Management (GEM)

4. Community Residential Care

5. Home Health Care

6. Adult Day Health Care

7. Homemaker / Home Health Aide Services

Eyeglasses and Hearing Aids

You are eligible for hearing aids and eyeglasses if you
- receive increased pension for regular aid and attendance or being permanently housebound, or
- receive compensation for a service-connected disability, or
- are a former prisoner of war, or
- received a Purple Heart medal

Otherwise, hearing aids and eyeglasses will be provided only in special circumstances, and not for normally occurring hearing or vision loss.

Foreign Medical Care

You may receive hospital and outpatient care outside the United States at VA expense, if necessary for:

- Treatment of a service-connected condition, or

- Medical services needed as part of a VA vocational rehabilitation program.

Veterans in Canada

Before using this benefit, veterans should register with:

VA Medical Center
ATTN: 04FC
215 N. Main Street
White River Junction, Vermont 05009-0001
Telephone number: 802-296-6379

Veterans in the Philippines

Before using this benefit, veterans should register with:

VA Outpatient Clinic
2201 Roxas Boulevard
Pasay City 1300
Republic of the Philippines
Telephone number: 011-632-833-4566

Veterans in Other Foreign Countries

Health services provided in foreign countries other than Canada and the Philippines fall under the jurisdiction of the Foreign Medical Program (FMP). The Health Administration Center administers this program.

If you are permanently relocating to a country under the FMP Office's jurisdiction, you are encouraged to notify the FMP Office when you have a permanent foreign mailing address. At that time, arrangements will be made for FMP registration and the mailing of detailed program material. Included in the program material will be an FMP Handbook which will provide detailed information on benefit coverage and limitations, how to select health care providers, and claim filing instructions.

Gulf War Illnesses

Gulf War veterans from Operations Desert Shield, Desert Storm, and Iraqi Freedom, are eligible for a complete physical exam under the Persian Gulf Registry program.

Veterans with conditions recognized by VA as associated with Gulf War service are eligible for enrollment in priority group 6, unless eligible for enrollment in a higher priority. Veterans who have general health questions about Gulf Service may contact VA's Gulf War Veterans Information Helpline toll free at 1-800-PGW-VETS

Home Health Services

Skilled home care is provided by VA or through contract agencies to veterans that are homebound with chronic diseases. Available home health services includes nursing, physical/occupational therapy, and social services.

Home Improvement and Structural Alterations (HISA)

VA provides grants to assist eligible veterans in making certain home improvements or structural alterations that are medically necessary, to:

- Allow entrance to or exit from the veteran's residence

- Use of essential lavatory and sanitary facilities

- Allow accessibility to kitchen or bathroom counters or sinks

- Improve entrance paths or driveways in immediate vicinity of home to improve access to the home for the veteran

- Improve electrical or plumbing systems made necessary due to installation of dialysis equipment in the home

There is a lifetime maximum on the benefit as follows:

- $4,100 for service-connected conditions

- $1,200 for non-service-connected conditions

This program is administered by the Prosthetics Service at VA Medical Center and does require medical documentation of necessity. Application is made on VA Form 10-0103.

Homeless Programs

VA offers special programs and initiatives specifically designed to help homeless veterans live as independently as possible. VA's treatment programs offer:

- outreach to veterans living on streets and in shelters
- clinical assessment and referral to medical treatment
- domiciliary care, case management, and rehabilitation
- employment and income assistance
- supported permanent housing

Ionizing Radiation Exposure Treatment and Registry Examination

VA offers Ionizing Radiation Registry Examinations at no charge to any veteran who participated in a "radiation risk activity."

In addition, veterans with certain conditions recognized by VA as associated with radiation exposure are eligible for enrollment in priority group 6, unless eligible for enrollment in a higher priority, and will receive care at no charge for conditions related to exposure.

Maternity Care

VA will provide maternity care including labor and delivery to female veterans, but is unable to provide care to the child after birth.

Medical Equipment and Aids

If you are receiving VA care for any condition VA will provide you needed prosthetic appliances, medical equipment or devices, such as artificial limbs, orthopedic braces or shoes, wheelchairs, crutches or canes.

Military Sexual Trauma Counseling

VA provides counseling and treatment to help male and female veterans overcome psychological trauma resulting from sexual trauma while serving on active duty. In addition to counseling, related services are available at VA medical facilities. Veterans will receive care at no charge for conditions related to Military Sexual Trauma.

For information regarding sexual trauma services, contact the Military Sexual Trauma Coordinator or Women Veterans Program Manager at your local

VA facility. Additional information is located at: http://www.appc1.va.gov/wvhp/page.cfm?pg=20

Non-VA Health Care Services

VA may authorize veterans to receive care at a non-VA health care facility when the needed services are not available at the VA health care facility, or when the veteran is unable to travel the distance to the VA health care facility. Non-VA care must be authorized by VA in advance. Veterans may also obtain services not covered in the benefits package through private health care providers at their own expense.

Nose / Throat Radium Treatment

Veterans who served as an aviator in the active military, naval, or air service before the end of the Korean conflict or received submarine training in active naval service before January 1, 1965 may have received nasopharyngeal radium treatment (NPR) while in the military. Some veterans who received this treatment may have head and/or neck cancer that may be related to the exposure. These veterans are provided care for this condition at no cost.

Veterans who remember being treated or think they were treated with nasopharyngeal radium should tell their physicians about it. Veterans who have health problems they think may be related to nasopharyngeal radium also are encouraged to contact the nearest VA medical center. More information can be found at http://www1.va.gov/opa/fact/99nasrad.html.

Nursing Home Care

VA will provide nursing home care if you are a veteran:

- Who requires nursing home care for your service-connected condition; or

- With a service-connected disability rating of 70 percent or more; or

- Who is rated 60 percent SC and unemployable

VA may provide nursing home care to other veterans if space and resources are available. Veterans who have a service-connected disability are given first priority for nursing home care.

Non-service-connected and 0% non-compensable service-connected veterans requiring nursing home care for any non-service-connected disability must complete an income and asset assessment, to determine whether they will be billed for nursing home care.

Project 112/SHAD Participants

Project 112 is the name of the overall program for both shipboard and land-based biological and chemical testing that was conducted by the United States (U.S.) military between 1962 and 1973. Project SHAD was the shipboard portion of these tests, which were conducted to determine:

(1) The effectiveness of shipboard detection of chemical and biological warfare agents;

(2) The effectiveness of protective measures against these agents; and

(3) The potential risk to American forces posed by these weapons.

Department of Defense (DOD) estimates that about 6,000 veterans may have been involved in Project 112/SHAD. VA provides a physical examination to veterans who participated in SHAD. Veterans with conditions recognized by VA as associated with Project Shad are eligible for enrollment in priority group 6, unless eligible for enrollment in a higher priority. In addition, veterans will receive care at no charge for conditions related to exposure.

Veterans may also call the SHAD Helpline at 800-749-8387 or send e-mail to VA at SHADHELPLINE@vba.va.gov . for information on obtaining a medical evaluation or filing a claim for disability benefits.

Readjustment Counseling

Veterans who served on active duty in a war or conflict may apply for counseling to assist in readjusting to civilian life. Veterans who served in the active military during the Vietnam Era, but not in the Republic of Vietnam, may also be eligible if they requested assistance before January 1, 2004.

Counseling is provided at Vet Centers. Nearest Vet Center locations can be found by calling 1-800-827-1000 or by going to http://www.va.gov/rcs/index.htm

Women Veterans Services

Women veterans are eligible for the same Medical Benefit Package as all veterans. In addition to the Medical Benefits Package, the Women's Program provides women's gender-specific health care; such as

- hormone replacement therapy
- breast care

- gynecological care

- maternity care

- limited infertility treatment (excludes in-vitro fertilization)

- The Sexual Trauma Treatment Center is also affiliated with the Women's Clinic, providing treatment for the psychological effects of sexual trauma.

For addition information regarding these services contact the Women Veterans Coordinator at your local VA health care facility.

APPENDIX A

CHRONIC LYMPHOCYTIC LEUKEMIA

VA To Grant Benefits To More Vietnam Veterans
January 23, 2003

WASHINGTON – Based upon a recently released review of scientific studies, Secretary of Veterans Affairs Anthony J. Principi has decided to extend benefits to Vietnam veterans with chronic lymphocytic leukemia (CLL).

"Compelling evidence has emerged within the scientific community that exposure to herbicides such as Agent Orange is associated with CLL," Principi said. "I'm exercising my legal authority to ensure the full range of VA benefits is available to Vietnam veterans with CLL."

The ruling means that veterans with CLL who served in Vietnam during the Vietnam War don't have to prove that illness is related to their military service to qualify for Department of Veterans Affairs disability compensation. Additionally, for more than 20 years, VA has offered special access to medical care to Vietnam veterans with any health problems that may have resulted from Agent Orange exposure, and this decision will ensure higher-priority access to care in the future.

The decision to provide compensation was based upon a recent report by the Institute of Medicine (IOM) that found among scientific studies "sufficient evidence of an association" between exposure to herbicides during the Vietnam War and CLL.

The IOM review, conducted at VA's request, was the latest in a series spanning the period since 1993 when the independent, non-governmental agency first published a report for VA that examined thousands of relevant scientific studies on the health effects of various substances to which American servicemembers may have been exposed in Vietnam.

"On the modern battlefield, not all injuries are caused by shrapnel and bullets," Principi said. "This latest IOM study and my decision to act upon it are the latest examples of VA's continuing efforts to care for the needs of our combat veterans."

VA requested the IOM panel of experts to focus on CLL in their report because of veterans' concerns that CLL shares some similarities with non-Hodgkin's lymphoma, which the IOM had previously connected to Agent Orange exposure.

Principi ordered the development of regulations to enable VA to begin paying compensation benefits once a final rule takes effect. Publication of that regulation is expected in the near future. VA will publish further details, when available, on its Web site at http://www.vba.va.gov/bln/21/benefits/herbicide/.

In the meantime, veterans with questions about health-care, compensation and survivor benefits may call a toll-free help line at 1-800-749-8387 for information. VA also encourages Vietnam veterans who have not done so to request a subscription to Agent Orange Review, VA's free newsletter that will keep them abreast of developments on this issue and other policies and scientific findings in the future.

Newsletter subscription information is available from the help line number above. Back issues and additional information about Agent Orange are available at another VA Web site at http://www.va.gov/agentorange/.

APPENDIX B

OTHER GROUPS ELIGIBLE FOR BENEFITS

In addition to those who served in the United States Military, there are also a number of other groups who are entitled to benefits.

U.S. Groups Who Provided Military-Related Service

A number of groups who have provided military-related service to the United States have been granted VA benefits. For the service to qualify, the Secretary of Defense must certify that the group has provided active military service. Individuals must be issued a discharge by the Secretary of Defense to qualify for VA bene-fits. Service in the following groups has been certified as active military service for benefits purposes:

- Women Airforce Service Pilots (WASPs).

- World War I Signal Corps Female Telephone Operators Unit.

- Engineer Field Clerks.

- Women's Army Auxiliary Corps (WAAC).

- Quartermaster Corps female clerical employees serving with the American Expeditionary Forces in World War I.

- Civilian employees of Pacific naval air bases who actively participated in defense of Wake Island during World War II.

- Reconstruction aides and dietitians in World War I.

- Male civilian ferry pilots.

- Wake Island defenders from Guam.

- Civilian personnel assigned to OSS secret intelligence.

- Guam Combat Patrol.

- Quartermaster Corps members of the Keswick crew on Corregidor during World War II.

- U.S. civilians who participated in the defense of Bataan.

- U.S. merchant seamen who served on blockships in support of Operation Mulberry in the World War II invasion of Normandy.

- American merchant marines in oceangoing service during World War II.

- Civilian Navy IFF radar technicians who served in combat areas of the Pacific during World War II.

- U.S. civilians of the American Field Service who served overseas in World War I.

- U.S. civilians of the American Field Service who served overseas under U.S. armies and U.S. army groups in World War II.

- U.S. civilian employees of American Airlines who served overseas in a contract with the Air Transport Command between Dec. 14, 1941, and Aug. 14, 1945.

- Civilian crewmen of U.S. Coast and Geodetic Survey vessels who served in areas of immediate military hazard while conducting cooperative operations with and for the U.S. Armed Forces between Dec. 7, 1941, and Aug. 15, 1945.

- Members of the American Volunteer Group (Flying Tigers) who served between Dec. 7, 1941, and July 18, 1942.

- U.S. civilian flight crew and aviation ground support employees of United Air Lines who served overseas in a contract with Air Transport Command between Dec. 14, 1941, and Aug. 14, 1945.

- U.S. civilian flight crew and aviation ground support employees of Transcontinental and Western Air, Inc. (TWA), who served overseas in a contract with the Air Transport Command between Dec. 14, 1941, and Aug. 14, 1945.

- U.S. civilian flight crew and aviation ground support employees of Consolidated Vultee Aircraft Corp. (Consairway Division) who served overseas in a contract with Air Transport Command between Dec. 14, 1941, and Aug. 14, 1945.

- U.S. civilian flight crew and aviation ground support employees of Pan American World Airways and its subsidiaries and affiliates, who served overseas in a contract with the Air Transport Command and Naval Air Transport Service between Dec. 14, 1941, and Aug. 14, 1945.

- Honorably discharged members of the American Volunteer Guard, Eritrea Service Command, between June 21, 1942, and March 31, 1943.

- U.S. civilian flight crew and aviation ground support employees of Northwest Airlines who served overseas under the airline's contract with Air Transport Command from Dec. 14, 1941, through Aug. 14, 1945.

- U.S. civilian female employees of the U.S. Army Nurse Corps who served in the defense of Bataan and Corregidor during the period Jan. 2, 1942, to Feb. 3, 1945.

- U.S. flight crew and aviation ground support employees of Northeast Airlines Atlantic Division, who served overseas as a result of Northeast Airlines' contract with the Air Transport Command during the period Dec. 7, 1941, through Aug. 14, 1945.

- U.S. civilian flight crew and aviation ground support employees of Braniff Airways, who served overseas in the North Atlantic or under the jurisdiction of the North Atlantic Wing, Air Transport Command, as a result of a contract with the Air Transport Command during the period Feb. 26, 1942, through Aug. 14, 1945.

- Honorably discharged members of the Alaska Territorial Guard during World War II.

WWI or WWII Veterans from Allied Countries

- Veterans of Czechoslovakia and Poland

- Former Czechoslovakian or Polish service members who served during WWI or WWII in combat with an enemy of the United States are eligible for VA health care benefits if:

  1. they also served in, or with, the Armed Forces of France or Great Britain during WWI or WWII, and
  2. have been citizens of the United States for at least 10 years, and
  3. who present satisfactory evidence of such military service

Veterans of Great Britain, Canada, Australia, New Zealand or South Africa

- WWI and WWII veterans of these countries who have disabilities attributable to, or aggravated by their military service may be eligible for VA health care services for their service-connected conditions only. Treatment must be authorized and reimbursed by the foreign government.

Filipino Veterans

VA health care benefits are now available for:

- Filipino Commonwealth Army Veterans,

- New Filipino Scouts, and

- Veterans recognized as belonging to organized Filipino Guerilla Forces

  1. who reside in the United States and

  2. who are citizens or lawfully admitted for permanent residence.

- Old Filipino Scouts are also eligible for VA health care benefits; however, they do not have to meet the citizenship and residency requirements.

Service-connected Filipino veterans receiving VA disability compensation at the full-dollar rate do not have to furnish proof to qualify for the benefit. Other Filipino veterans must provide one of the following pieces of evidence to be eligible for this benefit:

- A valid U.S. passport

- A birth certificate showing he or she was born in the U.S.

- A Report of Birth Abroad of a Citizen of the U.S. issues by a U.S. consulate abroad

- Verification by the U.S. Citizenship and Immigration Services to VA that the Filipino veteran is a naturalized citizen of the U.S.

- Verification by the U.S. Citizenship and Immigration Services to VA that a veteran is an alien lawfully admitted for permanent residence in the U.S.

Other Foreign Veterans

The VA may provide care to foreign veterans of conflicts after WWII if the veteran is from a nation that was an ally during WWI or WWII and the care is authorized by the respective government.

APPENDIX C

VETERANS INDUSTRY

Veterans Industry is a vocational rehabilitation program of the Department of Veterans Affairs that sub-contracts with many and diverse industries. The Veterans Industries programs provide temporary and permanent staffing for information technology, manufacturing, warehousing, construction, office support, retail and the services delivery industry. Veterans Industry also provides outsource support in assembly, packaging, sorting, grading, reclaiming, and recycling.

From over 108 locations throughout the country, these programs strive to produce high quality work on a timely basis at a competitive price. The well trained, professional staff provides state of the art vocational rehabilitation services and many of our individual programs are CARF accredited and members of IAPSRS. Veterans Industry officers are located within VA medical centers in most large metropolitan areas and many smaller communities.

The goals of the Veterans Industry are to provide:

- a realistic and meaningful vocational opportunity to veterans;

- encouraging successful reintegration into the community at the veterans' highest functional level.

To achieve this mission the Veterans Industry develops partnerships with companies who want high quality work completed on a timely basis at a competitive price. The expectation of quality, as demanded by industry, helps create and maintain our programs atmosphere of success.

The Veterans Industries "temp to hire" transitional work program allows a company to pre-screen veterans, observing them in action before making a decision regarding competitive employment.

How Can Veterans Industries Help Private Companies?

- By providing labor services for semi-skilled and unskilled positions in information technology, office management, clerical, retail, manufacturing and production, warehousing, manual labor, food services, etc...
- By providing professional rehabilitation support including staff education, task analysis and job modification, case management, and follow-along services.

    1. Assembly and sub-assembly
    2. Custom packaging
    3. Reclaiming and recycling
    4. Inspection, grading and sorting products for industry

What Veterans Industry Participation Offer Veterans

Participation in Veteran Industry programs offers the following benefits:
- realistic and meaningful vocational opportunities to veterans;

- encourages successful reintegration into the community at the veterans' highest functional level.

VI/CWT values all veterans with disabilities and feels that each veteran has rehabilitation potential, i.e. a maximum degree of self-sufficiency that can be attained through vocational and residential rehabilitation services that focus on strengths, needs, abilities, and preferences rather than illness and symptoms.

Veterans Industries programs develop an individual rehabilitation plan for each veteran. And depending on the specific program location, Veterans Industries provides a wide range of support services to the veteran. These include:

- Transitional Work Experience (temporary to permanent staffing)

- Sheltered Work Therapy (outsource fulfillment and sub contract work)

- Career Development/ Job Placement and Follow-along Services

- Employment Education and Job Readiness Training

- Vocational Assessment (situational)

- Transitional Residence (residential rehabilitation)

- Vocational Counseling and Case Management

Transitional Residence

The Veterans Industries/ Transitional Residence Program (VI/TR) is a work-based Psychosocial Residential Rehabilitation Treatment Program (PRRTP) offering a therapeutic residential setting for veterans involved in Veterans Industries/Compensated Work Therapy (VI/CWT). This program provides a rehabilitation-focused residential setting for veterans recovering from chronic mental illness, chemical dependency and homelessness.

VI/TR provides a bridge between hospitalization or intensive outpatient treatment and successful community reintegration. The program utilizes a residential therapeutic community of peer and professional support, with a strong emphasis on increasing personal responsibility and achievement of individualized rehabilitation goals.

VI/TR differs from other VA-operated residential bed programs in that participants contribute (using their VI/CWT earnings) to the cost of operating and maintaining their residences and are responsible for planning, purchasing and preparing their own meals.

(** CARF Accredited Programs)

VI/TR LOCATIONS

Albany, NY	American Lake, WA **
Atlanta, GA **	Battle Creek, MI
Bedford, MA **	Birmingham, AL
Biloxi, MS	Bonham, TX
Boston, MA **	Boston, MA (female veterans)
Brecksville, OH	Bronx, NY
Dallas, TX **	Danville, IL
Fort Meade, SD **	Gainsville, FL
Hampton, VA **	Hot Springs, SD
Kansas City, MO	Lebanon, PA **
Lyons, NJ **	Martinsburg, WV
Milwaukee, WI	N. Little Rock, AR **
Northampton, MA **	North Chicago, IL **
Oklahoma City, OK **	Palo Alto, CA **
Perry Point, MD **	Pittsburgh, PA **
Tomah, WI	San Francisco, CA **
Topeka, KS	West Haven, CT

Veterans Industries/Compensated Work Therapy (VI/CWT) Programs
* Indicates CARF Accredited Programs

- **Alabama**
  Tuscaloosa*
  Tuskegee*
  Birmingham

- **Alaska**
  Anchorage

- **Arizona**
  Tucson*
  Prescott

- **Arkansas**
  Little Rock*

- **California**
  Loma Linda*,
  Long Beach,
  San Diego*,
  Palo Alto*,
  San Francisco*,
  Sepulveda* and
  West Los Angeles*

- **Colorado**
  Colorado Springs,
  Denver

- **Connecticut**
  West Haven

- **Florida**
  Bay Pines
  Gainesville
  Tampa
  Miami
  West Palm Beach

- **Georgia**
  Atlanta

Augusta
Dublin

- **Hawaii**
Honolulu

- **Illinois**
Danville
Hines
North Chicago

- **Indiana**
Indianapolis*

- **Iowa**
Knoxville

- **Kansas**
Leavenworth
Topeka

- **Kentucky**
Louisville
Lexington

- **Maine**
Togus

- **Maryland**
Baltimore
Perry Point

- **Massachusetts**
Bedford*
Boston*
Brockton*
North Hampton*

- **Michigan**
Ann Arbor*
Battle Creek*
Iron Mountain

- **Minnesota**
  Minneapolis
  Saint Cloud

- **Mississippi**
  Biloxi*
  Jackson

- **Missouri**
  Columbia
  Kansas City
  Poplar Bluff
  St. Louis

- **Nebraska**
  Omaha

- **Nevada**
  Reno*

- **New Jersey**
  East Orange
  Lyons*

- **New Mexico**
  Albuquerque

- **New York**
  Albany*
  Bronx*
  Buffalo*
  Montrose*
  Syracuse*
  Bath*
  Brooklyn*
  Canandaigua*
  Northport*

- **North Carolina**
  Asheville*
  Salisbury

- **North Dakota**
  Fargo

- **Ohio**
  Chillicothe*
  Cleveland*
  Columbus
  Cincinnati
  Dayton*

- **Oklahoma**
  Oklahoma City

- **Oregon**
  Eugene*
  Portland
  Roseburg*
  White City*

- **Pennsylvania**
  Butler
  Coatesville*
  Lebanon*
  Pittsburgh*
  Wilkes Barre
  Philadelphia

- **Rhode Island**
  Providence*

- **South Carolina**
  Charleston
  Columbia*

- **South Dakota**
  Fort Meade*
  Hot Springs*

- **Tennessee**
  Memphis
  Mountain Home
  Murfreesboro

- **Texas**
  Bonham*
  El Paso
  Houston*
  Waco
  Temple*
  Dallas*
  Fort Worth*
  San Antonio*

- **Utah**
  Salt Lake City*

- **Vermont**
  White River Junction

- **Virginia**
  Hampton*
  Richmond
  Salem*

- **Washington**
  Tacoma*
  Walla Walla

- **Washington D. C.**
  District of Columbia*

- **West Virginia**
  Martinsburg*

- **Wisconsin**
  Milwaukee*
  Tomah*
  Madison

- **Wyoming**
  Sheridan

These states do not have VI/CWT Programs:

- Delaware

- Louisiana

- New Hampshire

- Idaho

- Montana

Companies interested in opportunities with Veterans Industries, contact:

Charles McGeough
National Marketing Director
Veterans Industries
4500 South Lancaster Road (122)
Dallas, Texas 75216
(800) 355-VAMC (8262)
(214) 857-0381
Fax: (214) 857-0382
Charles.McGeough@med.va.gov

Veterans interested in opportunities with Veterans Industries, contact:

Rick Lee
National Program Coordinator
590/302/116D Bldg 148
VA Medical Center (122)
Hampton, Virginia 23667
(757) 722-9961 Ext. 3624
Fax: (757) 728-3143
Rick.Lee@med.va.gov

APPENDIX D

SELECTED LAWS HAVING TO DO WITH THE VA

Ratings for Special Purposes

§3.350 Special monthly compensation ratings.

The rates of special monthly compensation stated in this section are those provided under 38 U.S.C. 1114.

(a) Ratings under 38 U.S.C. 1114(k). Special monthly compensation under 38 U.S.C. 1114(k) is payable for each anatomical loss or loss of use of one hand, one foot, both buttocks, one or more creative organs, blindness of one eye having only light perception, deafness of both ears, having absence of air and bone conduction, complete organic aphonia with constant inability to communicate by speech or, in the case of a woman veteran, loss of 25% or more of tissue from a single breast or both breasts in combination (including loss by mastectomy or partial mastectomy), or following receipt of radiation treatment of breast tissue. This special compensation is payable in addition to the basic rate of compensation otherwise payable on the basis of degree of disability, provided that the combined rate of compensation does not exceed the monthly rate set forth in 38 U.S.C. 1114(l) when authorized in conjunction with any of the provisions of 38 U.S.C. 1114(a) through (j) or (s). When there is entitlement under 38 U.S.C. 1114 (l) through (n) or an intermediate rate under (p) such additional allowance is payable for each such anatomical loss or loss of use existing in addition to the requirements for the basic rates, provided the total does not exceed the monthly rate set forth in 38 U.S.C. 1114(o). The limitations on the maximum compensation payable under this paragraph are independent of and do not preclude payment of additional compensation for dependents under 38 U.S.C. 1115, or the special allowance for aid and attendance provided by 38 U.S.C. 1114(r).

(1) Creative organ.

(i) Loss of a creative organ will be shown by acquired absence of one or both testicles (other than undescended testicles) or ovaries or other creative organ. Loss of use of one testicle will be established when examination by a board finds that:

(a) The diameters of the affected testicle are reduced to one-third of the corresponding diameters of the paired normal testicle, or

(b) The diameters of the affected testicle are reduced to one-half or less of the corresponding normal testicle and there is alteration of consistency so that the affected testicle is considerably harder or softer than the corresponding normal testicle; or

(c) If neither of the conditions (a) or (b) is met, when a biopsy, recommended by a board including a genitourologist and accepted by the veteran, establishes the absence of spermatozoa.

(ii) When loss or loss of use of a creative organ resulted from wounds or other trauma sustained in service, or resulted from operations in service for the relief of other conditions, the creative organ becoming incidentally involved, the benefit may be granted.

(iii) Loss or loss of use traceable to an elective operation performed subsequent to service, will not establish entitlement to the benefit. If, however the operation after discharge was required for the correction of a specific injury caused by a preceding operation in service. it will support authorization of the benefit. When the existence of disability is established meeting the above requirements for nonfunctioning testicle due to operation after service, resulting in loss of use, the benefit may be granted even though the operation is one of election. An operation is not considered to be one of election where it is advised on sound medical judgment for the relief of a pathological condition or to prevent possible future pathological consequences.

(iv) Atrophy resulting from mumps followed by orchitis in service is service connected. Since atrophy is usually perceptible within 1 to 6 months after infection subsides, an examination more than 6 months after the subsidence of orchitis demonstrating a normal genitourinary system will be considered in determining rebuttal of service incurrence of atrophy later demonstrated. Mumps not followed by orchitis in service will not suffice as the antecedent cause of subsequent atrophy for the purpose of authorizing the benefit.

(2) Foot and hand.

(i) Loss of use of a hand or a foot will be held to exist when no effective function remains other than that which would be equally well served by an amputation stump at the site of election below elbow or knee with use of a suitable prosthetic appliance. The determination will be made on the basis of the actual remaining function, whether the acts of grasping, manipulation, etc., in the case of the hand, or of balance, propulsion, etc., in the case of the foot, could be accomplished equally well by an amputation stump with prosthesis; for example:

(a) Extremely unfavorable complete ankylosis of the knee, or complete ankylosis of two major joints of an extremity, or shortening of the lower extremity of 3 1/2 inches or more, will constitute loss of use of the hand or foot involved.

(b) Complete paralysis of the external popliteal nerve (common peroneal) and consequent footdrop, accompanied by characteristic organic changes including trophic and circulatory disturbances and other concomitants confirmatory of complete paralysis of this nerve, will be taken as loss of use of the foot.

(3) Both buttocks.

(i) Loss of use of both buttocks shall be deemed to exist when there is severe damage by disease or injury to muscle group XVII, bilateral, (diagnostic code 5317) and additional disability making it impossible for the disabled person, without assistance, to rise from a seated position and from a stooped position (fingers to toes position) and to maintain postural stability (the pelvis upon head of femur). The assistance may be done by the person's own hands or arms, and, in the matter of postural stability, by a special appliance. (Authority: 38 U.S.C. 1114(k))

(ii) Special monthly compensation for loss or loss of use of both lower extremities (38 U.S.C. 1114(l) through (n)) will not preclude additional compensation under 38 U.S.C. 1114(k) for loss of use of both buttocks where appropriate tests clearly substantiate that there is such additional loss.

(4) Eye. Loss of use or blindness of one eye, having only light perception, will be held to exist when there is inability to recognize test letters at 1 foot and when further examination of the eye reveals that perception of objects, hand movements, or counting fingers cannot be accomplished at 3 feet. Lesser extents of vision, particularly perception of objects, hand movements, or counting fingers at distances less than 3 feet is considered of negligible utility.

(5) Deafness. Deafness of both ears, having absence of air and bone conduction will be held to exist where examination in a Department of Veterans Affairs authorized audiology clinic under current testing criteria shows bilateral hearing loss is equal to or greater than the minimum bilateral hearing loss required for a maximum rating evaluation under the rating schedule. (Authority: Pub. L. 88-20)

(6) Aphonia. Complete organic aphonia will be held to exist where there is a disability of the organs of speech which constantly precludes communication by speech. (Authority: Pub. L. 88-22)

(b) Ratings under 38 U.S.C. 1114(l). The special monthly compensation provided by 38 U.S.C. 1114(l) is payable for anatomical loss or loss of use of both feet, one hand and one foot, blindness in both eyes with visual acuity of 5/200 or less or being permanently bedridden or so helpless as to be in need of regular aid and attendance.

(1) Extremities. The criteria for loss and loss of use of an extremity contained in paragraph (a)(2) of this section are applicable.

(2) Eyes, bilateral. 5/200 visual acuity or less bilaterally qualifies for entitlement under 38 U.S.C. 1114(l). However, evaluation of 5/200 based on acuity in excess of that degree but less than 10/200 (§4.83 of this chapter) does not qualify. Concentric contraction of the field of vision beyond 5 degrees in both eyes is the equivalent of 5/200 visual acuity.

(3) Need for aid and attendance. The criteria for determining that a veteran is so helpless as to be in need of regular aid and attendance are contained in §3.352(a).

(4) Permanently bedridden. The criteria for rating are contained in §3.352(a). Where possible, determinations should be on the basis of permanently bedridden rather than for need of aid and attendance (except where 38 U.S.C. 1114(r) is involved) to avoid reduction during hospitalization where aid and attendance is provided in kind.

(c) Ratings under 38 U.S.C. 1114(m).

(1) The special monthly compensation provided by 38 U.S.C. 1114(m) is payable for any of the following conditions:

(i) Anatomical loss or loss of use of both hands;

(ii) Anatomical loss or loss of use of both legs at a level, or with complications, preventing natural knee action with prosthesis in place;

(iii) Anatomical loss or loss of use of one arm at a level, or with complications, preventing natural elbow action with prosthesis in place with anatomical loss or loss of use of one leg at a level, or with complications, preventing natural knee action with prosthesis in place;

(iv) Blindness in both eyes having only light perception;

(v) Blindness in both eyes leaving the veteran so helpless as to be in need of regular aid and attendance.

(2) Natural elbow or knee action. In determining whether there is natural elbow or knee action with prosthesis in place, consideration will be based on whether use of the proper prosthetic appliance requires natural use of the joint, or whether necessary motion is otherwise controlled, so that the muscles affecting joint motion, if not already atrophied, will become so. If there is no movement in the joint, as in ankylosis or complete paralysis, use of prosthesis is not to be expected, and the determination will be as though there were one in place.

(3) Eyes, bilateral. With visual acuity 5/200 or less or the vision field reduced to 5 degree concentric contraction in both eyes, entitlement on account of need for regular aid and attendance will be determined on the facts in the individual case.

(d) Ratings under 38 U.S.C. 1114(n). The special monthly compensation provided by 38 U.S.C. 1114(n) is payable for any of the conditions which follow: Amputation is a prerequisite except for loss of use of both arms and blindness without light perception in both eyes. If a prosthesis cannot be worn at the present level of amputation but could be applied if there were a reamputation at a higher level, the requirements of this paragraph are not met; instead, consideration will be given to loss of natural elbow or knee action.

(1) Anatomical loss or loss of use of both arms at a level or with complications, preventing natural elbow action with prosthesis in place;

(2) Anatomical loss of both legs so near the hip as to prevent use of a prosthetic appliance;

(3) Anatomical loss of one arm so near the shoulder as to prevent use of a prosthetic appliance with anatomical loss of one leg so near the hip as to prevent use of a prosthetic appliance;

(4) Anatomical loss of both eyes or blindness without light perception in both eyes.

(e) Ratings under 38 U.S.C. 1114 (o).

(1) The special monthly compensation provided by 38 U.S.C. 1114(o) is payable for any of the following conditions:

(i) Anatomical loss of both arms so near the shoulder as to prevent use of a prosthetic appliance;

(ii) Conditions entitling to two or more of the rates (no condition being considered twice) provided in 38 U.S.C. 1114(l) through (n);

(iii) Bilateral deafness rated at 60 percent or more disabling (and the hearing impairment in either one or both ears is service connected) in combination with service-connected blindness with bilateral visual acuity 5/200 or less.

(iv) Service-connected total deafness in one ear or bilateral deafness rated at 40 percent or more disabling (and the hearing impairment in either one of both ears is service-connected) in combination with service-connected blindness of both eyes having only light perception or less.

(2) Paraplegia. Paralysis of both lower extremities together with loss of anal and bladder sphincter control will entitle to the maximum rate under 38 U.S.C. 1114(o), through the combination of loss of use of both legs and helplessness. The requirement of loss of anal and bladder sphincter control is met even though incontinence has been overcome under a strict regimen of rehabilitation of bowel and bladder training and other auxiliary measures.

(3) Combinations. Determinations must be based upon separate and distinct disabilities. This requires, for example, that where a veteran who had suffered the loss or loss of use of two extremities is being considered for the maximum rate on account of helplessness requiring regular aid and attendance, the latter must be based on need resulting from pathology other than that of the extremities. If the loss or loss of use of two extremities or being permanently bedridden leaves the person helpless, increase is not in order on account of this helplessness. Under no circumstances will the combination of "being permanently bedridden" and "being so helpless as to require regular aid and attendance" without separate and distinct anatomical loss, or loss of use, of two extremities, or blindness, be taken as entitling to the maximum benefit. The fact, however, that two separate and distinct entitling disabilities, such as anatomical loss, or loss of use of both hands and both feet, result from a common etiological

agent, for example, one injury or rheumatoid arthritis, will not preclude maximum entitlement.

(4) Helplessness. The maximum rate, as a result of including helplessness as one of the entitling multiple disabilities, is intended to cover, in addition to obvious losses and blindness, conditions such as the loss of use of two extremities with absolute deafness and nearly total blindness or with severe multiple injuries producing total disability outside the useless extremities, these conditions being construed as loss of use of two extremities and helplessness.

(f) Intermediate or next higher rate. An intermediate rate authorized by this paragraph shall be established at the arithmetic mean, rounded to the nearest dollar, between the two rates concerned. (Authority: 38 U.S.C. 1114 (p))

(1) Extremities.

(i) Anatomical loss or loss of use of one foot with anatomical loss or loss of use of one leg at a level, or with complications preventing natural knee action with prosthesis in place, shall entitle to the rate between 38 U.S.C. 1114(l) and (m).

(ii) Anatomical loss or loss of use of one foot with anatomical loss of one leg so near the hip as to prevent use of prosthetic appliance shall entitle to the rate under 38 U.S.C. 1114(m).

(iii) Anatomical loss or loss of use of one foot with anatomical loss or loss of use of one arm at a level, or with complications, preventing natural elbow action with prosthesis in place, shall entitle to the rate between 38 U.S.C. 1114(l) and (m).

(iv) Anatomical loss or loss of use of one foot with anatomical loss or loss of use of one arm so near the shoulder as to prevent use of a prosthetic appliance shall entitle to the rate under 38 U.S.C. 1114(m).

(v) Anatomical loss or loss of use of one leg at a level, or with complications, preventing natural knee action with prosthesis in place with anatomical loss of one leg so near the hip as to prevent use of a prosthetic appliance, shall entitle to the rate between 38 U.S.C. 1114(m) and (n).

(vi) Anatomical loss or loss of use of one leg at a level, or with complications, preventing natural knee action with prosthesis in place with anatomical loss or loss of use of one hand, shall entitle to the rate between 38 U.S.C. 1114(l) and (m).

(vii) Anatomical loss or loss of use of one leg at a level, or with complications, preventing natural knee action with prosthesis in place with anatomical loss of one arm so near the shoulder as to prevent use of a prosthetic appliance, shall entitle to the rate between 38 U.S.C. 1114(m) and (n).

(viii) Anatomical loss of one leg so near the hip as to prevent use of a prosthetic appliance with anatomical loss or loss of use of one hand shall entitle to the rate under 38 U.S.C. 1114(m).

(ix) Anatomical loss of one leg so near the hip as to prevent use of a prosthetic appliance with anatomical loss or loss of use of one arm at a level, or with complications, preventing natural elbow action with prosthesis in place, shall entitle to the rate between 38 U.S.C. 1114(m) and (n).

(x) Anatomical loss or loss of use of one hand with anatomical loss or loss of use of one arm at a level, or with complications, preventing natural elbow action with prosthesis in place, shall entitle to the rate between 38 U.S.C. 1114(m) and (n).

(xi) Anatomical loss or loss of use of one hand with anatomical loss of one arm so near the shoulder as to prevent use of a prosthetic appliance shall entitle to the rate under 38 U.S.C. 1114(n).

(xii) Anatomical loss or loss of use of one arm at a level, or with complications, preventing natural elbow action with prosthesis in place with anatomical loss of one arm so near the shoulder as to prevent use of a prosthetic appliance, shall entitle to the rate between 38 U.S.C. 1114(n) and (o).

(2) Eyes, bilateral, and blindness in connection with deafness and/or loss or loss of use of a hand or foot.

(i) Blindness of one eye with 5/200 visual acuity or less and blindness of the other eye having only light perception will entitle to the rate between 38 U.S.C. 1114(l) and (m).

(ii) blindness of one eye with 5/200 visual acuity or less and anatomical loss of, or blindness having no light perception in the other eye, will entitle to a rate equal to 38 U.S.C. 1114(m).

(iii) Blindness of one eye having only light perception and anatomical loss of, or blindness having no light perception in the other eye, will entitle to a rate between 38 U.S.C. 1114(m) and (n).

(iv) Blindness in both eyes with visual acuity of 5/200 or less, or blindness in both eyes rated under subparagraph (2)(i) or (ii) of this paragraph, when accompanied by service-connected total deafness in one ear, will afford entitlement to the next higher intermediate rate of if the veteran is already entitled to an intermediate rate, to the next higher statutory rate under 38 U.S.C. 1114, but in no event higher than the rate for (o).

(v) Blindness in both eyes having only light perception or less, or rated under subparagraph (2)(iii) of this paragraph, when accompanied by bilateral deafness (and the hearing impairment in either one or both ears is service-connected) rated at 10 or 20 percent disabling, will afford entitlement to the next higher intermediate rate, or if the veteran is already entitled to an intermediate rate, to the next higher statutory rate under 38 U.S.C. 1114, but in no event higher than the rate for (o). (Authority: Sec. 112, Pub. L. 98-223)

(vi) Blindness in both eyes rated under 38 U.S.C. 1114(l), (m) or (n), or rated under subparagraphs (2) (i), (ii) or (iii) of this paragraph, when accompanied by bilateral deafness rated at no less than 30 percent, and the hearing impairment in one or both ears is service-connected, will afford entitlement to the next higher statutory rate under 38 U.S.C. 1114, or if the veteran is already entitled to an intermediate rate, to the next higher intermediate rate, but in no event higher than the rate for (o). (Authority: 38 U.S.C. 1114(p))

(vii) Blindness in both eyes rated under 38 U.S.C. 1114(l), (m), or (n), or under the intermediate or next higher rate provisions of this subparagraph, when accompanied by:

(A) Service-connected loss or loss of use of one hand, will afford entitlement to the next higher statutory rate under 38 U.S.C. 1114 or, if the veteran is already entitled to an intermediate rate, to the next higher intermediate rate, but in no event higher than the rate for (o); or

(B) Service-connected loss or loss of use of one foot which by itself or in combination with another compensable disability would be ratable at 50 percent or more, will afford entitlement to the next higher statutory rate under 38 U.S.C. 1114 or, if the veteran is already entitled to an intermediate rate, to the next higher intermediate rate, but in no event higher than the rate for (o); or

(C) Service-connected loss or loss of use of one foot which is ratable at less than 50 percent and which is the only compensable disability other than bilateral blindness, will afford entitlement to the next higher intermediate rate or, if the veteran is already entitled to an intermediate rate, to the next higher statutory rate under 38 U.S.C. 1114, but in no event higher than the rate for (o). (Authority: 38 U.S.C. 1114(p))

(3) Additional independent 50 percent disabilities. In addition to the statutory rates payable under 38 U.S.C. 1114(l) through (n) and the intermediate or next higher rate provisions outlined above, additional single permanent disability or combinations of permanent disabilities independently ratable at 50 percent or more will afford entitlement to the next higher intermediate rate or if already entitled to an intermediate rate to the next higher statutory rate under 38 U.S.C. 1114, but not above the (o) rate. In the application of this subparagraph the disability or disabilities independently ratable at 50 percent or more must be separate and distinct and involve different anatomical segments or bodily systems from the conditions establishing entitlement under 38 U.S.C. 1114(l) through (n) or the intermediate rate provisions outlined above. The graduated ratings for arrested tuberculosis will not be utilized in this connection, but the permanent residuals of tuberculosis may be utilized.

(4) Additional independent 100 percent ratings. In addition to the statutory rates payable under 38 U.S.C. 1114(l) through (n) and the intermediate or next higher rate provisions outlined above additional single permanent disability independently ratable at 100 percent apart from any consideration of individual unemployability will afford entitlement to the next higher statutory rate under 38 U.S.C. 1114 or if already entitled to an intermediate rate to the next higher intermediate rate, but in no event higher than the rate for (o). In the application of this subparagraph the single permanent disability independently ratable at 100 percent must be separate and distinct and involve different anatomical segments or bodily systems from the conditions establishing entitlement under 38 U.S.C. 1114(l) through (n) or the intermediate rate provisions outlined above.

(i) Where the multiple loss or loss of use entitlement to a statutory or intermediate rate between 38 U.S.C. 1114(l) and (o) is caused by the same etiological disease or injury, that disease or injury may not serve as the basis for the independent 50 percent or 100 percent unless it is so rated without regard to the loss or loss of use.

(ii) The graduated ratings for arrested tuberculosis will not be utilized in this connection, but the permanent residuals of tuberculosis may be utilized.

(5) Three extremities. Anatomical loss or loss of use, or a combination of anatomical loss and loss of use, of three extremities shall entitle a veteran to the next higher rate without regard to whether that rate is a statutory

rate or an intermediate rate. The maximum monthly payment under this provision may not exceed the amount stated in 38 U.S.C. 1114(p).

(g) Inactive tuberculosis (complete arrest). The rating criteria for determining inactivity of tuberculosis are set out in §3.375.

(1) For a veteran who was receiving or entitled to receive compensation for tuberculosis on August 19, 1968, the minimum monthly rate is $67. This minimum special monthly compensation is not to be combined with or added to any other disability compensation.

(2) For a veteran who was not receiving or entitled to receive compensation for tuberculosis on August 19, 1968, the special monthly compensation authorized by paragraph (g)(1) of this section is not payable.

(h) Special aid and attendance benefit; 38 U.S.C. 1114(r):

(1) Maximum compensation cases. A veteran receiving the maximum rate under 38 U.S.C. 1114 (o) or (p) who is in need of regular aid and attendance or a higher level of care is entitled to an additional allowance during periods he or she is not hospitalized at United States Government expense. (See §3.552(b)(2) as to continuance following admission for hospitalization.) Determination of this need is subject to the criteria of §3.352. The regular or higher level aid and attendance allowance is payable whether or not the need for regular aid and attendance or a higher level of care was a partial basis for entitlement to the maximum rate under 38 U.S.C. 1114(o) or (p), or was based on an independent factual determination.

(2) Entitlement to compensation at the intermediate rate between 38 U.S.C. 1114(n) and (o) plus special monthly compensation under 38 U.S.C. 1114(k). A veteran receiving compensation at the intermediate rate between 38 U.S.C. 1114(n) and (o) plus special monthly compensation under 38 U.S.C. 1114(k) who establishes a factual need for regular aid and attendance or a higher level of care, is also entitled to an additional allowance during periods he or she is not hospitalized at United States Government expense. (See §3.552(b)(2) as to continuance following admission for hospitalization.) Determination of the factual need for aid and attendance is subject to the criteria of §3.352.

(3) Amount of the allowance. The amount of the additional allowance payable to a veteran in need of regular aid and attendance is specified in 38 U.S.C. 1114(r)(1). The amount of the additional allowance payable to a veteran in need of a higher level of care is specified in 38 U.S.C. 1114(r)(2). The higher level aid and attendance allowance authorized by 38 U.S.C. 1114(r)(2) is payable in lieu of the regular aid and attendance allowance authorized by 38 U.S.C. 1114(r)(1).

(i) Total plus 60 percent, or housebound; 38 U.S.C. 1114(s). The special monthly compensation provided by 38 U.S.C. 1114(s) is payable where the veteran has a single service-connected disability rated as 100 percent and:

(1) Has additional service-connected disability or disabilities independently ratable at 60 percent, separate and distinct from the 100 percent service-connected disability and involving different anatomical segments or bodily systems, or

(2) Is permanently housebound by reason of service-connected disability or disabilities. This requirement is met when the veteran is substantially confined as a direct result of service-connected disabilities to his or her dwelling and the immediate premises or, if institutionalized, to the ward or clinical areas, and it is reasonably certain that the disability or disabilities and resultant confinement will continue throughout his or her lifetime.

§3.310 Proximate results, secondary conditions.

(a) General. Except as provided in §3.300(c), disability which is proximately due to or the result of a service-connected disease or injury shall be service connected. When service connection is thus established for a secondary condition, the secondary condition shall be considered a part of the original condition.

(b) Cardiovascular disease. Ischemic heart disease or other cardiovascular disease developing in a veteran who has a service-connected amputation of one lower extremity at or above the knee or service-connected amputations of both lower extremities at or above the ankles, shall be held to be the proximate result of the service-connected amputation or amputations. (Authority: 38 U.S.C. 501(a), 1110-1131)

Ratings and Evaluations; Service Connection

§3.303 Principles relating to service connection.

(a) General. Service connection connotes many factors but basically it means that the facts, shown by evidence, establish that a particular injury or disease resulting in disability was incurred coincident with service in the Armed Forces, or if preexisting such service, was aggravated therein. This may be accomplished by affirmatively showing inception or aggravation during service or through the application of statutory presumptions. Each disabling condition shown by a veteran's service records, or for which he seeks a service connection must be considered on the basis of the places, types and circumstances of his service as shown by service records, the official history of each organization in which he served, his medical records and all pertinent medical and lay evidence. Determinations as to service connection will be based on review of the entire evidence of record, with due consideration to the policy of the Department of Veterans Affairs to administer the law under a broad and liberal interpretation consistent with the facts in each individual case.

(b) Chronicity and continuity. With chronic disease shown as such in service (or within the presumptive period under §3.307) so as to permit a finding of service connection, subsequent manifestations of the same chronic disease at any later date, however remote, are service connected, unless clearly attributable to intercurrent causes. This rule does not mean that any manifestation of joint pain, any abnormality of heart action or heart sounds, any urinary findings of casts, or any cough, in service will permit service connection of arthritis, disease of the heart, nephritis, or pulmonary disease, first shown as a clearcut clinical entity, at some later date. For the showing of chronic disease in service there is required a combination of manifestations sufficient to identify the disease entity, and sufficient observation to establish chronicity at the time, as distinguished from merely isolated findings or a diagnosis including the word "Chronic." When the disease identity is established (leprosy, tuberculosis, multiple sclerosis, etc.), there is no requirement of evidentiary showing of continuity. Continuity of symptomatology is required only where the condition noted during service (or in the presumptive period) is not, in fact, shown to be chronic or where the diagnosis of chronicity may be legitimately questioned. When the fact of chronicity in service is not adequately supported, then a showing of continuity after discharge is required to support the claim.

(c) Preservice disabilities noted in service. There are medical principles so universally recognized as to constitute fact (clear and unmistakable proof), and when in accordance with these principles existence of a disability prior to service is established, no additional or confirmatory evidence is necessary. Consequently with notation or discovery during service of such residual conditions (scars; fibrosis of the lungs; atrophies following disease of the central or peripheral nervous system; healed fractures; absent, displaced or resected parts of organs; supernumerary parts; congenital malformations or hemorrhoidal tags or tabs, etc.) with no evidence of the pertinent antecedent active disease or injury during service the conclusion must be that they preexisted service. Similarly, manifestation of lesions or symptoms of chronic disease from date of enlistment, or so close thereto that the disease could not have originated in so short a period will establish preservice existence thereof. Conditions of an infectious nature are to be considered with regard to the circumstances of the infection and if manifested in less than the respective incubation periods after reporting for duty, they will be held to have preexisted service. In the field of mental disorders, personality disorders which are characterized by developmental defects or pathological trends in the personality structure manifested by a lifelong pattern of action or behavior, chronic psychoneurosis of long duration or other psychiatric symptomatology shown to have existed prior to service with the same manifestations during service, which were the basis of the service diagnosis will be accepted as showing preservice origin. Congenital or developmental defects, refractive error of the eye, personality disorders and mental deficiency as such are not diseases or injuries within the meaning of applicable legislation.

(d) Postservice initial diagnosis of disease. Service connection may be granted for any disease diagnosed after discharge, when all the evidence, including that pertinent to service, establishes that the disease was incurred in service. Presumptive periods are not intended to limit service connection to diseases so diagnosed when the evidence warrants direct service connection. The presumptive provisions of the statute and Department of Veterans Affairs regulations implementing them are intended as liberalizations applicable when the evidence would not warrant service connection without their aid.

§3.304 Direct service connection; wartime and peacetime.

(a) General. The basic considerations relating to service connection are stated in §3.303. The criteria in this section apply only to disabilities which may have resulted from service in a period of war or service rendered on or after January 1, 1947.

(b) Presumption of soundness. The veteran will be considered to have been in sound condition when examined, accepted and enrolled for service except as to defects, infirmities, or disorders noted at entrance into service, or where clear and unmistakable (obvious or manifest) evidence demonstrates that an injury or disease existed prior thereto. Only such conditions as are recorded in examination reports are to be considered as noted. (Authority: 38 U.S.C. 1111)

(1) History of preservice existence of conditions recorded at the time of examination does not constitute a notation of such conditions but will be considered together with all other material evidence in determinations as to inception. Determinations should not be based on medical judgment alone as distinguished from accepted medical principles, or on history alone without regard to clinical factors pertinent to the basic character, origin and development of such injury or disease. They should be based on thorough analysis of the evidentiary showing and careful correlation of all material facts, with due regard to accepted medical principles pertaining to the history, manifestations, clinical course, and character of the particular injury or disease or residuals thereof.

(2) History conforming to accepted medical principles should be given due consideration, in conjunction with basic clinical data, and be accorded probative value consistent with accepted medical and evidentiary principles in

relation to value consistent with accepted medical evidence relating to incurrence, symptoms and course of the injury or disease, including official and other records made prior to, during or subsequent to service, together with all other lay and medical evidence concerning the inception, development and manifestations of the particular condition will be taken into full account.

(3) Signed statements of veterans relating to the origin, or incurrence of any disease or injury made in service if against his or her own interest is of no force and effect if other data do not establish the fact. Other evidence will be considered as though such statement were not of record. (Authority: 10 U.S.C. 1219)

(c) Development. The development of evidence in connection with claims for service connection will be accomplished when deemed necessary but it should not be undertaken when evidence present is sufficient for this determination. In initially rating disability of record at the time of discharge, the records of the service department, including the reports of examination at enlistment and the clinical records during service, will ordinarily suffice. Rating of combat injuries or other conditions which obviously had their inception in service may be accomplished pending receipt of copy of the examination at enlistment and all other service records.

(d) Combat. Satisfactory lay or other evidence that an injury or disease was incurred or aggravated in combat will be accepted as sufficient proof of service connection if the evidence is consistent with the circumstances, conditions or hardships of such service even though there is no official record of such incurrence or aggravation. (Authority: 38 U.S.C. 1154(b))

(e) Prisoners of war. Where disability compensation is claimed by a former prisoner of war, omission of history or findings from clinical records made upon repatriation is not determinative of service connection, particularly if evidence of comrades in support of the incurrence of the disability during confinement is available. Special attention will be given to any disability first reported after discharge, especially if poorly defined and not obviously of intercurrent origin. The circumstances attendant upon the individual veteran's confinement and the duration thereof will be associated with pertinent medical principles in determining whether disability manifested subsequent to service is etiologically related to the prisoner of war experience.

(f) Post-traumatic stress disorder. Service connection for post-traumatic stress disorder requires medical evidence diagnosing the condition in accordance with §4.125(a) of this chapter; a link, established by medical evidence, between current symptoms and an in-service stressor; and credible supporting evidence that the claimed in-service stressor occurred. Although service connection may be established based on other in-service stressors, the following provisions apply for specified in-service stressors as set forth below:

(1) If the evidence establishes that the veteran engaged in combat with the enemy and the claimed stressor is related to that combat, in the absence of clear and convincing evidence to the contrary, and provided that the claimed stressor is consistent with the circumstances, conditions, or hardships of the veteran's service, the veteran's lay testimony alone may establish the occurrence of the claimed in-service stressor.

(2) If the evidence establishes that the veteran was a prisoner-of-war under the provisions of §3.1(y) of this part and the claimed stressor is related to that prisoner-of-war experience, in the absence of clear and convincing evidence to the contrary, and provided that the claimed stressor is consistent with the circumstances, conditions, or hardships of the veteran's service, the veteran's lay testimony alone may establish the occurrence of the claimed in-service stressor.

(3) If a post-traumatic stress disorder claim is based on in-service personal assault, evidence from sources other than the veteran's service records may corroborate the veteran's account of the stressor incident. Examples of such evidence include, but are not limited to: records from law enforcement authorities, rape crisis centers, mental health counseling centers, hospitals, or physicians; pregnancy tests or tests for sexually transmitted diseases; and statements from family members, roommates, fellow service members, or clergy. Evidence of behavior changes following the claimed assault is one type of relevant evidence that may be found in these sources. Examples of behavior changes that may constitute credible evidence of the stressor include, but are not limited to: a request for a transfer to another military duty assignment; deterioration in work performance; substance abuse; episodes of depression, panic attacks, or anxiety without an identifiable cause; or unexplained economic or social behavior changes. VA will not deny a post-traumatic stress disorder claim that is based on in-service personal assault without first advising the claimant that evidence from sources other than the veteran's service records or evidence of behavior changes may constitute credible supporting evidence of the stressor and allowing him or her the opportunity to furnish this type of evidence or advise VA of potential sources of such evidence. VA may submit any evidence that it receives to an

appropriate medical or mental health professional for an opinion as to whether it indicates that a personal assault occurred. (Authority: 38 U.S.C. 501(a), 1154)

§3.306 Aggravation of preservice disability.

(a) General. A preexisting injury or disease will be considered to have been aggravated by active military, naval, or air service, where there is an increase in disability during such service, unless there is a specific finding that the increase in disability is due to the natural progress of the disease. (Authority: 38 U.S.C. 1153)

(b) Wartime service; peacetime service after December 31, 1946. Clear and unmistakable evidence (obvious or manifest) is required to rebut the presumption of aggravation where the preservice disability underwent an increase in severity during service. This includes medical facts and principles which may be considered to determine whether the increase is due to the natural progress of the condition. Aggravation may not be conceded where the disability underwent no increase in severity during service on the basis of all the evidence of record pertaining to the manifestations of the disability prior to, during and subsequent to service.

(1) The usual effects of medical and surgical treatment in service, having the effect of ameliorating disease or other conditions incurred before enlistment, including postoperative scars, absent or poorly functioning parts or organs, will not be considered service connected unless the disease or injury is otherwise aggravated by service.

(2) Due regard will be given the places, types, and circumstances of service and particular consideration will be accorded combat duty and other hardships of service. The development of symptomatic manifestations of a preexisting disease or injury during or proximately following action with the enemy or following a status as a prisoner of war will establish aggravation of a disability. (Authority: 38 U.S.C. 1154)

(c) Peacetime service prior to December 7, 1941. The specific finding requirement that an increase in disability is due to the natural progress of the condition will be met when the available evidence of a nature generally acceptable as competent shows that the increase in severity of a disease or injury or acceleration in progress was that normally to be expected by reason of the inherent character of the condition, aside from any extraneous or contributing cause or influence peculiar to military service. Consideration will be given to the circumstances, conditions, and hardships of service.

§3.307 Presumptive service connection for chronic, tropical or prisoner-of-war related disease, or disease associated with exposure to certain herbicide agents; wartime and service on or after January 1, 1947.

(a) General. A chronic, tropical, prisoner of war related disease, or a disease associated with exposure to certain herbicide agents listed in §3.309 will be considered to have been incurred in or aggravated by service under the circumstances outlined in this section even though there is no evidence of such disease during the period of service. No condition other than one listed in §3.309(a) will be considered chronic.

(1) Service. The veteran must have served 90 days or more during a war period or after December 31, 1946. The requirement of 90 days' service means active, continuous service within or extending into or beyond a war period or which began before and extended beyond December 31, 1946, or began after that date. Any period of service is sufficient for the purpose of establishing the presumptive service connection of a specified disease under the conditions listed in §3.309(c) and (e).

(2) Separation from service. For the purpose of paragraph (a)(3) and (4) of this section the date of separation from wartime service will be the date of discharge or release during a war period, or if service continued after the war, the end of the war period. In claims based on service on or after January 1, 1947, the date of separation will be the date of discharge or release from the period of service on which the claim is based.

(3) Chronic disease. The disease must have become manifest to a degree of 10 percent or more within 1 year (for Hansen's disease (leprosy) and tuberculosis, within 3 years; multiple sclerosis, within 7 years) from the date of separation from service as specified in paragraph (a)(2) of this section.

(4) Tropical disease. The disease must have become manifest to a degree of 10 percent or more within 1 year from date of separation from service as specified in paragraph (a)(2) of this section, or at a time when standard accepted treatises indicate that the incubation period commenced during such service. The resultant disorders or diseases originating because of therapy administered in connection with a tropical disease or as a preventative may also be service connected. (Authority: 38 U.S.C. 1112)

(5) Diseases specific as to former prisoners of war. The diseases listed in §3.309(c) shall have become manifest to a degree of 10 percent or more at any time after discharge or release from active service. (Authority: 38 U.S.C. 1112)

(6) Diseases associated with exposure to certain herbicide agents.

(i) For the purposes of this section, the term herbicide agent means a chemical in an herbicide used in support of the United States and allied military operations in the Republic of Vietnam during the period beginning on January 9, 1962, and ending on May 7, 1975, specifically: 2,4-D; 2,4,5-T and its contaminant TCDD; cacodylic acid; and picloram. (Authority: 38 U.S.C. 1116(a)(4))

(ii) The diseases listed at §3.309(e) shall have become manifest to a degree of 10 percent or more at any time after service, except that chloracne or other acneform disease consistent with chloracne, porphyria cutanea tarda, and acute and subacute peripheral neuropathy shall have become manifest to a degree of 10 percent or more within a year after the last date on which the veteran was exposed to an herbicide agent during active military, naval, or air service.

(iii) A veteran who, during active military, naval, or air service, served in the Republic of Vietnam during the period beginning on January 9, 1962, and ending on May 7, 1975, shall be presumed to have been exposed during such service to an herbicide agent, unless there is affirmative evidence to establish that the veteran was not exposed to any such agent during that service. The last date on which such a veteran shall be presumed to have been exposed to an herbicide agent shall be the last date on which he or she served in the Republic of Vietnam during the period beginning on January 9, 1962, and ending on May 7, 1975. Service in the Republic of Vietnam includes service in the waters offshore and service in other locations if the conditions of service involved duty or visitation in the Republic of Vietnam. (Authority: 38 U.S.C. 501(a) and 1116(a)(3))

(b) Evidentiary basis. The factual basis may be established by medical evidence, competent lay evidence or both. Medical evidence should set forth the physical findings and symptomatology elicited by examination within the applicable period. Lay evidence should describe the material and relevant facts as to the veteran's disability observed within such period, not merely conclusions based upon opinion. The chronicity and continuity factors outlined in §3.303(b) will be considered. The diseases listed in §3.309(a) will be accepted as chronic, even though diagnosed as acute because of insidious inception and chronic development, except:

(1) Where they result from intercurrent causes, for example, cerebral hemorrhage due to injury, or active nephritis or acute endocarditis due to intercurrent infection (with or without identification of the pathogenic micro-organism); or

(2) Where a disease is the result of drug ingestion or a complication of some other condition not related to service. Thus, leukemia will be accepted as a chronic disease whether diagnosed as acute or chronic. Unless the clinical picture is clear otherwise, consideration will be given as to whether an acute condition is an exacerbation of a chronic disease. (Authority: 38 U.S.C. 1112)

(c) Prohibition of certain presumptions. No presumptions may be invoked on the basis of advancement of the disease when first definitely diagnosed for the purpose of showing its existence to a degree of 10 percent within the applicable period. This will not be interpreted as requiring that the disease be diagnosed in the presumptive period, but only that there be then shown by acceptable medical or lay evidence characteristic manifestations of the disease to the required degree, followed without unreasonable time lapse by definite diagnosis. Symptomatology shown in the prescribed period may have no particular significance when first observed, but in the light of subsequent developments it may gain considerable significance. Cases in which a chronic condition is shown to exist within a short time following the applicable presumptive period, but without evidence of manifestations within the period, should be developed to determine whether there was symptomatology which in retrospect may be identified and evaluated as manifestation of the chronic disease to the required 10-percent degree.

(d) Rebuttal of service incurrence or aggravation.

(1) Evidence which may be considered in rebuttal of service incurrence of a disease listed in §3.309 will be any evidence of a nature usually accepted as competent to indicate the time of existence or inception of disease, and medical judgment will be exercised in making determinations relative to the effect of intercurrent injury or disease. The expression "affirmative evidence to the contrary" will not be taken to require a conclusive showing, but such showing as would, in sound medical reasoning and in the consideration of all evidence of

record, support a conclusion that the disease was not incurred in service. As to tropical diseases the fact that the veteran had no service in a locality having a high incidence of the disease may be considered as evidence to rebut the presumption, as may residence during the period in question in a region where the particular disease is endemic. The known incubation periods of tropical diseases should be used as a factor in rebuttal of presumptive service connection as showing inception before or after service.

(2) The presumption of aggravation provided in this section may be rebutted by affirmative evidence that the preexisting condition was not aggravated by service, which may include affirmative evidence that any increase in disability was due to an intercurrent disease or injury suffered after separation from service or evidence sufficient, under §3.306 of this part, to show that the increase in disability was due to the natural progress of the preexisting condition. (Authority: 38 U.S.C 1113 and 1153)

§3.308 Presumptive service connection; peacetime service before January 1, 1947.

(a) Chronic disease. There is no provision for presumptive service connection for chronic disease as distinguished from tropical diseases referred to in paragraph (b) of this section based on peacetime service before January 1, 1947.

(b) Tropical disease. In claims based on peacetime service before January 1, 1947, a veteran of 6 months or more service who contracts a tropical disease listed in §3.309(b) or a resultant disorder or disease originating because of therapy administered in connection with a tropical disease or as a preventative, will be considered to have incurred such disability in service when it is shown to exist to the degree of 10 percent or more within 1 year after separation from active service, or at a time when standard and accepted treatises indicate that the incubation period commenced during active service unless shown by clear and unmistakable evidence not to have been of service origin. The requirement of 6 months or more service means active, continuous service, during one or more enlistment periods. (Authority: 38 U.S.C. 1133)

§3.309 Disease subject to presumptive service connection.

(a) Chronic diseases. The following diseases shall be granted service connection although not otherwise established as incurred in or aggravated by service if manifested to a compensable degree within the applicable time limits under §3.307 following service in a period of war or following peacetime service on or after January 1, 1947, provided the rebuttable presumption provisions of §3.307 are also satisfied.

- Anemia, primary.

- Arteriosclerosis.

- Arthritis.

- Atrophy, Progressive muscular.

- Brain hemorrhage.

- Brain thrombosis.

- Bronchiectasis.

- Calculi of the kidney, bladder, or gallbladder.

- Cardiovascular-renal disease, including hypertension. (This term applies to combination involvement of the type of arteriosclerosis, nephritis, and organic heart disease, and since hypertension is an early symptom long preceding the development of those diseases in their more obvious forms, a disabling hypertension within the 1-year period will be given the same benefit of service connection as any of the chronic diseases listed.)

- Cirrhosis of the liver.

- Coccidioidomycosis.

- Diabetes mellitus.

- Encephalitis lethargica residuals.

- Endocarditis. (This term covers all forms of valvular heart disease.)

- Endocrinopathies.

- Epilepsies.

- Hansen's disease.

- Hodgkin's disease.

- Leukemia.

- Lupus erythematosus, systemic.

- Myasthenia gravis.

- Myelitis.

- Myocarditis.

- Nephritis.

- Other organic diseases of the nervous system.

- Osteitis deformans (Paget's disease).

- Osteomalacia.

- Palsy, bulbar.

- Paralysis agitans.

- Psychoses.

- Purpura idiopathic, hemorrhagic.

- Raynaud's disease.

- Sarcoidosis.

- Scleroderma.

- Sclerosis, amyotrophic lateral.

- Sclerosis, multiple.

- Syringomyelia.

- Thromboangiitis obliterans (Buerger's disease).

- Tuberculosis, active.

- Tumors, malignant, or of the brain or spinal cord or peripheral nerves.

- Ulcers, peptic (gastric or duodenal) (A proper diagnosis of gastric or duodenal ulcer (peptic ulcer) is to be considered established if it represents a medically sound interpretation of sufficient clinical findings warranting such diagnosis and provides an adequate basis for a differential diagnosis from other conditions with like symptomatology; in short, where the preponderance of evidence indicates gastric or duodenal ulcer (peptic ulcer). Whenever possible, of course, laboratory findings should be used in corroboration of the clinical data.

(b) Tropical diseases. The following diseases shall be granted service connection as a result of tropical service, although not otherwise established as incurred in service if manifested to a compensable degree within the applicable time limits under §3.307 or §3.308 following service in a period of war or following peacetime service provided the rebuttable presumption provisions of §3.307 are also satisfied.

- Amebiasis.

- Blackwater fever.

- Cholera.

- Dracontiasis.

- Dysentery.

- Filariasis.

- Leishmaniasis, including kala-azar.

- Loiasis.

- Malaria.

- Onchocerciasis.

- Oroya fever.

- Pinta.

- Plague.

- Schistosomiasis.

- Yaws.

- Yellow fever.

Resultant disorders or diseases originating because of therapy administered in connec¬tion with such diseases or as a preventative thereof.

(c) Diseases specific as to former prisoners of war.

(1) If a veteran is a former prisoner of war, the following diseases shall be service connected if manifest to a degree of disability of 10 percent or more at any time after discharge or release from active military, naval, or air service even though there is no record of such disease during service, provided the rebuttable presumption provisions of §3.307 are also satisfied.

- Psychosis.

- Any of the anxiety states.

- Dysthymic disorder (or depressive neurosis).

- Organic residuals of frostbite, if it is determined that the veteran was interned in climatic conditions consistent with the occurrence of frostbite.

- Post-traumatic osteoarthritis.

- Atherosclerotic heart disease or hypertensive vascular disease (including hypertensive heart disease) and their complications (including myocardial infarction, congestive heart failure, arrhythmia).

- Stroke and its complications.

(2) If the veteran:

(i) Is a former prisoner of war and;

(ii) Was interned or detained for not less than 30 days, the following diseases shall be service connected if manifest to a degree of 10 percent or more at any time after discharge or release from active military, naval, or air service even though there is no record of such disease during service, provided the rebuttable presumption provisions of §3.307 are also satisfied.

- Avitaminosis.

- Beriberi (including beriberi heart disease).

- Chronic dysentery.

- Helminthiasis.

- Malnutrition (including optic atrophy associated with malnutrition).

- Pellagra.

- Any other nutritional deficiency.

- Irritable bowel syndrome.

- Peptic ulcer disease.

- Peripheral neuropathy except where directly related to infectious causes.

- Cirrhosis of the liver.

Authority: 38 U.S.C. 1112(b).

(d) Diseases specific to radiation-exposed veterans.

(1) The diseases listed in paragraph (d)(2) of this section shall be service-connected if they become manifest in a radiation-

exposed veteran as defined in paragraph (d)(3) of this section, provided the rebuttable presumption provisions of §3.307 of this part are also satisfied.

(2) The diseases referred to in paragraph (d)(1) of this section are the following:

(i) Leukemia (other than chronic lymphocytic leukemia).

(ii) Cancer of the thyroid.

(iii) Cancer of the breast.

(iv) Cancer of the pharynx.

(v) Cancer of the esophagus.

(vi) Cancer of the stomach.

(vii) Cancer of the small intestine.

(viii) Cancer of the pancreas.

(ix) Multiple myeloma.

(x) Lymphomas (except Hodgkin's disease).

(xi) Cancer of the bile ducts.

(xii) Cancer of the gall bladder.

(xiii) Primary liver cancer (except if cirrhosis or hepatitis B is indicated).

(xiv) Cancer of the salivary gland.

(xv) Cancer of the urinary tract.

(xvi) Bronchiolo-alveolar carcinoma.

(xvii) Cancer of the bone.

(xviii) Cancer of the brain.

(xix) Cancer of the colon.

(xx) Cancer of the lung.

(xxi) Cancer of the ovary.

For the purposes of this section, the term urinary tract means the kidneys, renal pelves, ureters, urinary bladder, and urethra. (Authority: 38 U.S.C. 1112(c)(2))

(3) For purposes of this section:

(i) The term radiation-exposed veteran means either a veteran who, while serving on active duty, or an individual who while a member of a reserve component of the Armed Forces during a period of active duty for training or inactive duty training, participated in a radiation-risk activity.

(ii) The term radiation-risk activity means:

(A) Onsite participation in a test involving the atmospheric detonation of a nuclear device.

(B) The occupation of Hiroshima or Nagasaki, Japan, by United States forces during the period beginning on August 6, 1945, and ending on July 1, 1946.

(C) Internment as a prisoner of war in Japan (or service on active duty in Japan immediately following such internment) during World War II which resulted in an opportunity for exposure to ionizing radiation comparable to that of the United States occupation forces in Hiroshima or Nagasaki, Japan, during the period beginning on August 6, 1945, and ending on July 1, 1946.

(D)   (1) Service in which the service member was, as part of his or her official military duties, present during a total of at least 250 days before February 1, 1992, on the grounds of a gaseous diffusion plant located in Paducah, Kentucky, Portsmouth, Ohio, or the area identified as K25 at Oak Ridge, Tennessee, if, during such service the veteran:

(i) Was monitored for each of the 250 days of such service through the use of dosimetry badges for exposure at the plant of the external parts of veteran's body to radiation; or

(ii) Served for each of the 250 days of such service in a position that had exposures comparable to a job that is or was monitored through the use of dosimetry badges; or

(2) Service before January 1, 1974, on Amchitka Island, Alaska, if, during such service, the veteran was exposed to ionizing radiation in the performance of duty related to the Long Shot, Milrow, or Cannikin underground nuclear tests.

(3) For purposes of paragraph (d)(3)(ii)(D)(1) of this section, the term "day" refers to all or any portion of a calendar day.

(iii) The term atmospheric detonation includes underwater nuclear detonations.

(iv) The term onsite participation means:

(A) During the official operational period of an atmospheric nuclear test, presence at the test site, or performance of official military duties in connection with ships, aircraft or other equipment used in direct support of the nuclear test.

(B) During the six month period following the official operational period of an atmospheric nuclear test, presence at the test site or other test staging area to perform official military duties in connection with completion of projects related to the nuclear test including decontamination of equipment used during the nuclear test.

(C) Service as a member of the garrison or maintenance forces on Eniwetok during the periods June 21, 1951, through July 1, 1952, August 7, 1956, through August 7, 1957, or November 1, 1958, through April 30, 1959.

(D) Assignment to official military duties at Naval Shipyards involving the decontamination of ships that participated in Operation Crossroads.

(v) For tests conducted by the United States, the term operational period means:

(A) For Operation TRINITY the period July 16, 1945 through August 6, 1945.

(B) For Operation CROSSROADS the period July 1, 1946 through August 31, 1946.

(C) For Operation SANDSTONE the period April 15, 1948 through May 20, 1948.

(D) For Operation RANGER the period January 27, 1951 through February 6, 1951.

(E) For Operation GREENHOUSE the period April 8, 1951 through June 20, 1951.

(F) For Operation BUSTER-JANGLE the period October 22, 1951 through December 20, 1951

(G) For Operation TUMBLER-SNAPPER the period April 1, 1952 through June 20, 1952.

(H) For Operation IVY the period November 1, 1952 through December 31, 1952.

(I) For Operation UPSHOT-KNOTHOLE the period March 17, 1953 through June 20, 1953.

(J) For Operation CASTLE the period March 1, 1954 through May 31, 1954.

(K) For Operation TEAPOT the period February 18, 1955 through June 10, 1955.

(L) For Operation WIGWAM the period May 14, 1955 through May 15, 1955.

(M) For Operation REDWING the period May 5, 1956 through August 6, 1956.

(N) For Operation PLUMBBOB the period May 28, 1957 through October 22, 1957.

(O) For Operation HARDTACK I the period April 28, 1958 through October 31, 1958.

(P) For Operation ARGUS the period August 27, 1958 through September 10, 1958.

(Q) For Operation HARDTACK II the period September 19, 1958 through October 31, 1958.

(R) For Operation DOMINIC I the period April 25, 1962 through December 31, 1962.

(S) For Operation DOMINIC II/ PLOWSHARE the period July 6, 1962 through August 15, 1962.

(vi) The term occupation of Hiroshima or Nagasaki, Japan, by United States forces means official military duties within 10 miles of the city limits of either Hiroshima or Nagasaki, Japan, which were required to perform or support military occupation functions such as occupation of territory, control of the population, stabilization of the government, demilitarization of the Japanese military, rehabilitation of the infrastructure or deactivation and conversion of war plants or materials.

(vii) Former prisoners of war who had an opportunity for exposure to ionizing radiation comparable to that of veterans who participated in the occupation of Hiroshima or Nagasaki, Japan, by United States forces shall include those who, at any time during the period August 6, 1945, through July 1, 1946:

(A) Were interned within 75 miles of the city limits of Hiroshima or within 150 miles of the city limits of Nagasaki, or

(B) Can affirmatively show they worked within the areas set forth in paragraph (d)(4)(vii)(A) of this section although not interned within those areas, or

(C) Served immediately following internment in a capacity which satisfies the definition in paragraph (d)(4)(vi) of this section, or

(D) Were repatriated through the port of Nagasaki. (Authority: 38 U.S.C. 1110, 1112, 1131)

(E) Disease associated with exposure to certain herbicide agents. If a veteran was exposed to an herbicide agent during active military, naval, or air service, the following diseases shall be service-connected if the requirements of §3.307(a)(6) are met even though there is no record of such disease during service, provided further that the rebuttable presumption provisions of §3.307(d) are also satisfied.

- Chloracne or other acneform disease consistent with chloracne

- Type 2 diabetes (also known as Type II diabetes mellitus or adult-onset diabetes)

- Hodgkin's disease

- Chronic lymphocytic leukemia

- Multiple myeloma

- Non-Hodgkin's lymphoma

- Acute and subacute peripheral neuropathy

- Porphyria cutanea tarda

- Prostate cancer

- Respiratory cancers (cancer of the lung, bronchus, larynx, or trachea)

- Soft-tissue sarcoma (other than osteosarcoma, chondrosarcoma, Kaposi's sarcoma, or mesothelioma)

  1: The term soft-tissue sarcoma includes the following:

- Adult fibrosarcoma

- Dermatofibrosarcoma protuberans

- Malignant fibrous histiocytoma

- Liposarcoma

- Leiomyosarcoma

- Epithelioid leiomyosarcoma (malignant leiomyoblastoma)

- Rhabdomyosarcoma

- Ectomesenchymoma

- Angiosarcoma (hemangiosarcoma and lymphangiosarcoma)

- Proliferating (systemic) angioendotheliomatosis

- Malignant glomus tumor

- Malignant hemangiopericytoma

- Synovial sarcoma (malignant synovioma)

- Malignant giant cell tumor of tendon sheath

- Malignant schwannoma, including malignant schwannoma with rhabdomyoblastic differentiation (malignant Triton tumor), glandular and epithelioid

- malignant schwannomas

- Malignant mesenchymoma

- Malignant granular cell tumor

- Alveolar soft part sarcoma

- Epithelioid sarcoma

- Clear cell sarcoma of tendons and aponeuroses

- Extraskeletal Ewing's sarcoma

- Congenital and infantile fibrosarcoma

- Malignant ganglioneuroma

2: For purposes of this section, the term acute and subacute peripheral neuropathy means transient peripheral neuropathy that appears within weeks or months of exposure to an herbicide agent and resolves within two years of the date of onset.

APPENDIX E

DEPENDENT INDEMNITY COMPENSATION

DIC is a monthly benefit paid to eligible survivors of a

- Military service member who died while on active duty, OR
- Veteran whose death resulted from a service-related injury or disease, OR
- Veteran whose death resulted from a non service-related injury or disease, and who was receiving, or was entitled to receive, VA Compensation for service-connected disability that was rated as totally disabling for at least 10 years immediately before death, OR
- since the veteran's release from active duty and for at least five years immediately preceding death, OR
- for at least one year before death if the veteran was a former prisoner of war who died after September 30, 1999.

Who is Eligible?

Spouse:

The surviving spouse is eligible if he or she:

- validly married the veteran before January 1, 1957, OR

- was married to a service member who died on active duty, OR

- married the veteran within 15 years of discharge from the period of military service in which the disease or injury that caused the veteran's death began or was aggravated, OR

- was married to the veteran for at least one year, OR

- had a child with the veteran, AND

- cohabited with the veteran continuously until the veteran's death or, if separated, was not at fault for the separation, AND

- is not currently remarried[62].

Children:

The surviving child(ren), are eligible if he/she is:

- not included on the surviving spouse's DIC
- unmarried AND
- under age 18, or between the ages of 18 and 23 and attending school[63].

Parents:

The surviving parent(s) may be eligible for an income-based benefit. See our fact sheet, Parents' DIC, or call the toll-free number below for more information.

How Much Does VA Pay?

The basic monthly rate of DIC is $993 for an eligible surviving spouse. The rate is increased for each dependent child, and also if the surviving spouse is housebound or in need of aid and attendance. VA also adds a transitional benefit of $250 to the surviving spouse's monthly DIC if there are children under age 18.

The amount is based on a family unit, not individual children. It is paid for two years from the date that entitlement to DIC commences, but is discontinued earlier when there is no child under age 18 or no child on the surviving spouse's DIC for any reason. Benefit rate tables, including those for

---

[62] A surviving spouse who remarries on or after December 16, 2003, and on or after attaining age 57, is entitled to continue to receive DIC.

[63] Certain helpless adult children are entitled to DIC. Call the toll-free number below for the eligibility requirements for those survivors.

children alone and parents, can be found on the Internet at http://www.vba.va.gov/bln/21/Rates, or call the toll-free number below.

How To Apply?

Claimants should complete VA Form 21-534 (*Application for Dependency and Indemnity Compensation, Death Pension and Accrued Benefits by a Surviving Spouse or Child*), and submit it to the VA regional office serving the claimant's area. Call the toll-free number below for information about supporting materials that VA may need to process a DIC claim.

APPENDIX F

ASSISTANCE FOR HOMELESS VETERANS

VA has many benefits and services to assist homeless veterans. Disability benefits, education, health care, rehabilitation services, residential care, and compensated work therapy are among the services we offer to eligible veterans.

The VA offers the following services and benefit programs for homeless veterans:

- **HEALTH CARE FOR HOMELESS VETERANS PROGRAMS (HCHV)** – operates at 135 sites, where extensive outreach, physical and psychiatric health exams, supported housing programs, Drop-In-Centers, compensated work therapy, treatment, referrals, and ongoing case management are provided to homeless veterans with mental health problems, including substance abuse.

- **DOMICILIARY CARE FOR HOMELESS VETERANS PROGRAM (DCHV)** – provides medical care and rehabilitation in a residential setting on VA medical center grounds to eligible ambulatory veterans disabled by medical or psychiatric disorders, injury or age and who do not need hospitalization or nursing home care.

- **INPATIENT & OUTPATIENT HEALTH CARE** -- VA medical centers provide inpatient treatment to thousands of homeless veterans each year. Hospitals and outpatient clinics provide eligible veterans with comprehensive physical and mental health care, alcohol and substance abuse treatment, rehabilitation treatment, and other specialized services.

- **READJUSTMENT COUNSELING CENTERS** -- These centers, also called Vet Centers, help veterans through community outreach. They offer specialized services, such as group, individual and family counseling, to help eligible veterans overcome psychological difficulties or to resolve conflicts that may be contributing to their homelessness. They also provide referral services, connecting veterans to VA programs and community services.

- **OUTREACH** -- The staff from VA regional offices, medical centers, vet centers, and special homeless programs regularly visit community shelters, agencies, and the streets to help thousands of homeless veterans each year.

- **BENEFITS AND ENTITLEMENTS** -- VA annually awards more than $17 billion in disability benefits to millions of veterans. In many instances, these payments are the major source of income to veterans and serve to prevent homelessness. VA's Fiduciary Program provides specialized case management to over 67,000 veterans, many of whom might be homeless without the services it provides.

- **ACQUIRED PROPERTY SALES FOR HOMELESS PROVIDERS** Program -- makes available properties VA obtains through foreclosures on VA-insured mortgages for sale to homeless provider organizations at a discount of 20 to 50 percent. Some of these properties are available for lease.

How Do You Get More Information?

Contact any VA medical center or regional office and a VA representative can provide information about VA benefits and services available to assist homeless veterans. They can also provide you with the address and phone number of the VA homeless program coordinator nearest you.

APPENDIX G

FORMER PRISONERS OF WAR (POWS)

Since World War I, more than 142,000 Americans, including 85 women, have been captured and interned as POWs. Not included in this figure are nearly 93,000 Americans who were lost or never recovered. Only one third of America's former POWs since World War I are still living (about 36,500). More than 90% of living former POWs were captured and interned during World War II. Over 21,000 former POWs are in receipt of compensation for service-connected injuries, diseases, or illnesses. In 1981, Congress passed Public Law 97-37 entitled "Former Prisoners of War Benefit Act." This law accomplished several things.

- It established an Advisory Committee on Former Prisoners of War and mandated medical and dental care.

- It also identified certain diagnoses as presumptive service-connected conditions for former POWs.

- Subsequent public laws and policy decisions by the Secretary of Veterans Affairs have added additional diagnoses to the list of presumptive conditions.

Presumptive Conditions for Former POWs

Today, former POWs are generally entitled to a presumption of service-connection for seven diseases, regardless of the length of captivity, if manifested to a degree of 10 percent or more after discharge or release from active military, naval or air service. These diseases are:

- Psychosis

- Any of the Anxiety States

- Dysthymic disorder, or depressive neurosis

- Post-traumatic osteoarthritis

- Cold Injury

- Stroke and Complications

- Heart Disease and Complications

If a former POW was interned for 30 days or more, the following additional diseases are presumed to be service-connected:

- Avitaminosis

- Beriberi

- Chronic Dysentery

- Cirrhosis of the Liver

- Helminthiasis

- Irritable Bowel Syndrome

- Malnutrition, including associated Optic Atrophy

- Pellagra and any other nutritional deficiency

- Peptic Ulcer Disease

- Peripheral Neuropathy, except where directly related to infectious causes

How should a former POW apply for VA Compensation?

Former POWs can apply for Compensation for their service-connected injuries, diseases or illnesses by completing VA Form 21-526 (*Veterans Application for Compensation or Pension*), and submitting it to the VA regional office serving their. They can also apply on the Internet at http://vabenefits.vba.va.gov/vonapp/main.asp.

Medical Benefits for POWs

The VA health care system affords priority treatment for former POWs. Those who have a service–connected disability are eligible for VA health care. This includes hospital, nursing home, and outpatient treatment. Former POWs who do not have a service-connected disability are eligible for VA hospital and nursing home care – without regard to their ability to pay.

They are also eligible for outpatient care on a priority basis – second only to veterans with service-connected disabilities. While former POWs are receiving treatment in an approved outpatient treatment program, they are eligible for needed medicines, glasses, hearing aids, or prostheses. They are also eligible for all needed dental care. There is no co-payment requirement for former POWs at VA pharmacies.

Benefits for Survivors of Former POWs

The major benefit that is available for survivors of former POWs is Dependency and Indemnity Compensation (DIC) which is a monthly benefit payable to the surviving spouse (and the former POW's children and parents in some cases) when the former POW:

- was a service member who died on active duty; or
- died from service-related disabilities; or
- died on or before September 30, 1999 and was continuously rated totally disabled for a service connected condition (including individual unemployability) for at least 10 years immediately preceding death; or
- died after September 30, 1999, and was continuously rated totally disabled for a service-connected condition (including individual unemployability) for at least 1 year immediately preceding death.

DIC is terminated for a surviving spouse who remarries, but can be resumed if the remarriage ends in death, divorce or annulment. Also, a surviving spouse who remarries on or after attaining age 57, and on or after December 16, 2003, can continue to receive DIC.

However, a surviving spouse who remarried before December 16, 2003, and on or after attaining age 57, must apply no later than December 15, 2004, to have DIC restored. VA must deny applications received after that date.

Related Benefits for Former POWs and Their Dependents/survivors?

The following are other significant VA benefits to which certain veterans may be entitled:

- disability pension,

- medical care,

- education and training, home loan guaranty, and burial benefits.

- Certain disabled veterans may be eligible for vocational rehabilitation and employment services, insurance, clothing allowance, special adapted housing assistance, and specially adapted automobile equipment.

- Certain dependents/survivors may be entitled to health care, death pension, education and training, home loan guaranty, and burial in a national cemetery.

Special Assistance Is Available to Former POWs?

Each VA Regional Office has a coordinator for former POWs. Any former POW who needs special assistance should ask to speak to the Former POW Coordinator. Additional former POW information is available at http://www.vba.va.gov/bln/21/Benefits/POW/index.htm.

APPENDIX H

HOME LOAN GUARANTY BENEFITS

VA-guaranteed loans are made by private lenders, such as banks, savings and loan associations, or mortgage companies. To get a loan, you apply to the lender. If the loan is approved, VA will guarantee part of it. The amount of VA's guaranty usually depends on the size of the loan. This guaranty protects the lender against loss up to the amount guaranteed by VA. The largest guaranty that VA can give a lender is $60,000. Lenders generally limit the maximum VA loan to $240,000, which is 4 times the maximum VA loan.

A VA-guaranteed loan offers a number of safeguards and advantages. For example, the interest rate on a VA loan is competitive with conventional rates with little or no down payment required. The loan guaranty can be used to:

- buy a home, a manufactured home, or a condominium

- buy a lot for a manufactured home

- build, repair or improve a home (including energy efficient improvements)

- refinance an existing loan

Eligibility

Generally, the following groups are eligible for Home Loan Guaranty Benefits[64]:

---

[64] There are certain other groups who may be eligible. For information about these groups, call VA toll free at the number shown below.

- veterans who were discharged since 9/16/40, under other than dishonorable conditions

- military personnel on active duty who have served a minimum period

- certain Reservists and National Guard members (until 9/30/09)

- surviving spouses of certain deceased veterans

How To Apply

You can apply for a VA-guaranteed loan through a private lender. If you need help in finding a lender, please visit the web site listed below. You will need a VA Certificate of Eligibility to prove to the lender you are eligible. If you don't have a Certificate, your lender can help you apply OR you can get one from the nearest Eligibility Center.

Related Benefits

- Restoration of Entitlement
- Release of Liability/Substitution of Entitlement
- Purchase of Repossessed Homes
- Veterans Mortgage Life Insurance
- Specially Adapted Housing
- Direct Loans to Native American Veterans

APPENDIX I

RECEIVING VA BENEFITS WHILE IN PRISON

VA can pay certain benefits to veterans who are incarcerated in a Federal, state or local penal institution. However, the amount we can pay depends on the type of benefit and reason for incarceration. Outlined below is general information about the benefits most commonly affected by imprisonment.

VA Disability Compensation

Your monthly payment will be reduced beginning with the 61st day of your imprisonment for a felony. If your payment before you went to prison was $210 or more, your new payment amount will be $108. If you were getting $108 before you were imprisoned, your new payment will be $54[65].

VA Disability Pension

If you are imprisoned in a Federal, State or local penal institution as the result of conviction of a felony or misdemeanor, such pension payment will be discontinued effective on the 61st day of imprisonment following conviction.

---

[65] If you are released from incarceration – participated in a work release or half-way house program, paroled, and completed sentence, your compensation payments will not be reduced.

Eligibility For VA Medical Care While Imprisoned

While incarcerated veterans do not forfeit their eligibility for medical care, current regulations restrict VA from providing hospital and outpatient care to an incarcerated veteran who is an inmate in an institution of another government agency when that agency has a duty to give the care or services.

However, VA may provide care once the veteran has been unconditionally released from the penal institution. Veterans interested in applying for enrollment into the VA health care system should contact the nearest VA health care facility upon their release.

Payments to Your Spouse, Children Or Dependent Parent(s) While Your Are Imprisoned

VA can take all or part of the amount of compensation you are not receiving and apportion it to your spouse, child or children and dependent parents on the basis of individual need. They should contact the nearest VA regional office for details on how to apply. They will be asked to provide income information as part of the application process.

Resumption of Benefit Payments Upon Release

Your award for compensation or pension benefits shall be resumed the date of release from incarceration if the Department of Veterans Affairs receives notice of release within 1 year from following release. Depending on the type of disability, VA may schedule you for a medical examination to see if your disability has improved. You will need to visit or call your local VA regional office for assistance.

APPENDIX J

SERVICE DISABLED VETERANS INSURANCE (RH)

Service-Disabled Veterans Insurance is life insurance for veterans with service-related disabilities. The basic program, which is called "RH Insurance", insures eligible veterans up to $10,000. A supplemental policy, called "Supplemental RH Insurance", gives certain disabled veterans extra coverage of up to $20,000.

Eligibility

You are eligible for RH INSURANCE if[66]:
- You left service after April 24, 1951, AND

- VA has notified you that you have a service-related disability, AND

- You are healthy except for your service-related disability, AND

- You apply within 2 years of being notified of your disability.

You are eligible for SUPPLEMENTAL RH INSURANCE if:
- You have RH Insurance, AND

---

[66] If the veteran is mentally incompetent, call the toll-free number below for information about eligibility and time limits.

- VA has notified you that you don't have to pay your insurance premiums (which is called a waiver[67]), AND

- You apply within 1 year of being notified of the waiver, AND

- You are under 65 years of age[68].

Cost

The cost varies depending upon your age, type of plan you select (term or one of several permanent plans), and the amount of coverage.

How To Apply

You can apply by using the following forms:

- VA Form 29-4364 to apply for basic RH Insurance

- VA Form 29-0188 to apply for Supplemental RH Insurance

- VA Form 29-357 to apply for a waiver of your RH Insurance premiums

---

[67] Waiver of RH Premiums - you may be eligible for a waiver if you become too disabled to work before your 65th birthday and stay that way for at least 6 consecutive months. (Premiums for Supplemental RH Insurance can't be waived.) Call the toll-free number below for information.

[68] In some cases, veterans over age 65 can apply. Call the toll-free number below for details.

APPENDIX K

NEW PHILIPPINE SCOUTS

Some benefits are also available to New Philippine Scouts (Non-Commissioned – Enlisted under PL 190, 79th Congress on or after October 5, 1945). These benefits are outlined below:

Benefit Programs For Veterans

Disability Compensation:
This is payable to a veteran with service-connected condition(s) rated at 10% or more. The veteran is also entitled to receive special allowance for a spouse who is in need of aid and attendance of another person if the veteran is evaluated 30% or more.

Clothing Allowance:
This is payable to a veteran who is entitled to receive compensation for a service-connected disability for which he or she uses prosthetic or orthopedic appliances that tends to wear out or tear clothing or whose service-connected skin condition requires prescribed medication which irreparably damages the veteran's outer garments.

Benefit Programs For Survivors

The following programs are available for survivors of New Philippine Scouts[69]:

---

[69] Payment of the above benefits shall be made at a rate of $0.50 for each dollar authorized per Sec 107(a), 38 USC.

- Dependency & Indemnity Compensation (DIC): Payable to eligible spouses, children and parents.

- Aid and Attendance (A&A): Payable to surviving spouses and parents receiving DIC if they are patients in a nursing home or require aid and attendance of another person.

- Housebound: Payable to surviving spouses qualified for DIC who are not so disabled as to require the regular aid and attendance of another person but who, due to disability, are permanently housebound.

- Dependents' Educational Assistance: Payable to children of veterans who are eligible under Chapter 35 benefits. Spouses are not eligible.

Benefit Programs That Are Not Available?

Certain benefit programs are not available to New Philippine Scouts:
- Non-service connected pension benefits for veterans and dependents;

- Hospitalization, nursing home care, domiciliary care, outpatient dental and medical care even though the veteran has service-connected conditions. However, while in the United States or its territories, the VA may furnish hospital and nursing home care and medical services to Commonwealth Army veterans for treatment only of their service-connected disabilities. (Sec. 1734, 38 USC);

- VA loans such as home loan guarantees and small business loans;

- Specially Adapted Homes;

- Automobile or Other Conveyances.

- Service-Disabled Veterans Insurance (RH);

- Burial and Funeral Expense Allowance;

- Plot or Interment Allowance;

- Burial Flag;

- Burial in national Cemeteries, and

- Headstones and Markers.

This information does not apply to officers who were commissioned in connection with the administration of Public Law 190 (Authority: 38 USC 107).

Commissioned officers (and their dependents) have the same benefits as United States veterans including payments in dollars.

APPENDIX L

BENEFITS AVAILABLE TO COMMONWEALTH ARMY (USAFFE) AND RECOGNIZED GUERILLAS

The term Commonwealth Army veteran means persons who served before July 1, 1946 in the organized military forces of the Government of the Philippines, while such forces were in the service of the U.S. Armed Forces pursuant to the military order of the President of the United States dated July 26, 1941. This includes among such military forces, organized guerrilla forces under commanders appointed, designated, or subsequently recognized by the Commander-in-Chief, Southwest Pacific Area, or other competent authority in the Army of the United States and who were discharged or released from service under conditions other than dishonorable.

Benefit Programs for Veterans

(1)   Disability Compensation[70] - payable to veterans with service-connected condition(s) rated at 10% or more.

(2)   Prisoners of War – POWs who were incarcerated for at least 30 days are entitled to a presumption of service-connected for disabilities resulting from

---

[70] On October 27, 2000, the President signed into law the Department of Veterans Affairs and Housing and Urban Development, and Independent Agencies Appropriations Act, 2001, Pub. L.106-377, 144 Stat. 1441. Section 501 of the Act amended 38 U.S.C. 107 to provide full-dollar rate compensation payments (rather than the half-dollar rate they were receiving) for benefits for certain Filipino veterans who are residing in the United States. The veterans must also be either United States citizens or lawfully admitted permanent resident aliens. This law covers only Commonwealth Army (USAFFE) and Recognized Guerrilla service (not New Philippine Scouts).

certain diseases if manifested to a degree of 10 percent at any time after active service, including psychosis and anxiety.

(3)　　　Clothing allowance - payable to a veteran who is entitled to receive compensation for a service-connected disability for which he or she uses prosthetic or orthopedic appliances that tends to wear out or tear clothing or whose service-connected skin condition requires prescribed medication which irreparably damages the veteran's outer garments.　Payment of the clothing allowance shall be made at a rate of $0.50 for each dollar authorized per Sec 107(a), 38 USC, for all Filipino veterans.

Benefit programs not available

- Non-service connected pension benefits for veterans and dependents;
- VA loans such as home loan guarantees and small business loans;
- Specially Adapted Homes;
- Automobile or Other Conveyances.

For More Information Call Toll-Free 1-800-827-1000

Benefit Programs for Survivors

- Dependency & Indemnity Compensation (DIC) - *payable to eligible spouses, children and parents if the veteran died in service, or died due to sickness or injury incurred in service.
- Aid and Attendance (A&A) – *payable to surviving spouses and parents receiving DIC if they are patients in a nursing home or require aid and attendance of another person.
- Housebound - *payable to surviving spouses qualified for DIC who are not so disabled as to require the regular aid and attendance of another person but who, due to disability, are permanently housebound.
- Dependents' Educational Assistance – payable to children of veterans who are eligible under Chapter 35 benefits.　Spouses are not eligible. Payments shall be made at a rate of $0.50 for each dollar authorized per 38 U.S.C., Section 3565(b)(1).

Payment of the above benefits shall be made at a rate of $0.50 for each dollar authorized per 38 U.S.C., Section 107(a).

Expansion of Health Care Benefits for Certain Filipino Veterans

On October 27, 2000, Public Law 106-377, The Department of Veterans Affairs and Housing and Urban Development and Independent Agencies Appropriations Act, 2001, was signed by the President, authorizing VA to provide hospital, nursing home and outpatient medical care to certain Filipino veterans in the same manner such care is provided to service-connected U.S. veterans[71].

Service-connected Filipino Commonwealth Army Veterans and those who were recognized by authority of the U.S. Army as belonging to organized Filipino Guerrilla forces, who reside in the United States and are citizens or lawfully admitted for permanent residence, are now eligible for the care as provided in Public Law 106-377[72].

---

[71] New Filipino Scouts are not covered by this change. NOTE: Title 38 United States Code Section 1734 provides that the VA may provide care for a service-connected disability of New Filipino Scouts within the limits of VA facilities.

[72] Old Filipino Scouts were not affected by this change since they are already eligible for VA health care on the same basis as U.S. veterans. Project 112 and Project SHAD

APPENDIX M

PROJECT 112 AND PROJECT SHAD

The Department of Defense (DOD) conducted a series of operational tests from 1962 to 1973 in support of Project 112. Project 112 was DOD's comprehensive program of chemical and biological warfare vulnerability tests which were conducted to determine how to protect U.S. troops against these health threats.

Project SHAD (Shipboard Hazard and Defense) was part of Project 112. These tests were primarily shipboard tests. SHAD tests were conducted to evaluate the effectiveness of shipboard detection of chemical and biological agents, the effectiveness of protective measures, and risks to U.S. forces. For the land-based tests, the purpose was generally to learn more about how chemical or biological warfare agents behave under a variety of environmental conditions. Biological and chemical warfare agents, simulants, tracers, and decontaminates were used.

How Are Project 112/SHAD Veterans Identified?

- DOD reports that about 6,000 veterans participated in these tests. Most veterans only participated in the shipboard tests (SHAD).

- DOD has collected, reviewed, and declassified many records. As medically relevant information was declassified, DoD provided VA with the test name, date, and location (for SHAD, the name of the ship). DoD also identified service members who participated in the tests, and may have been exposed to substances used.

Should Test Participants Be Concerned?

- Protective measures were used when biological or chemical warfare agents were tested. Prior research suggests that the other agents, tracers, chemical simulants, and decontaminants are unlikely to cause long-term health effects without signs of acute toxicity soon after exposure. Most veterans were exposed to only one or a few of these agents, but some veterans may have been involved in multiple tests and repeated exposures.

- DOD reports that no veteran is known to have become acutely ill from exposures during these tests. In a recent VA health care utilization review, no diagnosis stands out among Project 112/SHAD veterans. Since there is no known illness or diagnosis that stands out among Project 112/SHAD veterans, there is no "SHAD test" or examination at this time.

What Is VA Doing About Project 112/SHAD?

- The Veterans Benefits Administration (VBA) is contacting veterans identified by DOD, and urging them to have a clinical evaluation at the nearest VA medical center if they have any health concerns.

- VA offers all Project 112/SHAD veterans a complete "Primary Care New Patient History and Physical Examination" even if the veteran has previously received health care from VA. Documentation of each veteran's health condition may be important should future information on Project 112/SHAD indicate a need for concern.

- Each VA medical facility has a designated representative to provide information about Project 112/SHAD.

- VA contracted with the Institute of Medicine in September 2002 to conduct a three-year, three million dollar study of possible health effects associated with Project SHAD in order to ensure appropriate health care and assistance for veterans.

Must Test Participants Pay for a Clinical Evaluation?

Due to legislation enacted in late 2003, veterans will be exempt from co-payments for care or medications required for treatment of any health problem possibly related to participation in Project 112/SHAD. The initial clinical evaluation of health conditions possibly due to Project 112 is also free.

More Information or Assistance

VA -   Project 112/SHAD helpline: 1-800-749-8387
General benefits information: 1-800-827-1000
Internet: www.va.gov/shad/

DOD - Hotline: 1-800-497-6261
Internet:

http://www.deploymentlink.osd.mil/current_issues/shad/shad_intro.shtml

APPENDIX N

INDEX OF TERMS RELATING TO THE VA

A&A   Aid and attendance

AAO   Assistant adjudication officer

ACAP   Annual clothing allowance payment

Active Duty   Full-time service in the armed forces (other than active duty for training), full-time duty (other than for training purposes) as a commissioned officer of the regular or reserve corps of the Public Health Service, full-time duty as a commissioned officer of the National Oceanic and Atmospheric Administration, and service at any time as a cadet at the United States Military, Air Force, or Coast Guard academies or as a midshipman at the United States Naval Academy (38 U.S.C. §101(21); 38 C.F.R. §3.6 (1999)).

Advance on the Docket   A change in the order in which an appeal is reviewed and decided - from the date when it would normally occur to an earlier date.

Agency of Original jurisdiction   The VARO, hospital, or other field-level activity that renders initial benefits determinations. If a determination is adverse to a claimant, the claimant is required to file his or her Notice of Disagreement with that particular office (38 U.S.C. §7105).

Agent Orange Agent Orange was a defoliant used during the Vietnam War. Some known effects are listed in 38 CFR §3.309(e). For more detailed information and new changes see: Agent Orange Home Page   See   also   Spina   Bifida   below. http://www.vba.va.gov/bln/21/Benefits/Herbicide/index.htm

---

AGG   Aggravated in service

Aid & Attendance Allowance

An additional benefit paid to veterans, their spouses, surviving spouses and parents. This allowance is paid in all Compensation, DIC and Pension Programs. It is paid based on the need of aid and attendance by another person or by specific disability. Special Monthly Compensation (L) can at times be designated an aid & attendance benefit.

AIDS (Acquired Immune Deficiency Syndrome)

AIDS can qualify as a service connected disability. Improved Pension may also be paid if AIDS is the disability preventing the veteran from working.

http://www.va.gov/About_VA/Orgs/VHA/VHAProg.htm

AIRS   Appellate Index Retrieval System

ALJ   Administrative Law Judge

AMIE   Automated Medical Information Exchange

Annualization Twelve-month projection of income (countable income plus pension benefits) from the date of entitlement to pension, or from the effective date of change in income.

AO   Adjudication officer or Agent Orange

AOJ   Agency of Original Jurisdiction

APA   Administrative Procedures Act

Appeals   If you do not like a VA decision, most can be appealed. Start by contacting your nearest office. Appeals are first made to the office that made the decision. A hearing officer or decision review officer usually handles these cases. If the case is still in dispute it is then sent to the Board of Veterans Appeals (BVA). If it is not resolved there, it can be appealed outside the

Department of Veterans Affairs to the Court of Appeals for Veteran Claims (CAVC). http://www.va.gov/vbs/bva/index.htm

---

Appellant   An individual who has appealed an AOJ claim determination.

Application   On Line Application's are available for Compensation, Pension and Vocational Rehabilitation & Employment benefits. Your application may need supporting evidence and/or documents. (If any of the evidence is not immediately available, send in the application anyway. The date VA receives your application is important to you, if VA grants your claim. VA benefits payments usually will begin from that date regardless of when the claim is approved.) http://vabenefits.vba.va.gov/vonapp/

AR   Army regulation

Automobile Allowance & Adaptive Equipment

One automobile allowance is payable to certain very disabled veterans. Some reimbursement is possbile for adaptive equipment. Check with your nearest office before making any purchases.
http://www.vba-arms.intecwash.navy.mil/regs/38cfr/bookb/part3/s3_808.doc

---

AWOL   Absence without official leave

BCD   Bad conduct discharge

BCNR   Board for Correction of Naval Records

BMAO   Board medical advisor opinion

Board   The Board of Veterans' Appeals.

Board Member   An attorney, appointed by the Secretary of Veterans Affairs and approved by the President, who decides veterans' benefit appeals.

Board of Veterans' Appeals   The part of VA that reviews benefit claims appeals and that issues decisions on those appeals.

Burial   The Burial Benefit Program covers, burial, plot, internment, cremation, flags, representation at a funeral, transportation and headstone. Specific criteria govern each category.

Burial Allowance   A lump sum benefit paid to the party or parties who assume responsibility for the burial expense of the veteran.

BVA   Board of Veterans' Appeals

BVA Hearing   A personal hearing, held at the BVA office in Washington, D.C., or at a regional office, that is conducted by a member of the Board. A BVA hearing can be held by videoconference from some regional offices. Also see Travel Board Hearing.

C & P   Compensation and Pension

C&C   Confirmed and continued (rating decision)

C.F.R.   Code of Federal Regulations

CAVC   U.S. Court of Appeals for Veterans Claims

CBD   Chief Benefits Director

CD   Clemency discharge

Cemetery -   See the National Cemetery Administration's site or Burial above. http://www.cem.va.gov/

Cf.   Literally means "compare." Used when the cited authority supports a different proposition from the main one but nonetheless is similar or analogous enough that it should be looked at.

C-FILE   VA Claims Folder

CFR   Code of Federal Regulations

CHAMPUS   Civilian Health and Medical Program of the Uniformed Services

---

CHAMPVA   A health insurance is available from the Veterans Health Administration. See their CHAMPVA website for more information. http://www.va.gov/hac/champva/champva.html

---

Children   Children of veterans receive benefits based on two eligibility factors:

(1) whether the benefit program allows for payment for or to children and

(2) whether the veteran's relationship to the child can be proven.

http://www.vba-arms.intecwash.navy.mil/regs/38cfr/bookb/part3/s3_57.doc

---

Claim   A request for veterans' benefits.

Claim Number   A number assigned by VA that identifies a person who has filed a claim; often called a "C-number."

Claims File   Same as claims folder.

Claims Folder   The file containing all documents concerning a veteran's claim or appeal.

Clearly erroneous   A standard that Congress has rarely, if ever, used for court review of federal agency action. The Court interpreted this standard of review in its landmark decision in Gilbert v. Derwinski by stating that a finding is "'clearly erroneous' when although there is evidence to support it, the reviewing court on the entire evidence is left with the definite and firm conviction that a mistake has been committed.

Clothing Allowance   Prosthetic appliances and medications have an effect on clothing. If qualified, a veteran can receive a one time or yearly allowance for reimbursement

http://www.vba-arms.intecwash.navy.mil/regs/38cfr/bookb/part3/s3_810.doc

---

CMD   Chief medical director

COG   Convenience of the government

COLA   Cost-of-living adjustment

Committee for Research of Unit Records

(formerly the Environmental Support Group) Administered by the Army, Department of Defense repository of Vietnam military unit records originally compiled to document exposure of U.S. military units to Agent Orange in Vietnam. The function of the office has evolved to conduct research of military records to verify stressor events on behalf of veterans who file claims for service connection of post-traumatic stress disorder.

Comp. Compensation

Compensation This benefit program evaluates disability resulting from all types of diseases and injuries encountered as a result of military service. The degrees of disability that are determined by VA represent, as far as can practicably be determined, the average loss in wages resulting from such diseases and injuries and their complications in civil occupations. Generally, the degrees of disability specified are also designed to compensate for considerable loss of working time from exacerbations or illnesses.

http://www.vba-arms.intecwash.navy.mil/regs/38cfr/bookb/part3/s3_4.doc

---

Countable Income Almost any kind of payment from any source received during the twelve-month annualization period, with some exceptions (38 C.F.R. §§ 3.252(c), 271(a), and 3.272 (1999) (exclusions from income)).

Court of Veterans Appeals An independent court that reviews appeals of BVA decisions.

COVA U.S. Court of Veterans Appeals

CTA Centralized transcription activities

CUE Clear and Unmistakable Error

CWT Compensation work therapy

DC Diagnostic code

DD Dishonorable discharge

DD Form 214 Military Discharge/DD Form 214 - (Copy 4 - Member Copy) Those applicants who have a copy of their DD-214 are encouraged to provide a copy with their claim to expedite processing. Otherwise, VA will attempt to obtain verification from the service department

http://www.vba-arms.intecwash.navy.mil/regs/38cfr/bookb/part3/s3_203.doc

---

De Novo Review A decision maker's reviewing of a claim for the first time or without giving any deference to a previous decision maker's determination of the same claim.

DEA   Dependents' Educational Assistance

Death Compensation Benefits paid to the spouse or dependent children of a deceased veteran based on a period of wartime service by the veteran. Income limitations and net worth are factors in this benefit.

Decision The final product of BVA's review of an appeal. Possible decisions are to grant or deny the benefit or benefits claimed, or to remand the case back to the AOJ for additional action.

Dependency and Indemnity Compensation (DIC)

This benefit program pays a monthly payment to a surviving spouse, child, or parent of a veteran because of a service-connected death of a veteran.

http://www.vba-arms.intecwash.navy.mil/regs/38cfr/bookb/part3/s3_5.doc

---

Determination A decision on a claim made at the AOJ.

Diabetes Mellitus (Type II) As a presumptive condition for in-country Vietnam veterans see: Agent Orange Home Pagefor more detailed information.

http://www.vba.va.gov/bln/21/Benefits/Herbicide/index.htm

DIC   Dependency and indemnity compensation

Disability Compensation

This benefit program evaluates disability resulting from all types of diseases and injuries encountered as a result of military service. The degrees of disability that are determined by VA represent, as far as can practicably be determined, the average loss in wages resulting from such diseases and injuries and their complications in civil occupations. Generally, the degrees of disability specified are also designed to compensate for considerable loss of working time from exacerbations or illnesses.

http://www.vba-arms.intecwash.navy.mil/regs/38cfr/bookb/part3/s3_4.doc

---

Disability Examinations Worksheets

Physical examinations, when made by the VA, are done under criteria worked out by both the Veterans Health Administration and Veterans Benefits Administration.

http://www.vba.va.gov/bln/21/Benefits/exams/index.htm

Disability Severance Pay

By law, payment of VA compensation and military disability severance pay for the same medical condition or disability is prohibited. VA compensation will be withheld on a monthly basis until the total amount of military severance pay has been recovered.

http://www.vba-arms.intecwash.navy.mil/regs/38cfr/bookb/part3/s3_700.doc

---

DNA   Defense Nuclear Agency

Docket   A listing of appeals that have been filed with BVA. Appeals are listed in numerical order, called docket number order, based on when a VA Form 9 is received by VA.

Docket Number The number assigned to an appeal when a VA Form 9 is received by VA. By law, cases are reviewed by the Board in docket number order.

DOD   Department of Defense

DRB   Discharge Review Board

Drill Pay   By law, if you are an active member of the Selected Reserve or National Guard, your VA compensation will be withheld at the rate of one day of pay for each drill period served. Also, VA compensation is not payable while serving full-time on active duty.

http://www.vba-arms.intecwash.navy.mil/regs/38cfr/bookb/part3/s3_700.doc

---

DRO   Decision Review Officer

DSM IV   Diagnostic and Statistical Manual of Mental Disorders (4th ed.)

DVA   Department of Veterans Affairs

E.g.   Literally means "for example." When used within a citation, it means that the authority states the main proposition

---

EAD   Entry on active duty

EAJA   Equal Access to Justice Act

Education   VA has many educational assistance programs.

http://www.gibill.va.gov/

Education Benefits   Assistance paid by the VA for on-the-job, institutional, cooperative on-the-farm, or apprenticeship programs.

Effective Date   The date as of which the VA calculates its decision to grant, increase, reduce, suspend, or terminate benefits.

Eligibility Verification Report

Form used by the VA to verify continued recipient eligibility for income-based programs; intended to elicit net worth, dependency, and income information.

en banc   In the bench. Full bench. Refers to a session where the entire membership of the court will participate in the decision rather than the regular quorum. In the U.S. the Circuit Courts of Appeal usually sit in panels of judges but for important cases may expand the bench to a larger number, when they are said to be sitting en banc.

Environmental Support Group   (see United States Armed Services Committee for Research of Unit Records)

EOD   Entry on duty

EPC   End product control

ESG   Environmental Support Group (see USASCRUR)

Et al.   Literally means "and others." This abbreviation is affixed to the name of the first person mentioned in a group of names, such as when there is more than one author of a book or plaintiff in a lawsuit.

Et seq.   Literally means "and the following." Used when numerous pages or sections follow a citation to an authority and indicates that the pages of sections after the cited page or section should be included.

ETS   Expiration of term of service

EVR   Eligibility verification report

Examinations   Physical examinations, when made by the VA, are done under criteria worked out by both the Veterans Health Administration and Veterans Benefits Administration.
http://www.vba.va.gov/bln/21/Benefits/exams/index.htm

File   To submit in writing.

Filipino Veterans   New Philippine Scouts or Commonwealth Army (USAFFE) and Recognized Guerillas
http://www.vba.va.gov/bln/21/Milsvc/benfacts.htm#Fili

Flag   A United States Flag is available at the death of a veteran.
http://www.vba.va.gov/bln/21/Milsvc/benfacts.htm#BM06

FOIA   Freedom of Information Act

Foreign Services Program
http://www.vba.va.gov/bln/21/Foreign/index.htm

Former Prisoner of War (POW)
Former POWs often underwent experiences that severely affected their lives. VA works with this group of veterans to ensure that their needs are met.
http://www.vba.va.gov/bln/21/Benefits/POW/index.htm

Forms   VA forms have been organized for your use. Some are available via the web. http://www.vba.va.gov/pubs/forms1.htm

---

FR Index   Federal Register Index

Fraud   An intentional misrepresentation of fact, or the intentional failure to disclose pertinent facts, for the purpose of obtaining or retaining, or assisting an individual to obtain or retain, eligibility for VA benefits, with knowledge that the misrepresentation or failure to disclose may result in the erroneous award or retention of such benefits (38 C.F.R. §3.1(aa)(2) (1999)).

FTCA   Federal Tort Claims Act

GAF   Global Assessment of Functioning Scale

GAO   General Accounting Office

Garnishment   A statutory proceeding whereby a person's property, money, or credits in possession of, under control of, or owing by, another are applied to payment of a debt to a third person (Black's Law Dictionary 612 (5th ed. 1979)).

GC   General Counsel

GD   General discharge

Global Asset Functioning Scale (GAF)
The GAF is a 100-point tool rating overall psychological, social and occupational functioning of people over 18 years of age and older. It excludes physical and environmental impairment. The GAF is included in the Diagnostic and Statistical Manual of Mental Disorders, Fourth Edition, Text Revision (DSM-IV-TR) in the section on multi-axial assessments.
http://www.hadit.com/gaf.htm

GPO   Government Printing Office

GSW   Gunshot wound

Gulf War   The "Gulf War" began on August 2, 1990. Since an end of the conflict has not been declared by Congress, everyone who has been on active duty since it began may qualify as wartime veterans, regardless of duty assignment, when seeking VA benefits   http://www.va.gov/health/environ/persgulf.htm

----

HB   Housebound

HD   Honorable discharge

Health Care Programs for Elderly Veterans
The Veterans Health Administration offers many health care programs for elderly veterans. See the VHA web site on this issue. http://www.va.gov/seniors/health/

Hearing   A meeting, similar to an interview, between an appellant and an official from VA who will decide an appellant's case, during which testimony and other evidence supporting the case is presented. There are two types of personal hearings: Regional office hearings (also called local office hearings) and BVA hearings.

Hereinafter	Signals that an abbreviated version of the cited authority is used in subsequent citations to that authority. Usually used because the full title of the authority is so long that it would be burdensome to keep repeating it.

HISA	Home Improvement and Structural Alterations Program

HIV	Human immunodeficiency virus

HO	Hearing officer

Housebound	Cash payment paid over and above any other compensation or pension payment that may be due, for claimants who are substantially confined to their home or immediate premises (if institutionalized, then ward or clinical area) because of a disability or disabilities (see 38 C.F.R. § 3.351(e) (1999) (permanently housebound)). For compensation purposes, a claimant determined to be housebound because of his or her service-connected conditions is entitled to Special Monthly Compensation over and above the 100 percent compensation rate. For pension purposes, an amount over and above the maximum annual pension rate (MAPR) is paid to a claimant determined to be housebound. In making the determination for pension purposes, all conditions, whether service-connected or not, are considered.

Id.	Indicates that the citation is to the same authority that immediately precedes the citation. In other words, it literally means "same as immediately above."

IFP	In Forma Pauperis In the character or manner of a pauper. Describes permission given to a poor person (I.e. indigent) to proceed without liability for court fees or costs. An indigent will not be deprived of his rights to litigate and appeal: if the court is satisfied as to his indigence he may proceed without incurring costs or fees of court.

IG	Inspector General

IME	Independent medical expert

In re	Literally means "in the matter of."

In the Line of Duty

For an injury or disease to be considered to have been incurred or aggravated during a period of active military, naval, or air service, it must have occurred in the line of duty. If such injury or disease was the result of willful misconduct on the part of the veteran it will not be considered to have occurred in the line of duty. A service department's finding that injury, disease, or death occurred in the line of duty will be binding on the VA unless it is patently inconsistent with the requirements of laws administered by the VA. Requirements for a line of duty determination are not met if at the time the injury was suffered or disease contracted the veteran avoided duty by desertion or absence without official leave, was confined by court-martial involving an unremitted dishonorable discharge, or was confined under sentence of a civil court for a felony as determined under the laws of jurisdiction where the person was convicted by such court (38 U.S.C. §105 (1999)).

INC Incurred in service

Individual Unemployability

Total disability evaluation assigned to an individual because of any service-connected impairment (or combination of impairments) of mind or body that fails to meet the criteria for a total disability rating under the Schedule for Rating Disabilities but that nonetheless renders it impossible for that person to follow substantial gainful employment (38 C.F.R. §4.16 (1999)).

Infra Indicates that the authority cited is cited again later in the document

Insurance Life insurance benefits paid to the beneficiary designated on the policies at the time of a veteran's death under various government programs providing insurance to active-duty service personnel and veterans.

Issue A benefit sought on a claim or an appeal. For example, if an appeal seeks a decision on three different matters, the appeal is said to contain three issues.

IT Incentive therapy

IU Individual unemployability

IVAP　　　　　Income for VA purposes

JAG　　　　　member of Judge Advocate General's Corp

Local Office Hearing

A personal hearing conducted by an RO officer. A regional office hearing may be conducted in addition to a BVA hearing.

LOD　　　　　Line of duty

LSA　　　　　List of Sections Affected (C.F.R.)

MAPR　　　　Maximum annual pension rate

Maximum Annual Pension Rate

Maximum amount of pension payable to a veteran, reduced by the amount of the veteran's annual income and, in some instances, the annual income of other family members (38 U.S.C. §1521(b), (c); see 38 U.S.C. §1521(h)(1) (deduction of annual income of family members)).

Medal of Honor

The Medal of Honor award is paid by Compensation & Pension Service

http://www.vba-arms.intecwash.navy.mil/regs/38cfr/bookb/part3/s3_802.doc

---

Member of the Board

An attorney, appointed by the Secretary of Veterans Affairs and approved by the President, who decides veterans' benefit appeals.

Motion　　　　A legal term used to describe a request that some specific action be taken.

Motion for Reconsideration

The appellant's request that the BVA reconsider a final decision; in addition, the BVA can move on its own initiative to reconsider its decision ((38 C.F.R. § 20.1000 (1999).

Motion to Advance on the Docket

A request that BVA review and decide an appeal sooner than when it normally would based on the appeal's docket number order.

NA　　　　　National Archives

NAS   National Academy of Sciences

New and Material Evidences

a. A claimant must submit "new and material" evidence to reopen a previously disallowed claim.

(1) To qualify as "new" evidence under 38 CFR 3.156, evidence, whether documentary, testimonial or in some other form, must be submitted to VA for the first time. For example, a veteran injured while on duty may not have realized immediately that the condition required medical attention and may have sought treatment later that evening from a private physician. A compensation claim might later be denied if the service medical records contain no mention of treatment for the condition. Should the claimant subsequently submit proof of treatment by the civilian physician, that information would constitute new evidence on which the claim could be reopened.

(2) A photocopy or other duplication of information already contained in a VA claims folder does not constitute new evidence since it was previously considered; neither does information confirming a point already established, such as a statement from a physician verifying the existence of a condition which has already been diagnosed and reported by another physician. Even though such a medical evaluation is from a different doctor, it offers no new basis on which the claim might be reopened unless it contains new information, such as evidence that the condition first manifested itself earlier than previously established.

b. In order to be considered "material" under 38 CFR 3.156, the additional information must bear directly and substantially on the specific matter under consideration.

(1) For example, if VA has previously determined that a back condition claimed by a World War II veteran is not service connected, evidence that the claimant received treatment shortly after release from active duty might be considered new and material if VA had previously been unaware of that treatment. However, information addressing only the current severity of the condition submitted now, over 40 years after service, may not have a bearing on the issue of whether the condition was

incurred or aggravated during military service and does not warrant reopening the prior claim.

(2) Statements and affidavits attesting to the claimant's good character since his or her release from active duty are irrelevant if the issue is the character of the claimant's military service, but any new information offering mitigating circumstances for an action which resulted in an "other than honorable" discharge would address the specific issue under consideration and would warrant reopening the claim.

(3) A medical opinion is not material if it relies on historical facts which are wholly inaccurate.

c. A determination by VA that information constitutes "new and material evidence" means that the new information is sufficiently significant, either by itself or in connection with evidence already of record, that it must be considered in order to decide the merits of the claim fairly. It does not mean that the evidence warrants a revision of a prior determination.

d. A decision not to reopen a claim because the evidence submitted is not new and material is an appealable decision. The claimant must be furnished notice of procedural and appellate rights.

NHL   Non-Hodgkin's lymphoma

NOA   Notice of Appeal

NOD   Notice of Death or Notice of Disagreement

Non-service-connected

With respect to disability or death, a disability that was not incurred or aggravated, or a death that did not result from a disability incurred or aggravated, in the line of duty while the veteran was in the active military, naval, or air service (38 C.F.R. §3.1(1) (1999)).

Notice of Disagreement

A written statement expressing dissatisfaction or disagreement with a local VA office's determination on a benefit claim that must be filed within one year of the date of the regional office's decision.

NPRC   National Personnel Records Center

NSC	Non-service-connected
NSLI	National Service Life Insurance
NSO	National Service Officer
NVLSP	National Veterans Legal Services Program
OGC	Office of the General Counsel (VA)
OMPF	Official military personnel file
Op. G.C.	Opinion of the General Counsel
Op. Gen. Coun	Opinion of the General Counsel
Op. VA Gen. Counsel	Opinion of the General Counsel
OPC	Outpatient clinic
OPT	Outpatient treatment
PCT	Porphyria cutanea tarda (a liver dysfunction)
Pen.	Pension

Pension Monthly payments to a veteran who meets certain minimum wartime service requirements, who became permanently and totally disabled from disability or disabilities not related to military service, and who meets certain income and net worth limits.

per curiam By the court. A phrase used to distinguish an opinion of the whole court from an opinion written by any one judge. Sometimes it denotes an opinion written by the chief justice or presiding judge, or to a brief announcement of the disposition of a case by court not accompanied by a written opinion.

Permanent and Total Disability

For pension purposes, "all veterans who are basically unable to secure and follow a substantially gainful occupation by reason of disabilities which are likely to be permanent shall be rated as permanently and totally disabled" (38 C.F.R. §4.17 (1999); see also 38 C.F.R. § §3.340, 3.342 (1999)).

PIF   Pending issue file

PL   Public Law

PL/P.L.   Public Law

POA   Power of attorney

Post-traumatic Stress Disorder

Acquired mental condition manifested after the occurrence of an extreme traumatic event where the person's response involved intense fear, helplessness, or horror. Manifestations of the disorder include persistent reexperiencing of the traumatic event, avoidance of stimuli associated with the trauma or numbing of general responsiveness, and systems of increased arousal (Diagnostic and Statistical Manual of Mental Disorders 424 (4th ed. 1994)).

POW   Prisoner of war

PRES   Presumption

Presumptive Service Connection

The presumption that chronic, tropical, or prisoner-of-war related diseases, and diseases related to exposure to Agent Orange or ionizing radiation, have been incurred in service, even though there is no evidence of such disease during the period of service (38 C.F.R. § §3.307, 3.309 (1999)).

PT   Permanent total disability

PTSD   Post Traumatic Stress Disorder

Pub. L. No. Public Law

Pyramiding   Evaluation under the VA Schedule for Rating Disabilities of the same manifestation of a disability under various diagnoses (see 38 C.F.R. § 4.14 (1999) (prohibition against pyramiding)).

R.C.   Regional counsel (chief legal authority in a VARO)

RAD	Release from active duty
RE code	Reenlistment code

Regional Office

A local VA office; there are 58 VA regional offices throughout the U.S. and its territories.

Regional Office Hearing

A personal hearing conducted by an RO officer. A regional office hearing may be conducted in addition to a BVA hearing.

Remand   An appeal returned to the regional office or medical facility where the claim originated.

Representative

Someone familiar with the benefit claim process who assists claimants in the preparation and presentation of an appeal. Most representatives are Veterans' Service Organization employees who specialize in veterans' benefit claims. Most states, commonwealths, and territories also have experienced representatives to assist veterans. Other individuals, such as lawyers, may also serve as appeal representatives.

REPS   Restored Entitlement Program for Survivors

Restored Entitlement Program for Survivors

Program that restores certain social security survivors benefits to the surviving dependents of deceased veterans that were reduced or terminated by the Omnibus Budget Reconciliation Act of 1981 (Pub. L. No. 97-35).

RH   Insurance policy designation for veterans with service-connected disabilities

RI   Rating increase

RO   Regional Office

RO Hearing   A personal hearing conducted by an RO officer. A regional office hearing may be conducted in addition to a BVA hearing.

ROA   Record on Appeal

RPC	(VA) Records Processing Center (St.Louis)
RSFPP	Retired Services Family Protection Plan
SBP	Survivor Benefit Plan
SBP-MIW	Survivor Benefit Plan-Minimum Income Widow
SC	Service Connection

Schedule for Rating Disabilities

Title 38, part 4, of the Code of Federal Regulations, which provides a list of criteria for evaluation of all types of diseases and injuries encountered as a result of or incident to military service. The various percentage degrees of disability assigned to each disease or injury represent as far as can be practically determined the average impairment in earning capacity resulting from such diseases and injuries and their residual conditions in civil occupations. http://www.warms.vba.va.gov/bookc.html

SDN	Separation Designator Number
SDRP	Special Discharge Review Program

Secondary Service Connection

Disability that is proximately due to or the result of a service-connected disease or injury such that it is considered part of the original condition and thus also warrants service connection (38 C.F.R. §3.310 (1999)).

See	Precedes citation to authority that directly supports a proposition that logically follows from the authority but that is not explicitly stated by the authority.
See also	Precedes citation to authority in support of a proposition that is in addition to authority cited earlier in support of the same proposition
See Generally	Precedes citation to authority that provides helpful background information related to the proposition presented.

See, e.g.	Precedes citation to authority that supports a proposition that logically follows from the authority that is not directly stated by the authority and is useful as an example only.
Service-connected	With respect to a disability or death, a disability that was incurred or aggravated, or a death that resulted from a disability incurred or aggravated, in the line of duty in the active military, naval, or air service (38 C.F.R. §3.1(k) (1999)).
SF	Standard Form
SFW	Shell fragment wound
SGLI	Servicemen's Group Life Insurance
SIRS	Special Issue Rating System
slip op.	An individual decision of a court that is printed and published separately from a larger volume reporting many decisions of the court. Slip opinions are usually published when a decision is first issued or when no volume reporting many decisions exists.
SMC	Special Monthly Compensation
SMIB	Supplementary medical insurance benefit
SMP	Special Monthly Pension
SMR	Service Medical Record
SOC	Statement of the Case
SPCM	Special court-martial
SPD	Separation Program Designator
SPN	Separation program number
SRD	Schedule for Rating Disabilities
SSA	Social Security Administration
SSD	Social Security Disability Income

SSDI   Social Security Disability Income

SSI   Supplemental Security Income

SSOC   Supplemental Statement of the Case

Statement of the Case

Prepared by the AOJ, this is a summary of the evidence considered, as well as a listing of the laws and regulations used in deciding a benefit claim. It also provides information on the right to appeal an RO's decision to BVA.

STS   Soft tissue sarcomas

Subpoena   A command to appear at a certain time and place to give testimony upon a certain matter. A subpoena duces tecum requires the production of books, papers, records, documents and other materials (Black's Law Dictionary 1279 (5th ed. 1979)). Under 38 U.S.C. § 5711, the VA has authority to issue a subpoena requiring the production of records, documents and other material and the attendance of any witness within a radius of 100 miles from the place of the hearing.

Substantive Appeal   A completed VA Form 9.

Supplemental Statement of the Case

Prepared by the agency of original jurisdiction when additional pertinent evidence has been introduced, an amended decision has been made, or a material defect in the Statement of the Case has been discovered (38 C.F.R. §19.31 (1999).

Supra   Indicates that the cited authority is cited earlier in the document

----

TDHR   Texas Department of Human Resources

TDIU   Total Rating Based on Individual Unemployability

TDRL   Temporary Disability Retired List (uniformed service)

Temporary Disability Retirement List

Status of military personnel that are determined to suffer from a physical or psychological disability, not yet determined to be permanent in nature, but that nonetheless disqualifies them from active military duty. Periodic medical reviews of persons in this status are conducted to determine whether their conditions have improved such that they are fit to return to active military service, or whether they should be permanently retired for disability.

TIN   Transaction Identification Number

TPQ   Third-party query

Travel Board Hearing

A personal hearing conducted at a VA regional office by a member of the Board.

U.S.C.A.   United States Code Annotated

U.S.C.S.   United States Code Service

UCMJ   Uniform Code of Military justice

UD   Undesirable discharge

United States Court of Veterans Appeals

An independent court that reviews appeals of BVA decisions.

UOTHC   (Discharge) under other than honorable conditions

USASCRUR United States Armed Services Center for Research of Unit Records

----

USC   United States Code

USCCAN   United States Code Congressional and Administrative News

----

VA   Department of Veterans Affairs (also used for old Veterans Administration)

VA Form 9 This form, which accompanies the SOC, formally initiates the appeal process.

VACO   VA Central Office

VACOLS   Veterans Appeals Control and Locator System

VADEX   VA Index

VAMC   Veterans Administration Medical Center

VAOPC   VA outpatient clinic

VAR   VA regulation

VARO   VA regional office

VBA   Veterans Benefits Administration

VD   Venereal disease

VEAP   Veterans' Education Assistance Program

Veteran   A person who served in the active military, naval, or air service and who was discharged or released therefrom under conditions other than dishonorable (38 U.S.C. § 101(2)).

Veterans' Service Organization

An organization that represents the interests of veterans. Most Veterans' Service Organizations have specific membership criteria, although membership is not usually required to obtain assistance with benefit claims or appeals.

VGLI   Veterans' Group Life Insurance

VHA   Veterans Health Administration

VJRA   Veterans' Judicial Review Act of 1988

Vocational Rehabilitation

Services and assistance provided to eligible veterans with compensable service-connected disabilities to enable them to achieve maximum independence in daily living and, to the maximum extent feasible, to become employable and to obtain and maintain suitable employment (38 U.S.C. §3100).

VRO   Veterans Administration Regional Office

VSO   Veterans' Service Organization

Waiver of Overpayment

Determination by a regional office Committee on Waivers and Compromises not to collect an overpayment, or any interest thereon, because to do so would be against equity and good conscience (38 C.F.R. §1.962 (1999)).

Well Grounded

A well grounded claim requires three elements:

(1) a medical showing of a current medical condition;

(2) lay or in certain circumstances, medical evidence of disease or injury in service; and

(3) medical evidence showing a nexus between the asserted injury in service and the current disability.

Where medical evidence is required, medical journal articles alone will generally not suffice unless they are enhanced by a physician's opinion stating that the current disability was related, is likely to be related, could be related, or even possibly was related to service. A physician's opinion need not be conclusive to establish a well-grounded claim. Alternatively, both the second and third elements above can be satisfied by the submission of minimum evidence

(a) that the condition was "noted" during service or during an applicable presumption period;

(b) that there has been post service continuity of symptomatology (as to which lay opinion can suffice; and

(c) medical, or in some rare circumstances, lay evidence of a nexus between the present disability between the present disability and the post service symtpomatology.

Willful Misconduct

An act involving conscious wrongdoing or known prohibited action; willful misconduct involves deliberate or intentional wrongdoing with knowledge of or wanton and reckless disregard of its probable consequences. Benefits are not payable in cases where an injury, disease, or death was the result of willful misconduct (38 C.F.R. §§ 3.1(n), 3.301(b), (c) (1999)).

Writ of Mandamus

A writ of mandamus is an order issued by a court to compel an agency to act on a decision that has been unreasonably withheld. It is used in the VA context when the VA simply does nothing on a claim after you have asked that it be decided. It cannot be used to compel a particular result -- say, service connection -- only that the VA go up or down on it.

INDEX

B

C

E

F

N

O

P

Q

R

S

T

U

ABOUT THE AUTHOR

Ken Hudnall is a 100% disabled veteran who lives in El Paso, Texas. Though he has a law degree and a number of years experience dealing with the law and administrative regulations, for many years, he struggled to make sense out of the claims system of the Department of Veterans Affairs. Finally, he undertook a detailed study of the system and the result is the book that you have just read.

This book is not an attempt to practice law, or represent anyone in particular. This work is designed to educate those who are entitled to benefits from the Department of Veterans Affairs in obtaining those benefits.

Good luck.

CPSIA information can be obtained at www.ICGtesting.com
Printed in the USA
LVOW101432260212

270471LV00001B/211/A

9 780975 492390